The
Anarchist Encyclopedia
Abridged

The
Anarchist Encyclopedia
Abridged

edited by
Sébastien Faure

THIS EDITION EDITED AND TRANSLATED BY
Mitchell Abidor

The Anarchist Encyclopedia: Abridged

Translations and editorial expertise © 2019 Mitchell Abidor

This edition © 2019 AK Press (Chico, Edinburgh)

ISBN: 978-1-84935-306-9

E-ISBN: 978-1-84935-307-6

Library of Congress Control Number: 2018932236

AK Press

370 Ryan Ave. #100

Chico, CA 95973

United States

www.akpress.org

akpress@akpress.org

AK Press

33 Tower St.

Edinburgh EH6 7BN

Scotland

www.akuk.com

ak@akedin.demon.co.uk

The above addresses would be delighted to provide you with the latest AK Press distribution catalog, which features books, pamphlets, zines, and stylish apparel published and/or distributed by AK Press. Alternatively, visit our websites for the complete catalog, latest news, and secure ordering.

Cover illustration and design by Josh MacPhee | Antumbra Design

Printed in the USA

CONTENTS

Introduction 1
Preamble 17

Entries:
Altruism 19
Anarchy 21
Atheism 39
Bandit 51
Bolshevism 53
Bomb 67
Class struggle 69
Direct action 81
Direct action 87
Emancipation 89
Fascism 91
Flag 95
Guillotine 99
Heresy 101
Iconoclast 103
Illegalism 105
Individualism 111
Individualism (Individualist Anarchism) 113
Justice 117
Kabbalah 119
Leader 123
Morality 125
Nation 131
Organization 135
Police 141
Reformism, Reformist 147
Resistance 149
Revolution 153
Sabotage 179
Soldier 185
State 189
Synthesis 197
Terrorism 207
Terrorist Attacks 211
Theft 217
Violence (Reflections on) 225
Violence (Anarchist) 235
Vulture 247
War 255
Zeal 261

INTRODUCTION

In 1928, after decades in the movement, the universally respected elder of French anarchism, Sébastien Faure (known to all as "Sébast") published a pamphlet called *Le Synthèse anarchiste*: the anarchist synthesis. In it he called for the unity of the three dominant schools of anarchism: communist anarchism, anarcho-syndicalism, and individualist anarchism.

He wrote there that "it was natural and unavoidable that, having reached a certain development, an idea as vast as anarchism would attain this triple manifestation of life." Faure recognized that "each [school of anarchism] represents a force, a force it is not possible or desirable to bring down," each of them making an "indispensable contribution ... in the combat to be delivered."

After outlining the contributions of the three trends, he concluded that "nothing proclaims their incompatibility," that "the existence of these three currents in no way harms the total strength of anarchism," that "each has its place, its role, and its mission within the movement," and that "under these conditions, anarchism can be likened to what is called in chemistry a compound, that is, a body formed from the combination of several elements."

In the face of their ferocious enemies, capitalism, fascism, and Bolshevism, all anarchists must unite and realize that "the more divided we are, the weaker we are; the more united we again become and stand together, the stronger we will again become."

He addressed his comrades directly about the good that would come from uniting: "What great and mighty actions we could engage in and what lovely and noble campaigns we could undertake and lead to success with our fraternal hearts and arms united!"

When he wrote this, Faure was already three years into the production of the *Encyclopédie Anarchiste*, the *Anarchist Encyclopedia*, a massive work in four volumes and 2,893 pages that was, in book form, precisely the synthesis he called for in practice. Between the covers of these volumes we find, as we flip through its entries, articles on topics ranging from abdication to zoology, from onanism to Malthusianism, from abstentionism to the Sabbath. But more importantly, we find all of anarchism, not only its many schools, all allowed to present their cases uninhibitedly, but also the movement, the Idea in all its vigor, sharpness, confusion, goodness, and violence; all the goodness of its violence, and all the violence of its goodness. When publication was completed in December 1934, or at least this portion of the encyclopedia was published, for there was much more planned, those who read it were holding in their hands both a guide to action and a monument to a movement that even Faure recognized was in steep decline. It was in many ways the testament to a movement and a hope that had animated thousands, for which countless numbers had given their lives. There was no man more likely to produce this work than Sébastien Faure, and there was no one better qualified than he to do so.

II

Faure was born in 1855 to a bourgeois family in Saint-Etienne. He studied for the priesthood for a time, worked in commerce, did his military service, spent a year in England, worked for an insurance company, wed. It was only at age thirty that Faure entered what would be his true calling, that of a political activist, running as a candidate for the Parti Ouvrier in the legislative elections of 1885.

His marriage fell apart as a result of his political work (though much later he and his wife would reunite), and Faure moved to Paris where, by 1888, he was active in the capital's anarchist circles and quickly became a central figure of the movement. A gifted speaker, he embarked on his career as a professional lecturer, from which he would earn a significant part of his living for the rest of his days. As was often the case in the world of French anarchism, the war on religion was a frequent part of his activity, and he not only gave anti-religious lectures and wrote anti-religious pamphlets (most notably, *Twelve Proofs of the Non-Existence of God*) but also engaged in public debates with priests.

Faure defended illegalism, already an issue within the movement—though it would only become an explosive and divisive concern decades later with the acts of the Bonnot Gang—and attacked the celebration of May 1 for being taken under the control of politicians. During the wave of anarchist bombings in the early 1890s his position earned him the admiration of Auguste Vaillant, who had tossed a bomb into the Chamber of Deputies and, though the device failed to kill any of the deputies, had received the death sentence. Before being executed, Vaillant asked that his daughter be entrusted to Faure, who raised the child.

In 1894 Faure was considered a sufficient threat to be included in the Trial of the Thirty (though only twenty-six of the thirty accused actually appeared at the trial), an effort to put an end to anarchist propaganda and anarchism in France after Vaillant's attentat. Like almost all the defendants, who included Jean Grave, Emile Pouget (famous for his pamphlet advocating sabotage), and the art critic (and alleged bomber) Félix Fénéon, Faure was acquitted, and a year later he founded the weekly *Le Libertaire*, which would live a long life (with interruptions), distinguishing itself throughout by the catholicity of views expressed in its pages.

With the arrest, trial, and degradation of Alfred Dreyfus, Faure and the anarchist movement on a whole were not among those on the left in France who viewed the Dreyfus Affair as an intra-bourgeois issue (as even someone as decent as Jean Jaurès did at first), in part because the first Dreyfusard was one of theirs, Bernard Lazare.

Faure threw himself heart and soul into the defense of Dreyfus, and the first outlines of what would later become his anarchist synthesis can be seen in the even broader form of the Revolutionary Coalition he advocated for the defense movement, which would include republicans, freethinkers, socialists, revolutionaries, and anarchists in the fight against reaction.

Some of Faure's comrades who were tainted by Jew-hatred accused him and his colleagues in the newspaper *Le Journal du Peuple*, of being funded by Jews, but it did nothing to dissuade Faure in his fight both in defense of Dreyfus and later in his opposition to anti-Semitism (a cause to which he remained dedicated over the following decades), a sentiment particularly strong among the Blanquists. Nevertheless,

Faure's lifelong opposition to anti-Semitism did not prevent him from allowing passages tainted with anti-Semitism to enter the encyclopedia, particularly those in the entry on "Xenophobia," by the future Nazi Collaborator Achille Blicq. Ultimately a split appeared among anarchists, a more radical wing feeling that Faure had gone too far in his defense of the accused and had abandoned revolution. In the end, with the release of Dreyfus and the end of the Dreyfusard movement, Faure was forced to close down his newspaper and start *Le Libertaire* up anew.

The disgust caused by these internecine quarrels led Faure to withdraw from the movement, and he spent the next decade doing work on the pedagogical front, founding the libertarian colony La Ruche (The Hive), which lasted thirteen years and received much attention and support from the socialist and anarchist left.

While still running La Ruche, he also developed the idea "to organize the party of the revolution" which would unite "insurrectionary socialists," "revolutionary syndicalists and cooperators," and "the anarchists." The idea came to naught.

The arrival of World War I found Faure writing a four-page tract entitled "Towards Peace. An Appeal to Socialists and Syndicalists, Revolutionaries, and Anarchists," again demonstrating his drive for unity. He continued his pacifist activities during the war, during which time he founded and edited the newspaper *Ce Qu'il Faut Dire* (What Must Be Said), which was remarkably successful (selling as many as 20,000 copies) given the atmosphere of the times and the heavy hand of the censor. This paper, it should be said, was founded by Faure and the individualist Mauricius, another example of Faure's synthesis.

With the end of the war, Faure assumed his role as senior statesman of anarchism, which went untainted and unquestioned despite some disturbing controversy. Though he had been arrested for political activities with some frequency prior to 1914, in 1917 and 1921, according to the monumental *Dictionnaire biographique du movement ouvrier* (Biographical Dictionary of the Workers' Movement) edited by Jean Maitron, Faure was arrested for "gross indecency," or, to phrase it more accurately, sex crimes. In the first instance, he was arrested for rubbing against young girls at the flea market at Clignancourt, and then four years later for having accompanied two other men to a hotel in the company of minors. After the first arrest, his comrades published a pamphlet in his defense entitled, "An Infamy: The Underside of an Odious Machination. The Faure Affair." Whatever French anarchists thought of these arrests, it doesn't seem to have noticeably impacted Faure's political activities or reputation.

During the Bolshevik revolution he initially offered the successful revolutionaries qualified support, which he soon retracted (lively debate on the topic appeared in *Le Libertaire*). While continuing to give public lectures he also set up a print shop, La Fraternelle, whose address at 55 rue Pixérécourt, in the working-class Belleville quarter in the 20th arrondissement, would also serve as the address of the *Anarchist Encyclopedia* when he began that project in 1925. In 1922, Faure founded yet another review, *La Revue Anarchiste*, which lasted thirty-five issues, until 1925, and as in all of Faure's projects, opened its pages to all the tendencies of anarchism. He also published a journal dedicated to the international movement, *La Revue Internationale Anarchiste*.

The subsequent years were spent fighting for and defending the anarchist synthesis alongside Voline, and founding the Association des Fédéralistes Anarchistes as the organized body representing the idea, which was opposed by the group known as the platformists, part of the Union Anarchiste Communiste, led by Piotr Archinov. (Archinov also wrote articles for the *Anarchist Encyclopedia*, specifically the important articles on Bolshevism and democracy, the former of which is included below.) The battle between the two tendencies was harsh, and was only settled by unity between the two sides (though their organizations' names had changed in the meanwhile) in the Union Anarchiste.

The Spanish Civil War found Faure working actively in support of the anarchists, spending two weeks in Catalonia, visiting Durruti, and reporting on events there in *Le Libertaire* and the French language newspaper of the CNT *L'Espagne antifasciste*. The Spaniards, in recognition of Faure's lifetime commitment to anarchism, named a children's colony and a centurion of their international fighters after the Frenchman.

With the beginning of World War II, Faure joined the exodus from Paris, taking refuge in Royan. Though he wanted to return to

Paris, his health didn't allow it, and he spent his final two years in the seaside resort town. It was there he was buried.

III

The origins and object of the *Anarchist Encyclopedia* were explained in a mailing to potential contributors and in a special supplement to issue no. 4 of *La Revue Internationale Anarchiste*.

Nettlau, the great historian of the anarchist movement and biographer of Bakunin, was asked to participate in the project. As Faure wrote, the *Anarchist Encyclopedia* "is impossible without your figuring and truly being numbered among its collaborators." (In the event, Nettlau did contribute articles, including one on "terrorist attacks," included in this selection.)

The notice aimed at potential subscribers is a wide-ranging document.

The go-ahead for the encyclopedia was given at an assembly of the Groupe Internationale Anarchiste, held on January 21 and 25, 1925. When presented with Faure's proposal for an encyclopedia, the group unanimously decided that it would adopt the project, realize it as soon as possible, entrust the directorship of the editorial and administrative services to Faure, assist "our comrade" in his administrative and editorial tasks, and involve anarchist circles in all countries. The committee that adopted this measure was international but was predominantly French, Italian, and Spanish, or Spanish speaking. Only one American appears on its editorial committee, a misspelled "E. Goldmann."

The four existing volumes of the encyclopedia are but a pale shadow of the original intent. As designed, there would have been five parts:

1. The anarchist dictionary, explaining "the principles, concepts, tendencies, and methods of anarchist thought and action."

2. The historical aspect of anarchism "country by country and an overall view of the various national movements."

3. The life and works of "the principal militants having belonged to or belonging to the anarchist movement."

4. "The life and works of men who without having been anarchists properly speaking nevertheless … contributed to the struggle for human liberation."

5. A catalogue of anarchist books and pamphlets.

Faure related in the prospectus how the project had been one he long considered, but "for thirty years my activities as a militant have been spent in speeches, conferences, newspaper articles, and popular agitation. Constantly on the road, I couldn't even dream of undertaking a labor of this nature." Already 67 years old at this time, "my age and the state of my health no longer allowing me to carry out propaganda work that demand strength and endurance I no longer possess. I have thus substituted and will increasingly substitute written propaganda for spoken."

A lifetime's experience of anarchist activity taught Faure the need for something like the *Anarchist Encyclopedia*. For him, the "methodical" nature of the encyclopedia, its "simple, clear, precise, and lively form within the grasp of all" was necessary because, though anarchists "have a way of conceiving, feeling, judging, willing, and acting that is only theirs," he admitted that he had "many times regretfully observed that for most [anarchists] these opinions are confused, are all higgledy-piggledy, lacking in classification, order, or method." *The Anarchist Encyclopedia* intended to add to the knowledge base of anarchists and serve to impose on this knowledge "all the strength and clarity desirable."

For the man who conceived the encyclopedia, it was intended as "neither a catechism nor a gospel," but rather "a unique and complete anthology that anarchists can use to both educate themselves and as a source when writing or giving speeches."

In a promise that unfortunately was not kept, the readers were told that *The Little Anarchist Encyclopedia* (as the original documents call it) "will have an international character, like the anarchist movement and doctrine themselves." In the end, though, there were only a small number of non-French contributors (like the Russians Voline and Archinov), only Errico Malatesta and Max Nettlau did not live in France during the encyclopedia's gestation period. The work, Faure wrote, would first be published in French for practical and financial reasons, but "translated bit by bit, this work will appear in Spanish and Italian and, if possible, in other languages." This, unfortunately, never occurred.

The impulse and purpose behind the encyclopedia were also explained in a notice sent to potential contributors. Faure admitted that "a work of this scope cannot be that of one man alone and, what is more, to justify its title of *Anarchist Encyclopedia* it is indispensable that this monument be owed to the fraternal collaboration of all the anarchist thinkers, theoreticians, writers, and agitators who contribute to propagating around the world the only Idea that will liberate humanity."

After asking the recipients to choose from a list of words beginning in "A" he recommends how articles should be written: "Given that this is an exposé of the principles, theories, concepts, tendencies, and methods of anarchist thought and action, it would be interesting, useful, and even indispensable to draw freely from our abundant anarchist literature the passages in which ... our writers, those of both yesterday and today, have most clearly explained themselves.

The encyclopedia as a cross-generational work was clearly important to Faure: "In this form of judiciously chosen quotations and excerpts our dear departed will become, like the living militants, collaborators in the *Anarchist Encyclopedia*."

On a more down-to-earth subject, Faure informs the writers that they will be paid 25 francs a page (by some rough estimates, the equivalent of $25 today). "I request you consider this not as a salary worthy of the work you will accomplish, even less as a lure capable of stimulating your assistance, but rather as a feeble retribution proportionate to our possibilities and, even more, as testimony of gratitude and solidarity."

The committee behind the encyclopedia announced that it would appear in 36 issues of 48 pages each, for a total of 1,728 pages (missing the mark by almost 1300 pages) "the matter of 36 normal sized volumes of 300 pages." It would be available by subscription, the price running from 10.50 francs for three issues to 126 francs for all 36. Faure and his comrades didn't want price to be an object in the decision whether or not to subscribe to the *Encyclopedia*. "We don't want the subscriber who is able to pay 126, 84, 42, or 21 francs to have any advantage over those who can only pay 10.50. Doesn't the latter have as much need as the former of anarchist bread?"

The prediction was that the production of the *Anarchist Encyclopedia* would cost 216,000 francs and take three years, with 80,000 francs needed to get it off the ground (72,000 for production costs, 8,000 for publicity). 45,000 of this was expected to come from charitable contributions, the rest from subscriptions. Subscribers were informed (perhaps reassured) that issues would arrive with the envelope containing "no external indication that will make it known to the post office that this is the *Anarchist Encyclopedia*." The work would not be available at newsstands, since the charges owed newsstand distributors would eat too much into the revenue from the encyclopedia and the damage done to returned copies would make them a pure loss.

A comparison of the words that were planned to appear in the encyclopedia and those that actually did reveals that the plan was followed closely. So exhaustive a work could not possibly have been completed in three years. In fact, since the work was pursued alphabetically we can approximately track its progress through Faure's correspondence with a collaborator on the *Encyclopedia*, Charles Hotz. In a letter dated February 5, 1926, Hotz informs Faure that he is sending him the article on "bonté," kindness. So, one year into the encyclopedia the letter "B" was not yet completed. In December 1927 Hotz is still discussing with Faure how to treat the words "poésie," "presse," "rhétorique," "roman" (novel), and "satire," so we can again see that the process did not proceed without delays and hindrances.

The complete Encyclopedia—or at least this part of it—appeared in December 1934. None of the other planned elements was ever worked on, nor were translations into foreign languages done. But it can at least be said that the prediction in the initial prospectus that "this publication will mark an important date in the history of the international anarchist movement" was shown to be true.

IV

There were approximately 115 contributors to the *Anarchist Encyclopedia*. Among them were names in the first rank of international anarchism, men like Errico Malatesta, already 72 at the time the *Anarchist Encyclopedia* was begun and who would die in 1932, before seeing it completed. His entry on "organization" is discussed below. The embodiment of anarchism, Malatesta was a prolific writer and a tireless agitator, entering the struggle at age 14 and sending much of his life in exile in Egypt, England, Switzerland, and France.

Voline, born Boris Eichenbaum, who accompanied Makhno in his fight with the Bolsheviks and who authored the classic *The Unknown Revolution* worked with Faure, as did his fellow Makhnovtsi, Piotr Archinov, who eventually broke with anarchism after battling Voline and Faure on the organizational question and returned to the Soviet Union, where he wrote an attack on his former beliefs in 1935. He was later executed there for "attempting to restore anarchism" in 1937.

Max Nettlau, the historian and theoretician; Emile Armand and Hem Day, long-time spokesmen for individualist anarchism; even Charles Rappoport, a founding member of the French Communist Party, all appear in these pages.

However, the bulk of the encyclopedia was written by lesser-known names, some of which deserve to be remembered. People like the physician Fernand Elosu, an anarchist from Bordeaux who collaborated with Faure in his educational work, wrote for Faure's anti-war newspaper *Ce Qu'il Faut Dire* during World War I, stood with the Zimmerwaldians in the fight against the war, and wrote several articles for the *Encyclopedia*, including his moving condemnation of violence (included in this collection) with its words that anarchism "is not an idea that has found bayonets. It's an idea that has smashed bayonets." A man of great nobility, he had perhaps joined the PCF sometime in the 1930s and was the president of the Society of Friends of the USSR in Bayonne, which earned him an arrest for "attempting to reconstitute the Communist Party" in 1940. He offered to serve the prison term of another comrade imprisoned at the same time, and died shortly thereafter of pneumonia.

There was perhaps no more fascinating contributor to the *Anarchist Encyclopedia* than the sadly unknown Madeleine Pelletier, who signed her articles "Doctoresse Pelletier," using the feminine form of the noun "doctor." Professionally and politically, Pelletier's career was a dizzyingly colorful one. Born to a poor family of shopkeepers in Paris in 1874, Pelletier was close to the anarchists in her youth, though this first encounter with the movement was short lived. Influenced by

Louise Michel, she was at the same time a feminist, a principle she never strayed from throughout her life. An autodidact, she succeeded in being admitted to medical school but was refused admission as an intern at the psychiatric hospitals of the city of Paris, since as a woman she had no right to vote and a condition for the internship was the possession of political rights. A public campaign succeeded in her obtaining the position, making her the first woman to do so. Even Pelletier's appearance was a cause for complaint about her. As we see in photos of her, she had a fondness for men's suits and even wore bowler hats, though her response to criticism was that "my attire tells men: I am your equal."

Though clearly a progressive, in the early twentieth century Pelletier was a strong supporter of anthropometry, the pseudo-science that measures skulls as an indication of intelligence, writing that "the relationship [of skull measurement] with intellectual development is no longer in doubt today."

In 1904 she requested admission to the Masonic Lodge La Philosophie Sociale, one of the few open to women, but her campaign to open all lodges to women resulted in her encountering strong opposition and her departure from Masonry.

The doctor attempted to combine her feminism with socialism, participating in the more radical wing of French socialism, behind Jules Guesde, but when they showed a lack of interest in feminism she moved to the furthest left faction within the party, behind Gustave Hervé. Though unable to vote or hold office, she ran for parliament, receiving 340 votes.

After World War I, which she considered an imperialist war, Pelletier began a collaboration in the anarchist press, writing on women's liberation, population control, and anti-militarism, though she was not yet an anarchist. In fact, she was a founding member of the PCF, and was in fact part of the far left of the newly formed Communist Party where she also edited the party's women's newspaper, *La Voix des femmes*. Though delegated by the paper for a women's conference in Moscow, she was unable to obtain a passport and so traveled there clandestinely, writing a book on her experiences there.

An active propagandist for communism and the Soviet Union, by the mid-twenties she became disillusioned with the Soviet experiment and dedicated her activities to the anarchist and pacifist movements. Writing on "morality" in the *Anarchist Encyclopedia*, (included in the selections below) she said that "Morality's primordial function seems to be the protection of property. The categorical imperative is a psychic gendarme."

A longtime advocate of legal abortion and birth control, her idea on matters sexual were, to say the least, eccentric. At a debate in 1935 she discussed "devirginization," asking "Is the wedding night legal rape? Should virgins be de-virginized scientifically before marriage?"

In 1939, living in dire poverty, she was denounced for carrying out illegal abortions at her home on rue Monge in the Latin Quarter. Found guilty, she was judged to be mentally irresponsible and was committed to the asylum of Vaucluse, where she died.

A list of her works sums up her ideas: *The So-Called Psychological Inferiority of Women* (1904); *The Admission of Women to Freemasonry* (1905); *Women in Struggle for Their Rights* (1908); *The Sexual Emancipation of Women* (1911); *Celibacy: A Superior State* (n.d.); *The Feminist Education of Girls* (1914); *The Virgin Woman* (1933); and *Sexual Rationalization* (1935). It would not be until the 1990s that Pelletier began receiving scholarly attention.

Not every contributor would be as consistent and upright. Nor would the opinions expressed in it accord with reality. Achille Blicq, in an entry on "Xenophobia" that was written late in the process and does not appear in this collection, when nationalist frenzy was sweeping Europe, said that: "Borders, ever more unstable, are disappearing in many places in expectation of the day when their existence will come to an end, while a powerful current of mutual sympathy and fraternal mutual assistance, motivated by the clear notion of the shared interests of the workers of all nations, are irresistibly leading humanity towards the creation of one sole and immense fatherland that will be formed by men become free and independent, as well as more loving and in solidarity."

Blicq himself, like his fellow contributor, Georges Yvetot would not escape the German Occupation with his reputation unblemished. Yvetot, while still proclaiming himself to be an anarchist, was named to a collaborationist committee designed to help workers who had been victims of Allied bombings. He died before the committee could actually accomplish anything, but did give an interview to a Collaborationist newspaper. Blicq's case was more clear-cut, since he was appointed "Aryan administrator" of a confiscated Jewish firm, and also wrote to the Commissariat for Jewish Questions requesting information about a Jewish-owned clinic. Sued after the war by the returned owner of the firm Blicq administered, Maitron's *Biographical Dictionary* reports the police as saying that he lived "in a luxurious home … [and] enjoyed quite important pecuniary means." He suffered no consequences for his wartime activities.

V

There is perhaps no greater tribute to the openness with which Faure dealt with the entries in the *Encyclopedia*, to his willingness to stand by his ideas whatever that might bring, than in a debate hidden in plain sight within its pages.

As we noted above, the anarchist synthesis was Faure's guiding principle, both in his larger actions in his final years and in the compiling of the encyclopedia. There is even an entry (included in this volume) for "Synthesis (anarchist)," written by Voline who, along with Faure, not only edited the encyclopedia but advocated for the synthesis. Voline wrote in a pamphlet that it is "precisely anarchism as an understanding of the world and life which, in its very essence, is profoundly synthetic and profoundly imbued with the living and creative principle that is the motive force of life." As a result, it must "seek to become the great living synthesis of the different elements of life, established through scientific analysis and fecundated by the synthesis of our ideas. … [I]t must do this if it wishes to be the precursors of the truth, the true non-falsified factor and not a bankrupter of liberation and of human progress that the dozens of sullen 'isms,' each more narrow, more shut off, and further from the truth than the other, can clearly not become."

Voline's entry, in making the case for unity within the anarchist movement, explains its roots in his own failed experience in Russia after the 1917 Revolution where "already materially weak … in relation to other political and social currents anarchism was further weakened at the time of the Russian Revolution as a result of internecine quarrels that tore it apart." Voline explains that syndicalism "establishes the basis for the organization of the social revolution"; libertarian communism, "the basis for organization of the new society being formed"; and individualism, "the total emancipation and the happiness of the individual being the true goal of the social revolution and the new society."

For Voline the conclusion is clear: "The dismemberment of the anarchist idea into several currents has fulfilled its role. It is no longer of any use. Nothing can justify it any longer. It is leading the movement into an impasse. ... It is a matter of gluing the separated elements back together, of finding again and consciously reconstructing the abandoned synthesis."

He ended by dismissing the endless disputes within the movement: "As for the disputes and polemics between petty chapels each preaching 'its' truth alone, they can only arrive at the continuation of the current chaos, at interminable internecine quarrels and the stagnation of the movement."[1]

VI

Even in this incomplete form, minus the other planned volumes, the *Anarchist Encyclopedia* is a staggering performance. It is a tribute to the optimism of its contributors—both of funds and articles—that during a period when fascism was on the rise, when Communism had become the movement of choice for the majority of revolutionaries, they both undertook and completed this compendium of anarchist thought.

One can imagine the difficulty in selecting entries from as imposing a collection as this. The small sample collected here was chosen based on the topics discussed, on their current and/or historic interest. As a result, some well-known (or at least better-known) contributors were omitted, figures like Paul Reclus or Augustin Souchy or André Lorulot or Manuel Devaldès or Victor Méric, et cetera. Those omitted also demonstrate the catholicity of the *Anarchist Encyclopedia*.

1. It is worthy of note that Voline's case for the anarchist synthesis does not only rely on political considerations, but are augmented by arguments drawn from science based on the need for "an equilibrium of certain elements as being the bio-physical essence of life," which is "confirmed by physico-chemical scientific experiments." Scientism was an important element of all schools of anarchism, its purest example perhaps Kropotkin's attempt to found the idea on mutual aid as opposed to the Darwinian struggle for existence. If Marxists founded the inevitable victory of the working class in the class struggle, anarchists found the inevitability of a stateless, classless society proved by nature and science.

In some instances there were multiple entries for a given subject (like "Violence" with four). In cases like these the choice was purely subjective: the most interesting one was chosen. Most interesting, but not always the best-written. Many of the contributors were militants and not intellectuals. Someone like Achille Blicq was a prolific contributor to the encyclopedia, but frankly not a very good writer, seeming to think every paragraph should be composed of a single sentence. I have attempted to maintain the styles (such as they are) of the writers, only modifying for comprehensibility.

This selection is but a pale reflection of the original and should be taken as both a tool for study and action and a tribute to men and women who spent their lives in service to the Idea.

***

All footnotes are mine unless otherwise noted. Some of the selections contain sentiments that were barely acceptable in the 1930s and are totally unacceptable today (including and especially some language that is racist or antisemitic). I have left them as they were written. Similarly, the contributors wrote in a gendered language, and their references to man and mankind have been left as they were in the original versions.

—MITCHELL ABIDOR

PREAMBLE

The ANARCHIST ENCYCLOPEDIA is under the direction of Sébastien Faure. Its composition was ensured by

Anarchist theoreticians, militants, and writers;
Syndicalist theoreticians, militants, and writers;
Revolutionary theoreticians, militants, and writers;
Non-party specialists and technicians.

***

Well-being for all!
Freedom for all!
Nothing through force, everything through free agreement!
Tis is the ideal of the anarchists.
None *clearer*, more *humane*, or more *elevated* exists.

***

The *Anarchist Encyclopedia* is not a commercial undertaking; it is a work of libertarian education.

***

Those who wrote it and those who publish it only have in mind the satisfaction—which they place above all else—of propagating the sentiments and convictions that animate them and to which they have dedicated their lives.

***

This work is fraternally dedicated to all those who, braving privations, slander, and persecution work, wherever they might be, to assure and hasten the advent of an anarchist society.

***

The Anarchist Encyclopedia is aimed at the millions of pariahs of all nationalities who suffer from the hateful social organization of which, materially and morally, they are the victims. They will find enlightenment within it and will draw from it the energy that will be necessary to them when, animated by the Spirit of Revolt, they will resolve to free themselves.

***

Neither Gods nor Masters!

***

You who are bent beneath the yoke of the state, capital, and churches, know that *salvation lies within you, is entirely within you, and nowhere else but within you!*

—SÉBASTIEN FAURE

Altruism (from the Latin alter, other) It is wrong to see this word as the antonym of egoism: they are two heads under the same hat. Altruism is the name egoism assumes to avoid being recognized; it is the garb it adopts when it fears recognition. All the varieties of altruism, or so-called love of one's neighbor, can be reduced to egoism. It was the courtier La Rochefoucauld who was right and not the pedants, rosewater idealists, fanatics, advice givers, and others who professed vigor and were animated by excellent intentions and rotten with optimism. They want to make others happy against their will. In certain circles it is the done thing to "refute"—and with what arguments!—the author of the *Maxims*. At school leaving exams old, grumpy examiners systematically flunk those "little young ones" who dare share La Rochefoucauld's opinions. It is forbidden to have a personal opinion on this, as on so many other subjects. It is a given that altruism is the most elevated of virtues, distinguishing man from the animals.

Altruism, as it is practiced, is profoundly immoral: it is a lie. The altruism of the weak, of slaves, of the infirm (both intellectually and physically) is the source of boundless ills: the altruism of submission, obedience, and passivity. It is altruism that engenders the international conflicts it claims to deplore. Crime and ignorance, resignation, servitude, and the acceptance of humiliation are perpetuated under cover of altruism. What altruists grant with the greatest ease are promises. The rule that, "It is better to give than receive" should have the same value in morality as in right. Yet altruism gives nothing in exchange for the self-abdication it demands of its beneficiaries. Alms are a diminution. Altruism above all benefits those who practice it. It is a pretext for banquets, decorations, and entertainments in poor taste. The chimera of altruism is made real through the devastation it wreaks. Mutualism, solidarism, pacifism, et cetera do not leave the realm of abstraction and are expressed in hollow phrases that onlookers take for reality. Altruism is the opposite of love, which is sincerity.

Anarchy (from the Greek "a-" without and "arche," command, power, authority) A preliminary observation: the object of this *Anarchist Encyclopedia* is making known the totality of political, economic, philosophic, and moral concepts that have anarchism as either their departure or end points. Over the course of this work and in their proper place, the many theses embracing a careful and complete study of this subject will be laid out. It is thus only by methodically and coherently comparing and combining the sections of this *Encyclopedia* that the reader will achieve complete understanding of anarchy, anarchism, and the anarchists.

Consequently, in this article I will present only a concise and synthetic overview of what constitutes the essence of anarchy and anarchism. For details—and it is appropriate to note that some are of great importance—the reader is requested to consult the various words defined in the text.

Etymologically, the word "anarchy" (which should be written An-Archy) means the status of a people, or more accurately still, of a social environment, without government.

As an ideal and a social realization, anarchy is a modus vivendi in which, rid of all legal and collective constraints dependent on the public force, the individual's only obligations will be those imposed on him by his own conscience. He will have the ability to give himself over to whatever inspires him personally. He will enjoy the right to try out whatever experiences he considers desirable or fertile. He will freely commit to contracts of all kinds which, always temporary and revocable and reversible, will connect him to his fellows, and, not desiring to subject anyone to his authority, he will refuse to submit to the authority of anyone else.

Sovereign master of himself, of the meaning he gives his life, of the use of his faculties, knowledge, and productive activity, and of his relations based on sympathy, friendship, and love, the individual will organize his existence as he sees fit, expanding in all directions, flourishing, enjoying in all he does his full and entire freedom. He will experience no limits other than those assigned him by the freedom—full and entire as well—of other individuals.

This modus vivendi implies a social regime from which in law and fact any idea of wage labor and the wage earner, of capitalist and proletariat, of master and servant, of governor and governed, will be banished.

One can understand that, defined in this way, the word anarchy has been insidiously and ultimately diverted from its exact meaning; that it was over time taken to mean disorder and, in most dictionaries and encyclopedias, this is the only meaning that is given: chaos, overturning, confusion, waste, disarray, disorder.

Apart from the anarchists, all philosophers, all moralists, all sociologists—including democratic theoreticians and socialist doctrinaires—assert that in the absence of a government, of legislation and repression that ensures respect for the law and punishes any infractions of the latter, there can only be disorder and criminality.

And yet ... don't moralists and philosophers, statesmen and sociologists, notice the frightful disorder that reigns in all domains despite the authority that governs and the law that represses? Are they so lacking in critical sense and spirit of observation that they fail to see that the more regulation is increased, the more the network of legislation is tightened, the greater the extent of the field of repression, the more immorality, abjection, crimes, and misdemeanors increase?

It is impossible that these theoreticians of order and professors of morality seriously and honestly think of confusing the atrocities, horrors, and monstrosities whose revolting spectacle lays before our eyes with order.

And it is even more impossible (for there are degrees in the impossible) that in order to attenuate and *a fortiori* make these infamies disappear that these same learned men take the virtue of authority and the force of the law for granted.

To make such a claim would be pure madness.

The law has but one goal: justifying and then sanctioning all the usurpations and iniquities upon which rest what those who profit from these iniquities and usurpations call the social order. The holders of wealth crystallized the original legitimacy of their fortune in the law; the holders of power have raised to the height of an immutable and sacred principle the respect owed to the fortunate few by the masses, as well as the power and majesty with which they are crowned. One can dig as deeply as one wants into those monuments of hypocrisy and violence that are the legal codes—that are every legal code—without finding a single one that is not in favor of these two historical and circumstantial facts, which people attempt to convert into natural and foreordained facts: property and authority. I leave to the official Tartuffes and the professionals of bourgeois charlatanry all legislative matters concerned with morality. Legislation, in a society based on property and authority, is not capable of being anything but the humble servant and shameless accomplice of both the latter and the former. [...]

***

The concept [of anarchism] plunges its roots into the deep soil of history, experience, and reason. Its roots cannot be destroyed. It is still possible for masters to cut them as they tear through the crust of prejudices that covers them and prevents them from appearing before the eyes of all. And yet, deep within the bowels of the old world of oppression, ignorance, poverty, hatred, and ugliness, they persist in growing in robustness and reach.

***

Anarchy is not a religion: there is no revelation as its departure point. It has no part in dogmatic affirmation; it repudiates the *a priori*; it does not accept unproven ideas.

It is at one and the same time a doctrine and a way of life. It is a doctrine inspired by the never-ending evolution of individual and collective arrangements that constitute the life of individuals and collectivities, a life that takes account of this ceaseless transformation and reflects it in its doctrine.

It is a doctrine because history, experience, and reason have taught us certain truths whose correctness, always confirmed by observation and the scrupulously impartial examination of facts, is no longer arguable. These truths themselves are concordant. Not only do they not combat each other, but they unite and lend each other a hand: they are linked. Already powerful and resilient on their own, each of these truths lends the others—nearby or distant—a recrudescence of strength and toughness. It is this assemblage of certainties that forms and solidifies the doctrine, about whose fundaments all of the tendencies of anarchism—however numerous they might be—are unanimous and inseparable.

A certain number of guiding principles emanate from this doctrine that, applied to life, determine the social environment the anarchists want to establish.

On one hand, there is the study and observation of individual and social life that provide the truths and certainties upon which our anarchist doctrine is constructed. On the other hand, there are the guiding principles that, proceeding from this doctrine, must preside over the organization of individual and social life that we call "anarchy."

The doctrine emanates from the individual living in society; this is the theoretical aspect of anarchy. Then, as a rule of life, anarchy emanates from the doctrine and determines the social environment and its countless adaptations: this is the practical aspect of anarchy.

Socially, anarchy can be summed up in two words: free agreement. If this phrase seems too short, if one wishes it were more explicit, I will say, in order to be clearer and more precise, "Freedom through agreement," or even better, "Freedom for each through the agreement of all." Freedom is the alpha and omega, i.e., the beginning and end points of the theory. Free agreement is the beginning and end point of practice. Or, "Freedom is the doctrine; Agreement is life."

But this must be expanded upon a bit. Here is the essential demonstration: All philosophers and sociologists who have seriously and impartially studied human nature have remarked that the goal of all of an individual's aspirations, desires, movements, and activities is the satisfaction of one or many needs. There is no real need to engage in profound philosophical, biological, or sociological studies to reach this conclusion. Each and every one of us can do so.

To this first observation must be added the following: the satisfaction of a need procures a sensation of pleasure for the person feeling it, while the non-satisfaction of this need causes him pain. This second observation is also one that each of us can make and about which there is no doubt.

From these two observations, the second of which is nothing but the logical continuation of the first, we conclude that the individual, in seeking the satisfaction of his needs, has in mind the pleasure he finds in doing so and, consequently, we affirm that man seeks happiness.

Thus, the search for happiness becomes the goal that is the aim of any living being.

This is an important point, one we consider fundamental for anarchy.

But human beings do not live in isolation. They group together with beings of their species; they live in society.

We are thus led to pass from the individual to the social.

If the individual forms groups, it is first because it is in his nature, so he feels the need to do so; and secondly, he does so because he instinctively seeks to increase his happiness through the support and protection he hopes to find in his fellows.

The conclusion to be drawn from this is that the goal of grouping together in society is the increase of the happiness of those who constitute it. In other words, the social should contribute to bringing the individual closer to his goal of happiness. Society's raison d'être is thus ensuring the happiness of its members.

And so, we are now in possession of a second important and fundamental element of anarchy.

Let us cast a rapid glance behind us, as much to see the distance covered by our reasoning as to knit our two observations tightly together.

First observation: the individual seeks happiness through the satisfaction of his needs. Second observation: the goal of society is that of ensuring and increasing the happiness of all its members. Thus, the happiness of the individual is the goal of individual life and the happiness of all the individuals living in society is the goal of social life.

I have now reached the third of the observations that, connected to the others, brings us to the first of the certainties upon which anarchist doctrine rests.

Of all the forms of society, the worst is necessarily that which strays furthest from the goal to be attained: the happiness of the individuals who compose it. Of all the forms of society, the best is necessarily that which brings us closest to this goal. The most criminal society is that in which the proportion of the unhappy is highest, and the ideal society is that in which all those who compose it will be happy. Social progress—true, positive, unarguable progress—is not, cannot be anything but the gradual ascent towards that ideal society.

This is our third observation.

As we did a second ago, let us go back a few steps, or rather, let us stop a minute and bring together our three observations:

1. The individual seeks happiness;

2. Society's goal is to procure it for him;

3. The best form of society is that which brings us closer to this goal.

We now have the first of our certainties.

We will now seek the second.

Let us ask ourselves this question: Until today, have the many forms of society that have succeeded each other met the goal that any social grouping must assign itself: the happiness of all its members?

At this point history enters the scene and carries with it the lessons of the past.

And so, we must consult history.

Supported by abundant and authentic documentation, it provides us with proof that the immense majority of individuals were and are unhappy.

I think I have no need to insist on this point. I will continue and will pose two "whys" that flow from each other:

a. Why were individuals unhappy? Because the immense majority were deprived of the ability to satisfy their needs.

b. Why were they deprived of this ability?

• Because for centuries and centuries a certain number of men seized control of all riches and all its sources to the detriment of other men.

- Because the owning class had issued laws legitimizing and consolidating their spoliations.

- Because they organized governmental authority and forces whose role was that of subjugating the despoiled, preventing them from rebelling, and, in case of revolt, punishing them.

- Because this owning class and these masters dreamed up religions, whose goal was imposing on the dispossessed and the enslaved submission to laws, respect for masters, and resignation to their own misfortune.

- Because this hoarding of wealth, this legislation, this power and this religion were powerfully united against the multitude of the exploited and oppressed, who were thus deprived of the ability to eat their fill, to speak, to write, to assemble as they wish, to think and act freely.

- Because property was the authority of a class over things; the state the authority over bodies; the law the authority over consciences; and religion the authority over minds and hearts.

- Because all those who did not belong to the dominant class—in whose hands were gathered capital, the state, the law, and religion—formed an immense class of poor people, subjects, citizens, and the resigned.

- Because physically, intellectually, and morally this multitude was reduced to slavery.

- Because in a word, it wasn't free.

This class did not own yesterday and does not possess today the freedom to satisfy the needs of its body, its mind, and its heart.

This is what both history and experience tell us if they are consulted honestly, attentively, and impartially.

They say that in past and present societies, by far the most numerous class was unhappy because it wasn't free, and the situation is the same today.

The cause of all evil is authority in all the forms I have enumerated. The remedy thus consists in smashing all the gears of this authority—capital, state, law, and religion—and the founding of an entirely new society based on freedom.

This then is the second certainty. I will connect it to the first, at which point we will have the entire doctrine.

First certainty: Man seeks happiness; society's end is to ensure it; the best form of society is that closest to this goal.

Second certainty: Man is happy insofar as he is free to satisfy his needs; the worst of societies is thus that in which he is least free; consequently, the best is that in which he is most free. The ideal is one where he will be completely so.

Conclusion: anarchist doctrine can be summed up in one word, Freedom.

***

But I said that anarchy is 1) a doctrine and 2) a way of life. We will now move from the first to the second, from theory to practice, from the principle to its realization, from doctrine, which inspires and motivates, to life, which fulfills.

It goes without saying that the birth of anarchy (a social state without a government, without a state, without authority, and without constraint) can only follow upon the death of the current social state.

Here begins the second part of my demonstration. History, experience, and reasoning, the three abundant sources from which man draws all useful truths, initially led us to condemn without appeal all societies practicing a regime based on authority and the need to establish a social environment founded on freedom.

And so I imagine the revolution completed: authority is reduced to dust and we are now living in freedom. We have destroyed and now must reconstruct. What will we do?

The half-mad (if they are sincere I can't describe them in any other way) still contemplate the bizarre coupling of the two contradictory principles of freedom and authority. They dream of basing the freedom of all on the authority of some, as if it were possible for authority to give birth to freedom and favor the development of the latter! The anarchists combat this absurdity with implacable logic and ferocious energy. They rise up against any attempt at an authoritarian restoration; they oppose any attempt to resurrect power in any form. They end up carrying the day against their adversaries and smashing their final resistance. This is the more or less lengthy period during which the most pressing duty and the most urgent demand is to defend the victorious libertarian revolution against the return of the supporters of authority, including what to them is its most intolerable, most absurd, and most dangerous form: the dictatorship of the proletariat.

The defenders of the revolution finally understand that two contradictory things cannot mate since they are mutually exclusive, and that consequently, social authority can no more achieve individual liberty than individual freedom can emerge from social authority.

The bankruptcy and the need for the abolition of the authority principle have been definitively established. All that is left is to give the freedom principle a living and fertile reality.

Let us examine more closely the problem to be resolved, not losing sight of the fact that we presuppose the smashing of governmental authority by the triumphant revolution. The individual has been freed of his chains and has become free, that is, in possession of the ability to satisfy his needs and so to be happy.

But, as a social being, living and participating in life in common, we must specify what he will bring to his peers and what he will receive from them; under what conditions and to what extent he will collaborate in the satisfaction of the needs felt by all and will participate in the satisfaction of his own needs.

The problem is both pressing and urgent.

How to resolve it? One must not think of resorting to force, violence, and constraint, all of which are forms of authority, but rather to kindness, persuasion, and reason, which are varieties of freedom.

Let us pause, then, at reason.

But again, reason must impose itself on its own, by virtue of its own strength, by the influence of its prestige alone, and not through threats or sanctions.

And so we seek, we experiment, we consult, we examine the results of its various modes of application, and agreement appears, presents itself, and is recommended by its results, in so doing carrying the day.

Nature's example in this regard is eloquent and demonstrative. Everything there is agreement, freely accepted and spontaneous through affinities and characteristics shared among individuals or units of the same species. Things infinitely small, virtually dust, seek each other out, attract each other, combine and form nuclei. These nuclei in turn seek each other out, attract each other, combine and form organisms. These organisms seek each other out, attract each other, combine, and form ever vaster organisms.

[...]

This is the method of free and spontaneous agreement: The smallest unit, the individual, seeks and attracts others, combines with them in an original nucleus and forms the commune. The communes, in turn, seek each other out, combine and form a more vast and complex organization: the nation.

We then have agreement between the individuals and families who constitute the communal nucleus; agreement between the communes that constitute the regional organism; agreement between the regions that constitute the national organization; agreement from low to high, at all levels; agreement everywhere.

The people living under libertarian communism seek each other out, attract each other, combine and form an organization even more vast than the nation.

The day when all nations will be living under libertarian communism they will necessarily seek each other out, will inevitably attract each other, and will combine in forming an immense international organism, uniting all. This will constitute the global realization of freedom for all through agreement among all.

What must not be lost sight of is that it is no longer a matter, as in the past, of an organization with the widest reach, of a central organization that, through absorption or annexation, through constraint or war brings about the suppression of intermediary organizations and nuclei to arrive at the crushing of individual molecules. On the contrary, it is the individual molecule that, through agreement, extension, and development, adheres to the closest molecules and forms a nucleus with them. Then passing through increasingly vast organisms, with the circle of agreement growing ever-larger, it unites the totality of individual molecules in an ever more intense, fertile, and joyful life.

This is a picture of libertarian communist life, of the freedom of each as a result of the agreement of all.

***

Anarchy is fundamentally individualist. Governments, religions, fatherlands, and moralities have this in common, that in the name of the so-called higher interests of these institutions, the true interests of the individual have always been and continue to be unrecognized, violated, and sacrificed. Governments repress, oppress, and pressure the individual. Religions deprive him of the faculty of thinking freely and reasoning judiciously. Fatherlands push him into the carnage of war against his will. Moralities create the most inept obligations, and those obligations most contrary to his natural expansion and normal life weigh on him. Through ignorance and cowardice, through force and repression, all of these authoritarian institutions create in the masses the slave mentality and the herd-like habits the dominant classes need to perpetuate the regime of which they are the sole and insolent beneficiaries. Anarchy wants to shield all human beings from the multitude of physical, intellectual, and moral constraints of which they are victims. It denies society the right to sovereignly dispose of those who compose it. It declares that the vague term "society" corresponds to nothing outside the individuals who alone give it a living and concrete reality. It certifies that without that tangible, palpable unity, the Individual, society would be a non-existent totality and an expression stripped of any positive meaning. These are assertions so manifestly clear that one feels a certain shame in formulating them for fear of being accused of pushing against an open door.

But it must not be thought that if anarchism is, at its heart, individualist it should follow that anarchism condemns the individual to isolation and that it cuts the bonds that unite him to his fellows.

The opposite is the case, and it is impossible to conceive a social environment in which the relations connecting all the representatives of the species would be more numerous and more solid than under anarchy. The fundamental contradiction is that today the individual is imprisoned in a network of obligations and constraints forged in the name of the state, property, religion, morality, the family, the fatherland, and other hobby-horses. These constraints turn him into a slave who is forced to participate in a large number of associations, complicities, and contracts that he was not free to decide upon, not having been consulted. This same individual, having become free in an anarchist society, will have the latitude to dispose of himself in all regards, his only obligations being those he deliberately and consciously contracted. Under an authoritarian regime the bonds chaining men to each other are rigid, artificial, and mandatory; in anarchy the only valid contracts uniting people will be those freely agreed to, and these contracts will always be flexible, natural, freely accepted, and freely broken. [...]

***

People have long likened, if not confused, the tendencies and aspirations of collectivist or communist collectivism to those of anarchism. There were many reasons for this parallel, some of which are:

1. Socialism and anarchism rose up against bourgeois society. In both cases the slogan was that it was above all necessary to be rid of the latter and we'll see later on what will replace it. For years, socialists and anarchists attacked with equal fervor and virulence the bourgeoisie's institutions, government, property, fatherland, religion, and morality, whose ruin they both pursued.

2. The favored few, having an interest in causing and maintaining this confusion between socialism and anarchism, unscrupulously distorted the theories, unrestrainedly slandered the theoreticians, and persecuted without distinction socialist and anarchist agitators. Did they turn to the well-to-do? In that case they accused the socialists of wanting to substitute for the established order a society in which, held back neither by a moral brake nor material

authority, unleashed appetites would be given free rein to steal, lay waste, rape, and murder. Did they address the disinherited? They asserted that anarchists and socialists, the former openly and the latter underhandedly, only worked for the social revolution in order to dispossess the rulers and the wealthy so they could enjoy power and wealth.

3. The socialists themselves, while defending themselves from any comparison to the anarchists, willingly allowed it to be understood—especially during electoral periods, when they begged for working-class suffrage—that all in all there was no irreducible opposition between socialism and anarchism, but on the contrary many affinities and important points of contact; that the divergences above all (some said exclusively) resided in the problem of the tactics to be employed, and that despite it all, even though their paths and methods might differ, the goal was the same: the suppression of antagonistic classes and the replacement of the political state by an organism of registration rather than repression, aimed at assuming the administration of things, the welfare of each, and liberty for all. The number of workers who, indoctrinated in this way, fell into the trap and allowed themselves to be enlisted as voters and members of collectivist and communist parties is incalculable.

4. In keeping with the rule of impartiality we have imposed on ourselves here, it should be added that a good number of socialists spoke sincerely when they expressed themselves in this way. They were for a long time few in number. The favors of so-called universal suffrage went to the monarchist or republican parties of social conservatism, and the socialist militants, with the exception of a few more clear-sighted and ambitious leaders, viewed the electoral struggle and parliamentary activity strictly as means of propaganda and agitation. But since then, things have changed.

These various circumstances quite clearly explain the confusion I am discussing. Reality fades gradually away with this confusion and today the stark and profound rupture has occurred between anarchy, or libertarian communism, and authoritarian socialism (the socialist and communist parties).

Both of these doctrines emerged from the period of experimentation that all social ideas, given birth to by historical conditions, traverse. Socialism and anarchism currently form two totally distinct and even opposed movements as to their bases, methods, actions, and goals.

They are separated by an abyss, the socialists and communists wanting to conquer the state and have it serve their ends, the anarchists wanting to annihilate the state.

Let us go into some detail. Socialism builds on the authority principle and, in practice, logically arrives at the reinforcement of this principle, since the state, once in the power of the socialists, has a mandate to centralize and monopolize political and economic power.

To start with, the socialist and communist parties of all countries assert that society cannot live without the authority principle they declare indispensable to organization and agreement. The freedom of each, they say, must end where the freedom of all begins. But in the absence of laws, of rules that fix this limit between the freedom of each man and that of others, every man will be naturally led to extend his own freedom at the expense of the rest. These encroachments will constitute so many abuses, injustices, and inequalities, which will provoke endless conflicts and, lacking an authority with the ability to resolve these conflicts, they will be resolved by force and violence alone.

The strongest will abuse their strength against the weakest, and the most cunning, the most mischievous, will abuse their wiles against the most sincere and honest.

Having posited this, authoritarian socialists add that it is folly to conceive of a social organization without laws, without regulations.

Above all, they base themselves on the needs of economic life. If each is free to choose his type of labor and to work or do nothing, some will work a great deal, others less, and others still not at all. The lazy will be at an advantage in relation to the hard-working. If everyone is free to consume as he would like, with no control or verification, there are those who will set up housing in the nicest apartments and take the most beautiful furniture and clothing and the choicest morsels, while others will be forced to be happy with what is left over. This will not be and should not be acceptable. Laws and regulations are needed to establish the amount to be produced by everyone, at least the number of hours he must work and the proportion of what is produced that fall to him. If not, there will be waste, discord, and famine.

The authoritarian socialists add: "If everyone is free to do as he pleases, all he pleases, and only what pleases him, there will be an unhindered overflowing of passions, the triumph of vice, and impunity for all crimes." They conclude that authority is necessary, that a government is indispensable, and that laws and regulations are needed in all their rigor. And that consequently a public force (police and soldiers) is necessary for the suppression of riots and to arrest the guilty, as are tribunals to judge them, and sentences to punish them.

Even so, even those socialists and communists most enamored of the notion of the state declare that a day will definitely come when, having gradually been transformed, men will become conscious, will have an enlightened sense of responsibility, and will become reasonable and brotherly. At that moment authority will disappear and make way for anarchy, which, they admit, is the most elevated and just ideal, one they consider the end point of social evolution.

In conclusion, they say: "Let us begin by overturning the capitalist regime. First let us expropriate the bourgeoisie and socialize the means of production, transport, and exchange. Let's organize labor on a new basis, and afterward we'll see to the rest."

The anarchists reply: "Capitalist society is built on individual property and the state. Property would have no power or value if the state wasn't there to defend it. It is a serious error to think that capital is the sole agent of discord between men living in society. The structure of power plays every bit as much a divisive role. Capital divides them into two classes: the haves and the have-nots. The state also divides them into two classes; the rulers and the ruled. The owners of capital abuse their wealth to exploit the proletarians; the holders of political power abuse their authority to enslave the people.

"Doing away with the capitalist regime while maintaining the state means making only half a revolution, or not even making it at all, for authoritarian communism will require a formidable army of functionaries in the legislative, judiciary, and executive spheres. The order advocated by authoritarian communism will involve incalculable expenses. It will abolish neither classes nor privileges.

"The French Revolution thought it had abolished the privileges of the nobility; it did nothing but transmit them to the bourgeoisie. This is what authoritarian communism will do: it will wrest their privileges from the bourgeois and transfer them to the leaders of the new regime.

"These latter will form a new class of the privileged. Charged with making laws, with elaborating regulations, with punishing their violation, the mass of functionaries whose occupation this will be will form a separate caste: it will produce nothing and sponge off those who will assure production. There will be a rush of insatiable appetites and envies fighting over power, the best posts, and the most profitable sinecures. There will be a mad scramble over the pickings.

"A few years after the revolution we'll see the same discord, the same inequalities, the same competition, and finally, under the pretext of order, the same disorder and waste. Nothing will have been done and everything will have to be started over again, with this difference, that while the capitalist regime is disqualified, rotten, and on the eve of bankruptcy, which means it can be overthrown without any great difficulty, the authoritarian communism that will replace it will have its youth going for it and its future ahead of it.

"All of history pronounces a sentence on the authority principle. Under different forms, names, and labels, authority has always been synonymous with tyranny and persecution. Not only has it never protected or guaranteed freedom but it has always violated, deprecated, and slandered it.

"Trusting authority to ensure the freedom of all and to contain itself within the limits of justice is pure madness."

And to finish with the subject, the anarchists tell the socialists and communists:

"You want to impose everything by force; we want to establish everything through reason. You believe only in violence; we trust only persuasion. You conceive order from above; we conceive it from below. You intend everything to be centralized; we intend for everything to be federalized. You go from the compound to the simple, from the general to the particular, from number to unity; i.e., from society to the individual. We go from the simple to the compound, from the particular to the general, from the unit to number, i.e., from the individual, the sole tangible, living, palpable reality, to society, the totality of individuals. You base shared freedom on the subjection of each; we base the freedom of all on the independence of each.

"When we will be capable of overturning bourgeois society we will at the same time destroy capital and the state. This will be no more difficult a task than overturning one and not the other, because they sustain each other and at present form a single whole.

"Since you recognize that freedom is desirable and that libertarian communism is the noblest and most just ideal, the best and surest means of realizing this ideal is to combat and not to strengthen the authority principle, which is its negation. [...]"

***

Anyone who lends an attentive ear to the sinister cracking of the social edifice could boldly predict its imminent collapse. The crisis the world is currently confronting, a crisis as broad as it is deep, is so serious that it does not fool sensible people of any party, any class, or any continent. In the east and the west, in the north and the south the malaise grows, discontent increases, fear mounts. The old European powers that, through their economic and military organization, conquered an immense colonial empire in other parts of the world view with fear the revolt of the peoples they thought they'd forever colonized, that is, enslaved. The hour approaches when these populations, determined to take their own destinies in hand will wrest the territories occupied by their conquerors and proclaim their independence.

Ancient belief systems, spread by the imposters of all religions, see their prestige constantly shrink and human consciousness, for so long a prisoner of ignorance, superstition, and fear, is liberating itself from the captivity it has so greatly suffered under. The impotence of political parties is glaringly obvious and the rotting of states is there for all to see. The world of labor has become conscious of the intolerable iniquity of a social organization in which, though it produces all, it possesses nothing. From the cottage of the peasant to the slum of the workers crushed by endlessly accruing fiscal charges there rises a protest that is timid today but will be furious tomorrow. Everywhere, absolutely everywhere the spirit of revolt is replacing the spirit of submission. The vivifying and pure wind of liberty is rising; it is on the march and nothing will stop it. The moment approaches when violent, tempestuous, and fearsome, it will hurl like a hurricane and blow away all authoritarian institutions as if they were straw.

Evolution is moving in this direction. It is leading humanity toward anarchy.

—SÉBASTIEN FAURE

Atheism   The word atheism is formed from two Greek words: "a," the negative particle, and the noun "theos," god. Atheism is the theory of those who do not recognize any kind of god, any being higher than human nature, any intelligence regulating the movements of the universe and intervening in the affairs of men.

The opposite of atheism is theism, one of whose forms is deism.

An atheist, who does not want an all-powerful on earth (an authoritarian government) must necessarily reject the idea of an omnipotent master to which everything must be subject. He must, if he is conscious, declare himself an atheist in the common meaning of the term, but that does not suffice if one wants to understand the difficulties this word has forever raised and the idea people seem to have adopted about it.

Atheism has incited hatred, the scorn of those who have not understood either its philosophy, its morality, or its history. To begin with, we will quote the opinions of several well-known authors:

– "Atheism is an unnatural and monstrous opinion, difficult to establish in the human mind, however deranged it might be." (Montaigne)

– "There is no atheism except in coldness, egoism, and degradation." (Madame de Staël)

– "If atheism does not spill the blood of men it's less from love of peace than from indifference to the good." (J. J. Rousseau)

– "A proof that atheism is not rooted in the heart is the itch to spread it. When one doesn't mistrust one's opinions one has no need of seeking supports and defenders." (A. Bacon)

All of these phrases from philosophers are hollow and in a few words one can undo their effect. In this article, we hope to demonstrate that there is no basis for these objurgations thrown in the face of atheists.

Let us look at the phrase of the celebrated English philosopher, author of the *Novum Organum*. What party doesn't seek to gain converts? Do they not all have newspapers and books to defend their ideas? Aren't Christians the first ones to preach in their churches, to send out missionaries? Should we think that they all doubt the dogmas they teach? But we know that there are Christians, or simply theists, thoroughly convinced of the dogmas they seek to spread.

"Atheism," said Bossuet, "impoverishes humanity and robs it of its greatest possessions: God, the soul, and immortality."

To which we respond that the existence of none of these goods has been scientifically proven and that every free mind can legitimately doubt or even deny their existence. All religious sects claim that atheism leads to evil, that atheists are necessarily vicious men who adopted atheist ideas in defiance of a divinity justly offended by their scandalous life.

We will not stop here to ask the definition of the words "virtue," and "vice" whose definitions vary with every individual, every country, every epoch, every profession.

Believers affirm that among the direct causes of atheism are lack of education, depraved societies, and a licentious life. But anyone who has taken the trouble to study it with an open mind recognizes that atheists are perhaps those the most virtuous, the most honorable, the most devoted to humanity. Who can be compared to the Reclus brothers, those models of everything good, though clearly anarchists and atheists. How noble are Kropotkin, Bakunin, Chernyeshevsky, Myshkin, Shelley, Carlyle, Holcroft, Owen, and William Morris, all of whom fought for atheism and freedom! And in France, have we not seen men like Sylvain Maréchal, Lalande, Laplace, Helvétius, and Berthelot, all of them models of virtue and science? We will see later in this study that since the most ancient of times, since Confucius, Lao Tse, since Gautama Shakyamuni, called the Buddha, since the ancient Greek philosophers up till our time atheists and agnostics (who, for me, are atheists, since they do not affirm the existence of a God) far from being wantons or dishonest were models of all that is praiseworthy.

The statistics of prisons and penitentiaries in the United States prove that these establishments are full of pious men raised in religious environments who maintained theist ideas all their lives, while atheists, numerous in the population, are virtually unknown among the pensioners of the state. If atheists can be found among them they are men sentenced for political reasons, as advocates of anarchist ideas, or for clearly blasphemous speech, which is forbidden by the law of several American states and even in English legislation. Even today, it is enough to publicly deny God for theist judges to sentence a speaker to months of detention, which happened not too long ago to the propagandist Gott, sentenced to several months of prison for having distributed atheist pamphlets, even though his name means God. The poor man died in prison.

Bradlaugh, the great English orator, who had incited so much hatred and exposed himself to so many judicial proceedings by his atheist speeches, was expelled from the House of Commons because he declared during the elections that the name of God meant nothing to him. Being the idol of the working-class population of Northampton he was re-elected after every invalidation and succeeded in having the mandatory oath abolished in England.

Bradlaugh had written that conscious atheism provides more possibilities for human happiness than any system based on theism, and that the life of true atheists is more virtuous because more humane than those of believers in the divinity, the humanity of believers often being neutralized by the faith with which this humanity is necessarily constantly in conflict.

"Correctly understood, atheism is not simple incredulity, a cold and arid negation. On the contrary, it is a fertile affirmation of all proven truth, containing within it the positive assertion of the most elevated human activity." (*A Plea for Atheism*)

The atheist doesn't say, "There is no God," for it is impossible to prove a negative. He says, "I don't know what you mean by God; I have no idea what that is. For me, the word God is a sound that provides me with no clear or distinct affirmation. I do not deny God because I cannot deny what I have no concept of and about which the concept of believers is so imperfect that they are incapable of defining it for me. But if one wants to define God as an existence other than the existence of which I am a part, I affirm that such a God is impossible."

The initial difficulty of every religious polemic is, in fact, defining the word "God." It is equally impossible to affirm or deny a proposition unless between the affirmer and the negator there is an agreement on the meaning of every word of the proposition. Bradlaugh said: "I find this word frequently employed by educated individuals who have earned a reputation in various branches of the sciences, more to disguise their ignorance than to explain what they know." Various theist sects attribute meanings to this word, but these meanings often contradict each other. Among Jewish monotheists, Trinitarian Christians, Socinians, or Unitarians, among the ancient polytheists and Calvinists, the word God in each case expresses an idea absolutely irreconcilable with those of other sects.

When believers seek to reach an agreement about a definition they arrive at nothing. When the theist affirms that God is a different being, separate from the material universe; when he adorns this hypothetical being with numerous attributes (omniscience, omnipotence, omnipresence, immutability, immortality, perfect kindness) the atheist can respond: "I deny the existence of such a being because this theist definition is self-contradictory and contrary to daily experience." […]

"God is the name men have given their ignorance from the beginning of time until today" (Max Nordau, *Man's Morality and Evolution*). If one speaks to an atheist of God the Creator he answers that the concept of creation is impossible. It is impossible for us to imagine that nothing can become something or that something can become nothing. The words creation and destruction denote a change in phenomena; they do not denote the origin or cessation of the substance.

The theist who speaks of God creating the universe must suppose that this God drew it from within himself or that he produced it out of nothing. But the theist cannot view the universe as the evolution of the deity, because this would identify the universe with the deity, which would be pantheism ("pan" from the Greek "all" and "theos," God). There would be no distinction of substances, and no creation. The theist also cannot view the universe as created out of nothing, since according to him the deity is necessarily eternal and infinite. The existence of an eternal and infinite God excludes the possibility of the concept of the void that must be filled with the created universe. No one can think of a point in the vastness or duration and say: here is the separation point between the creator and the created. It is equally impossible to conceive an absolute beginning and an absolute end of existence.

The atheist affirms that he knows the effects, that the latter are both causes and effects, the causes of effects they preceded and effects of causes that precede them. There is, thus, no creation and no creator.

Not a single believer has any idea other than that of an anthropomorphic God (i.e., one in human form). All depict God in the form of an old man seated on a throne and floating in the clouds.

Raphael and the painters of the Renaissance painted him as an old man with a long beard, flying through the air in his enormous robe. In church paintings, even those by painters of genius like Michelangelo, we see the deity painted in flesh and blood, sometimes his head surrounded by a halo, a holdover from the cult of the sun, sometimes forming the center of a triangle.

In my trips to Russia I often saw peasants who, before removing their hats when entering a church, sought the image the Orthodox usually have in a corner of their room, and when they didn't see the icon asked *"Gdie bigh?"* (where is God?). For them, this piece of painted wood in a gilded frame was actually God, a portrait of God. [...]

The Bible speaks to us of Gods (Elohim, plural of El, the Semitic God) creating light before the sun and forming with his hands first a hermaphrodite being, male and female, then, in a second account of creation, Yahweh (the God of a tribe of Sinai) formed an isolated being and, while he slept, tore out a rib to create a woman. He planted trees expressly to make his creatures succumb to temptation. From his heaven he can't see what's happening in the garden of Eden and descends in order to stroll about and watch over the conduct of the two spouses, sewing garments for them. God makes himself visible to Moses face to face, while another time he only shows his back. God engraves the commandments in stone with his finger, while elsewhere he struggles an entire night with Jacob on the banks of Jabbok and is defeated by the man. God is thus a material being.

All the holy books of the East that speak of Gods depict them as beings, as superior humans. The New Testament says that God is spirit, which means absolutely nothing, since for most men light and heat are spirits, when they are nothing but manifestations of the movements of matter. What in psychology is called spirit is nothing but one of the functions of the brain, thus a manifestation of matter. God would then be material, something as absurd as it is impossible. [...]

***

Let us now examine the so-called proofs of the existence of God. The first argument that every Christian throws out in a discussion with an atheist is that of Fénelon and Bossuet that has been repeated ad nauseam: a clockmaker is needed to make a watch, a painter a painting, an author for everything, and I call that author God, thus God exists. This argument has no more worth than a soap bubble. If a creator was needed to create the world, who created this creator and the creator of this creator, and so on to infinity. The theist proof is nothing but a petition of principle, for it is the assertion of creation because this creator exists; but this original creator cannot be, for it can always be pushed further back to another creator and, what is more, creation has not been proved and probably never will be, for science does quite well without the idea of creation.

Fénelon thought he'd said all that had to be said by opposing the idea of God to chance. But chance might well only be a God, while science, as it exists today, recognizes laws, not chance; these laws are eternal to the extent we can deduce them through observation. There is thus no God. Fénelon's arguments are at times pure childishness, for example: "If water was more or less dense than it is it could not support ships," which is the same as saying that the waters were created to carry ships and not that ships were invented to navigate on waters.

"If the earth were more or less hard than it is it could not be cultivated and it could not support man." Always the famous principle: It is God who created all this for Man, for the good of Man, God's favorite. Poisonous snakes, wild beasts, scorpions, bugs, fleas, pathogenic bacteria, typhoid fever, leprosy, tuberculosis, cancerous flies, et cetera, were thus created for the divinity's beloved?

All of Fénelon's book, which in my days was used in philosophy classes, is filled with arguments as strong as that on the density of waters, the beauty of nature, and the instincts of animals. Fénelon writes things as astonishing as this: "All the qualities of persons and things come from God; intelligence is a quality; thus, God gives us intelligence, thus God exists."

The same goes for our clearest ideas and common sense. The same goes for our higher thoughts. A moment's reflection would suffice for a child to see the weakness of such an argument. It is always the petition of principle. The Bishop of Cambrai begins by accepting a superior being's design instead of proving to us that this supreme intelligence exists.

Another equally ridiculous argument is that of the beauty of the human body. "If the head were smaller than it is it would be out of proportion with the rest of the machine. If it were larger, aside from being disproportionate and deformed, it would weigh down the neck and would risk causing man to fall over in whichever direction he would lean."

The author was unaware of all the monstrous animals, the plesiosaurus, the pterodactyl, et cetera, who were given the absurd name of antediluvian and who probably existed for thousands of years, as long as climatic conditions allowed them to nourish themselves though their bodies, according to our modern ideas, were disproportionate and poorly conditioned. After having read Fénelon no intelligent reader could fail to recognize that no valid proof of God's existence can be found there.

So-called metaphysical proofs are no better. The Catholic apologist J. J. Auguste Nicolas, in his *Philosophical Studies of Christianity* (4 volumes in 8, 1842–1845 and often reprinted) thought he had discovered a new proof of God's existence. For him the best demonstration of this existence is that man conceived the very idea of divinity. Every other idea is related to matter: qualities and defects, beauty and ugliness, are always the result of a tacit comparison. But God can be compared to nothing. This argument is false, since for the immense majority of beings who believed or still believe in God, this deity is truly a being or, as the Bible says, a living God. Only material beings are endowed with life. It was only quite late that human intelligence raised itself—if we can speak in this way—to the idea of a spirit that was endowed with all the functions of a human being. Listen to two Christians converse and you'll hear them speak of God's eye, God's finger, the hand of God, God's spirit, God's will, God's anger, et cetera....

Christian apologists give man's idea of the infinite as proof of God's existence. But man, in general, does not reason about the infinite. For the theist God is finite, since he is limited by the universe, or for the believer by the earth and the sky, i.e., by the clouds and the atmosphere. Since it is impossible for two bodies to occupy the same space, God cannot exist if he is infinite, since matter is limited and the infinite spirit would have to be limited by the space occupied by matter.

An argument often used is the assertion that human beings universally recognize the existence of God. But modern travelers have discovered many tribes that have no idea of a superior being governing the earth and the heavens. James Frazer's great work *The Golden Bough* gives many examples of this total absence of knowledge of God. True Buddhists, who are atheists, number in the millions; the disciples of Confucius also know no God. Among modern scientists it is rare to find theists. All true scientists, like Berthelot, Lalande, Laplace, Tyndal, Huxley, Haeckel, Ostwald, et cetera, are either purely and simply atheists or positivists or agnostics, the latter two declaring that since human intelligence cannot discover primary causes they abstain from any concern with them. Theists, since they do not accept a God according to the common notion and general definition, they are atheists in reality. [...]

We now know that everything in the universe is in movement, that all the molecules of bodies are held together by the movement of these molecules and that there is no need of a higher being to sustain this movement or guide it: it is an immutable law of nature. The discoveries of Becquerel, Curie, Le Bon, Rutherford, Carnot, Meyer, Herz, Helmholz, Roentgen, Gresnel, et cetera, have amply demonstrated this. The so-called proof by final causes is equivalent to saying that God created the universe to serve man, which is what theologians preach. Many philosophers have dared declare they were totally ignorant of God's goal. Atheists respond that the universe has no destination and cannot have one. [...]

Let us now return to the arguments against God's existence. They cannot be called proofs since, as we already said, a negative cannot be proved, but it can be proved that the idea of an omnipotent and good God is absurd. The reasoning of Epicurus, the famous Greek philosopher, remains unbeatable. Here it is, as we know it from the refutation of the Church Father Lactantius: God exists, it is thus one thing or the other: 1. God knows that evil exists, wants to prevent it, and can't … Such a God would be powerless, thus inadmissible. 2. God does not know that evil exists … Such a God would thus be blind and ignorant, thus inadmissible. One sees no other possible hypothesis. Thus, God does not exist.

Believers were incensed by Epicurus's dilemma. They want it to be believed that evil exists because in Eden the first man disobeyed, and that this evil serves to improve man. This punishment inflicted on all the descendants of the guilty parties is awful enough to make one doubt the existence of so atrocious a God. But in nature everything suffers: all animals, from the biggest to the microscopic suffer from birth to death. Even plants suffer and decay, raw nature not escaping transformations and what we call death.

Molecules and metals as well are gradually transformed, so there is suffering everywhere. An immutable and good God cannot exist. It is true that philosophers, like Baron de Colins and his disciples believe, like Descartes, that animals have no feelings, that they are machines. This theory is not supported by close observation of animals, and in any event, doesn't a machine itself break down, and can't we consider labor a punishment? It is true that it does not have the nerves and brain that allow living beings to recognize pain, but matter transforming and spoiling is proof that evil exists everywhere, even though animals did not eat the apple with Eve.

Christian Scientists, who have so many followers in America as well as Europe, claim that suffering is not real, that it is a consequence of our imagination. Those who dare say this have never visited a hospital or a madhouse; they have never heard the cries of the ill and wounded. These Christian Scientists have never healed real pain, any more than have visits to pilgrimage places. Once auto-suggestion ceases to work, the pain returns.

And so, evil exists and a God who would have created it, knew it and wanted it, is incomprehensible, impossible.

If God doesn't not know that evil exists then he is even more absurd: he would resemble a God of the Bible who doesn't know what is happening in the earthly paradise and is forced to stroll there to see what the newlyweds are up to. It would be as if Jupiter descended to

earth to pass judgment on the abominations committed there and punished humans with the flood of Deucalion and Pyrrhus for the crime of
King Lycaon. Only those with narrow minds could accept a God like
that of the Bible or the Metamorphoses.

If there is a God, why are there so many religions? Priests claim
that their God is the sole true God. Yet there are an infinite number
of religions. If there were a God, would He not have seen to it that all
humans recognize Him? Dr. Carret sums up this objection thusly:

> There are three possibilities: 1) There is a God. This God wanted to
> manifest himself to humans and the number of religions proves he
> did not succeed. In this case God is powerless, thus inadmissible. All
> religions are then absurd and all their Gods false. 2) There is a God.
> This God did not want to be known to us and cares not a whit for
> our adoration. In this case, all religions are absurd and all their Gods
> false, for none resemble the real God. 3) There is no God. In this
> case, all religions are absurd. No other supposition is possible.

Atheists make use of other arguments to combat belief: the impos-
sibility of free will; the non-existence of an immortal soul; the difference between will and free-will, et cetera. All of this should be subject
of another article in the encyclopedia.

The Spiritualists, who are so active today, many of whom don't
believe in God, believe in the survival of the soul after death. The Insti-
tut Métaphysique of Paris and the Society for Psychical Research of
London seek to prove this survival, but none of their experiments have
proved anything up till now, and none of the manifestations the meta-
physicians speak of have produced anything convincing. We can admit
that the soul is nothing but a function of the brain, and as soon as death
occurs the soul is no more and the molecules of the brain disintegrate.
There is no possibility of immortality.

There is thus no more a soul than there is a God, and Epicurus's
reasoning remains unshakeable.

Friends of good food are called Epicureans. Without being ascetic
one can love the good and be devoted to mankind, and this is what
Epicurus wanted. Happiness for him resided in the satisfaction of
intellectual and moral good.

His disciple Lucretius, in his great poem *De Natura Rerum*, makes this clear.

In all periods, history was forced to recognize the perfect honesty of atheists. Antiquity cited as models of virtue atheists like Diagoras of Mio, who was part of the school of Leucippe, Theodore, and Euhemerus from the school of Syrenius, Strato of Lampsacus, Metrodoros, Plysemos, Hermachos, Polystratus, Basilides, and Protarchus.

We can also include among the atheist all the philosophical schools from Thaies (Anaximander, Anaxagoras, Achellaos) up to Socrates, who was sentenced to death on an accusation of atheism. Among atheists we also must include Heredite, Empedocles, Democritus, Pyrrhon, and the entire Skeptic school (Timon, Aenesdemus, et cetera) and the Stoic school (Zeno, Aristo of Chios, Cleantes, et cetera).

Atheism was always accepted by the enlightened spirits of antiquity, but the establishment in most states of an official religion occasionally prevented the teaching of the doctrine. Governments always made use of their authority and resorted to persecution to crush the terrible negation that at one and the same time shook religion and respect for the state.

Under penalty of death or ruin, atheists were forced to put a brake on their honesty. Montaigne, La Boétie, Charron, Giordano Bruno, and Vanini were atheists, but they didn't dare proclaim this, and the last two paid with their lives for the doubts they expressed about God's existence.

In the eighteenth-century Helvétius, d'Holbach, d'Alembert, and Diderot were atheists, Voltaire and Rousseau, often accused of being atheists were deists, as was Robespierre. On the other hand, Marat, Babeuf, and Buonarroti were atheists, for which their names were sullied by reactionary writers.

The socialists of the early nineteenth century had not yet shaken off the theist spirit, though the word God had no great significance for them.

In Germany, Kant, Schopenhauer, Nietzsche, and their disciples did not recognize a God.

Karl Marx, Engels, Lassalle, and Kautsky were atheists, as were the Hegelians and the democratic socialists. But so as not to shock the masses they abstained from attacking the theist idea.

There are a great many Catholic priests and Protestant pastors who do not believe in God, but out of cowardice and fear of losing their livelihood or their social position they don't make known what they think. I've noted this many times, and some of these frauds have admitted this to me. They continue to preach what they consider lies. One can only pity these men who are dishonest with themselves.

How much they differ from Lalande, the great scientist and continuer of Sylvain Maréchal's *Dictionary of Atheists*. Though looked on askance by Napoleon because of his opinions, he wrote: "I take more pride in my progress in atheism than I am in that which I've made in astronomy. The spectacle of the sky seems to everyone to be proof of God's existence. When I was nineteen this is what I believed. Today I see in it nothing but matter and movement."

—G. BROCHER[1]

---

1. Gustave Brocher (1850–1931). Son of a Fourierist, Brocher studied theology and was a pastor in England for three years. Upon returning to France he became active in revolutionary circles and was the secretary of the organizing committee of the International Anarchist Congress of 1881. He remained active until his death and was noted as a free-thinker.

Bandit (from the Italian *bandito*) According to the bourgeois definition of the word, a bandit is an individual in open revolt against the law who lives off armed attacks. The bourgeoisie doesn't fail to catalog all rebels under the epithet of bandit, all those who don't bend their necks beneath its yoke. This is done to attract public reprobation to rebels and discredit them in the eyes of the unthinking mass. Among the individuals designated under the name of bandits, a distinction must be made. There are those who attack bourgeois property with the sole goal of appropriating this property to themselves without expending any effort and are animated by the same vices and the same egoism as the owning class. These bandits do not interest us very much. Only the means employed to enjoy wealth are different, but the mentality remains the same. But there is another category of bandits we are prepared to defend, come what may. These are the unfortunates who, in order to have something to eat or to escape intolerable tyranny, wage war on society. The latter are victims of the current state of affairs and they cannot be blamed for resorting to extreme solutions.

For anarchists, they are no longer bandits but rather unfortunates who defend their right to live, their share of sunshine and light. They are victims who rebel and no longer want to accept the burden of poverty. They should be pitied and assisted and not condemned like wild beasts.

Does this mean there are no bandits on this earth, true bandits? Not at all. Society is unfortunately infested with unscrupulous vultures who spread poverty and death: these are the exploiters of all kinds, legal bandits who steal from their contemporaries under the complicitous eye of the gendarmes. Bandit: the factory manager who enriches himself on the backs of the workers who toil their lives away and who they allow to die like dogs the day when, old and worn out, they can no longer resist the fatigue of the workshop. Bandit: the banker who tricks poor devils, takes their hard-earned savings from them, and ruins them through stock market speculation. Bandit: The statesman who unleashes a war in which naïve workers will be massacred. These are the real bandits, those we must never cease unmaking.

Bolshevism It is since the revolution of 1917 that this phenomenon—Bolshevism—has acquired international celebrity. Before then, the name of Bolshevism was barely known outside Russian "professional" revolutionary circles, where it was considered the left fraction of the country's Social Democratic movement. Nevertheless, even before the revolution, this fraction represented a vigorous political party, solidly attached to the revolutionary worker's movement, aspiring to dominate it while at the same time adhering to the slogans of revolution and bourgeois democracy. The depth, the élan of the Russian Revolution of 1917 provided a constellation of political parties excellent terrain to tempt fortune, to take their chances in the favorable atmosphere of a social cataclysm unprecedented in human history. The Bolshevik Party was one of the parties in this constellation. It, too, took part in the race for happiness.

The complete collapse of the agrarian and industrial regime of old Russia—a collapse that made the ascendant march of the revolution predictable—forced this party to abruptly change its social democratic tactics and pushed it to a political boldness it had never dared consider before: the seizing of political power based on social upheaval.

The success of the revolution allowed it to solidly establish itself in power and arrogate to itself the position of master of the entire Russian Revolution. This fact suggested the idea that Bolshevism was the most revolutionary left wing of the Russian workers' movement, which had carried off victory over capitalism.

Widespread in bourgeois circles, as well as in certain revolutionary milieu unaware of the true situation, and supported by the Bolsheviks own demagogy, this idea is, however, completely erroneous.

Bolshevism is the direct heir and the powerful spokesman for not the revolutionary aspirations of the revolutionaries of the working class and the peasantry but of the political struggle that for a century was carried out by the stratum of Russian democratic intellectuals (the democratic "intelligentsia") against the tsarist political system with the aim of conquering certain political rights for itself.

In order to establish the genealogy as well as the social, class nature of Bolshevism, it is indispensable that we examine, even if only briefly, the emancipatory movement in Russia in general.

For centuries, the revolutionary movement in Russia advanced via two separate currents: one, younger, emerged directly from within enslaved labor. The other had its source in the democratic intellectual circles of Russian society, circles that had formed later and, in comparison with the workers and peasants, enjoyed considerable social and economic privileges but that were hostile to the tsarist political regime because of its absolutism.

The first popular current of the movement had a social character. It was a revolt of the world of labor against its social subjection and it aimed at the overturning of the very foundations of this subjugation. Such was the famous revolt of Stenka Razin in the seventeenth century, a revolt that raised up millions of peasants of the Volga, the Don, and other regions for the extermination of agrarian lords and nobles in the name of "a free peasant kingdom." The Pugachev rebellion of the eighteenth century was similar, and under serfdom countless smaller scale peasant riots and insurrections had the same character. Finally, in their meaning and tendencies, the immense strike movements of the proletariat of the cities that formed rapidly in the second half of the nineteenth century were of the same nature, movements that between 1900–1903 took on pan-Russian dimensions.

The other current of the Russian revolutionary movement, issued from democratic intellectual circles, had a political character. Its fundamental and unwavering goal was that of a transformation of the absolutist tsarist system into a constitutional or democratic republican one.

The uprising of the Decembrists on December 14, 1825 can be considered the beginning of this insurrectionary movement, a date on which a group of officers, at the head of the regiments under their orders, attempted a coup d'état in support of the constitution. The insurrection was drowned in blood by Tsar Nicholas I, but once unleashed the movement could not be stifled. On the contrary, the generations that followed it continued and deepened it. The most remarkable stages of this movement were the Narodnitchestvo and the Narodovoltchestvo.

The Narodnitchestvo (1860–1870) was a movement whose essential trait was a kind of pilgrimage to the deepest depths of the peasant mass. Thousands of young people belonging to the privileged classes abandoned their families and careers, broke with their class, dressed like peasants or workers, and went off into the countryside to live and work as simple peasants, while at the same time doing propaganda work. They sought to awaken in the peasant masses an interest in political slogans for a political revolution of democratic intellectuals.

The Narodovoltchestvo was the high point of the revolutionary movement of the intelligentsia. At that time, the movement had become socialist in character and slogans. It produced a magnificent series of heroic natures who, by their idealism and self-sacrifice in the struggle against tsarism, rose above the caste interests of the intelligentsia and moved closer to the broader interests of labor. Such were Sofia Pereskovaya and others. The clandestine organization Narodnaia Volia (The People's Will), created at this time (1879) delivered bitter combat against tsarism. This combat, which ended with the assassination of Tsar Alexander II (on March 11, 1881), brought about the destruction of Narodnaia Volia and the advent of a horrific regime of political reaction under the reign of Tsar Alexander II. This result was predictable, for Narodnaia Volia was nothing but a small clandestine and conspiratorial organization that, while exhorting the peasants to insurrection, had practically none of the organized and powerful peasant masses behind it and was consequently forced to limit itself to its own means and activities.

The failures of these small, conspiratorial organizations, as well as the penetration of Marxist ideas into Russia, led to the creation in Russian intellectual circles of a new current that in the struggle against tsarism wanted to orient itself, not toward the fractured peasant masses, as had been the case until then, but exclusively toward the urban proletariat. "The revolution in Russia will only succeed as a movement of the working class. If not, it will never occur." It is thus, in the words of Plekhanov, that the new current formulated its departure point in the struggle against tsarism. The young proletariat of the cities, newborn in Russia, offered fertile ground to their movement. The first social democratic group (The Liberation of Labor) was founded in 1880. Fifteen to eighteen years later almost every industrial center of

Russia already had a social democratic organization led by professional politicians recruited from the intelligentsia.

The first congress of these organizations, which led to the creation of the Russian Social Democratic Labor Party, took place in 1898.

A few years later, a serious split occurred in the party. At the Second Congress in London in 1903, the party split into two opposed currents, the majority left and the minority right. The immediate cause of the split was the famous plan for organization proposed by Lenin. The majority (in Russian: *bolshsintsvo*) of the party's members followed Lenin, from which their name, Bolsheviks and its derivative, Bolshevism. The term was thus a result of chance (Bolshevism from *bolshinstvo* = majority). Nevertheless, a solidly determined content hid behind this chance term.

The fundamental idea of Bolshevism, developed by Lenin, was the following: "The working masses are simply the bearers of rebellious instincts of revolutionary energy. By its nature it is incapable of an organizing, creative role. This latter task falls to the group of enlightened revolutionaries dedicated to the idea of revolution. Consequently, the first duty of the party of enlightened revolutionaries is that of establishing its hegemony over the masses. This hegemony is only possible on condition the party itself be constructed on the principle of the strictest centralization. The party must be an organism at the center of which functions a fine-tuned mechanism taking all decisions regarding the party, tolerating no friction, not a single grain of sand. This mechanism is the central committee of the party. Its will and decisions are law for the party."

This was the thesis that served as a basis for the construction of the Bolshevik party.

Recruiting its members largely from among the revolutionary intelligentsia, educating them in the atmosphere of the underground and extreme conspiratorial methods (no other atmosphere ever existed in Russia), grafting onto it the psychology specific to professional revolutionaries, Bolshevism thus prepared cadres accustomed to considering themselves the infallible guides of the proletariat, thanks to their enlightened minds and the revolutionary experience from which alone can emerge the emancipation of the masses. This inevitably left the road open to the inauguration of the dictatorship, first over the party, and then over the masses. Indeed, Lenin's project, which broke Russian social-democracy into two fractions, already introduced the principle of dictatorship into the ranks of the party. [...] From its first days, the Bolshevik party established internally the dictatorship of the Central Committee. Shortly thereafter, this dictatorship began to spread over the working masses.

Thus, a powerful political party appeared and developed on the field of the revolutionary movement of the intelligentsia, founded on centralism and the most rigorous discipline, filled with an unshakable faith in its infallibility, and aspiring with all its will to become the master of the entire Russian revolutionary movement. This party was the direct successor to those of the previous stages of the revolutionary movement of the Russian intelligentsia. It was closely and immediately related to all these movements. Throughout its existence, until the revolution of 1917, it acted under the slogans typical of the movement of this intelligentsia: the Constituent Assembly, a democratic republic, parliament, et cetera. This circumstance is of great importance for whoever wants to understand the true role and intentions of Bolshevism in the Russian Revolution.

In the meanwhile, the popular current of the revolutionary movement continued along its way, manifesting itself from time to time in acts typical of a social movement. Already, in the revolution of 1905–1906, the workers and, even more, the peasants demonstrated little interest in the political demands of democracy. They made their presence felt through acts of a social character: the peasantry by the forcible seizing of seigneurial domains, the workers by the founding in some locales of soviets (councils) of workers' deputies. Both actions were the expression of profound social and revolutionary tendencies inherent in the laboring masses and distinguished them from democratic tendencies. The ten years of tsarist and agrarian reaction that followed the debacle of the revolution of 1914–1917 only developed and strengthened these tendencies in the masses.

In the revolution of 1917, after the first obstacle—tsarist absolutism—was destroyed, these tendencies emerged with all the energy they had accumulated over the centuries and formed a determined, inevitable mass movement aimed at the overthrowing of the agrarian and industrial regime of Russia.

Despite the efforts of many democratic parties, including the Social-Democratic Party and the Socialist-Revolutionaries, to squeeze the revolutionary events into the framework of a bourgeois democratic republic, the peasants and workers rallied behind the powerful slogan, "Land to the peasants! Factories to the workers!" Yes, from the first days of the political turmoil (March 1917) the fate of the country's agrarian and industrial regime was decided. All of working class and peasant Russia was engaged in full reconstructive activity. With the force and the rapidity natural to the spontaneous activity of the masses, Soviets of workers' and soldiers' deputies were consciously created in all cities. In all factories and workshops, in manufacturing and extractive industries, revolutionary committees were created as organs guiding and assisting the working-class masses in their action. All of this was carried out independently and outside of political organizations. In a revolutionary act the peasants seized domains of landowners by force, and the agrarian question, discussed for decades in the programs of the different political parties, found a practical solution in the revolutionary acts of the peasant masses in May, June, July, and August of 1917. Peasant soviets were created in the villages.

The Bolsheviks' attitude at that moment was extremely hesitant. Their central leading group, with Lenin at the head, had just arrived from abroad where all its members had spent the previous eight years as émigrés. Lenin saw perfectly well that the events would not stop with the overthrowing of the tsarist political system, that things would go further. But where would they go? Neither Lenin nor his comrades could predict this. This is why the Bolsheviks' attitude was ambiguous during the first months that followed the coup d'état of March 1917. On one hand they sang half in chorus with the masses, rallying behind their social watchwords. On the other, they did not totally break with the political watchwords of bourgeois democracy. (At that time their party was still called the Bolshevik Social Democratic Party.) From this flowed their wavering, undecided attitude; from this their slogan "control of production," substituted for that of the masses: "the factories to the workers." From this too flowed their slogan of a Constituent Assembly, in contradiction with the masses' "the social revolution."

It was only several months later—a critical and decisive period, one where it became increasingly evident that social upheaval was inevitable—that the Bolsheviks decided in favor of this upheaval, but, as we will soon see, with the sole goal of attaining power, of profiting by this upheaval. It was then that Lenin changed his party's name, baptizing it the Communist Party (instead of Social Democratic Party) seeking in doing so to separate himself in the eyes of the masses from his colleagues on the right—the minority Mensheviks and the Socialist Revolutionaries—who continued to defend the principle of the bourgeois democratic republic, and who with each passing day increasingly compromised themselves in the eyes of the revolutionary masses. It was then that Lenin began to find the anarchists were in the right, that he began to speak of his spiritual closeness to them in the negation of parliamentarism, democracy, and statism (with certain reservations concerning the latter), as well as in a series of other important problems of the social revolution. But as later events would show, his only goal was finding allies among the anarchists and ensuring himself the sympathy of the masses.

The mass movement, both that of prior to October as well as that of October, which aimed at the overthrow of the capitalist system in Russia, needed elements capable of resolutely guiding them ideologically and organizationally, elements that would assist this movement in succeeding and achieving the masses' aspirations: the construction of a free and egalitarian worker and peasant regime. This task, that of guiding the mass movements, at bottom fell strictly to anarchism, the true bearer of ideas of social revolution. But due to their usual lack of organization, which weakened the libertarian movement in all countries, the Russian anarchists showed themselves to be ill-prepared and unable to fulfill their mission. Leadership and the preponderant influence over events throughout the country in the meanwhile passed over to the Bolsheviks. Having definitively lined up on the side of social upheaval, the latter unleashed decisive attacks against the capitalist system. They led all their available forces within the working class and the army in a bitter struggle against the bourgeoisie and their government (called "Provisional Revolutionary"). They had fully appreciated the colossal importance and power of the soviets of workers' deputies, created directly by the masses and immediately become fortresses of labor in its struggle with capital. They deployed all their energy to conquer them. But already they substituted for the idea of social revolution that of "soviet power," having launched the slogan, "All Power to the Soviets!" When the moment arrived that the majority of members of the central soviets were supporters of Bolshevism, the Bolsheviks struck the decisive blow: they overthrew the socialist-bourgeois coalition government, basing themselves on the Soviets as guiding organs of the revolution. The essential role of the system of Soviets of Workers' and Soldiers' Deputies was later spoken of appreciatively by Lenin, who said that if the masses had not created the soviets the Bolsheviks would never have achieved power.

As a consequence of the revolution, power naturally was placed in the hands of the Bolsheviks, become its principal leaders. The revolutionary activity of the Bolsheviks came to an end at this moment and was replaced by clearly counter-revolutionary activity.

Having seized power, the Bolsheviks methodically set out to adapt the political and social regime of the entire country to the regime of their party. Constructed on principles of absolute centralism and military discipline, this party became the model, the outline according to which the Bolsheviks began to construct Russia's new economic and social system. A gigantic statist and bureaucratic machine was formed, which set out to guide, to lead, all the economic, political, and social activity of the entire people, to concern itself with all their needs, to control their entire life, their way of thinking, et cetera.

And so it was that the project for organization proposed by Lenin in 1913, according to which the dictatorial leadership of all party life and activity would be concentrated in the hands of the Central Committee, was now applied on the scale of revolutionary Russia.

***

The creative economic and social activity of the Bolsheviks is divided into two periods, that of state communism and the NEP.

The essential trait of the Bolsheviks' statist communism was the nationalization of industry and commerce. As concerns the land, the Bolsheviks, unable at first to subdue the peasants with the assistance of "physical" methods, signed the decree socializing land. With this act they sought to ensure themselves of the active assistance of the peasant masses in the struggle against Kerensky's provisional government. "Let them [the provisional government] try to catch us now," Lenin said upon signing, after the October coup d'état, the decree on the socialization of land. Later, as the Bolsheviks' authority was reinforced, the decree was replaced by that of the tenant farming of land and by other decrees of the Council of Peoples' Commissars.

The nationalization of industry and commerce signified that the state was henceforth the owner and organizer of all the country's industry and commerce. In the future it would be the state that would direct and regulate the least detail of the economic and commercial process. The elaboration of tariffs, the wage scale, the hiring and firing of workers, arrangements within enterprises—all these measures would be the inalienable rights of the state. The goal would be attained with the assistance of the statization of professional workers' organizations, which would thus become organs of police control of the workers.

However, there was no change in the character, in the essence of industry. The principles of wage labor, of a wage scale, and of surplus value left by the worker in the hands of he who hires him, remained. Industry retained its previous capitalist forms and essence.

As for commerce, there too Bolshevik nationalization completely preserved the principle of "buying/selling," limiting itself in this realm to the establishment of a state monopoly.

As for the realm of agrarian relations, the Bolsheviks limited themselves there, during the period of state communism, to taking "excess wheat" from peasants, which signified that their entire provisions were taken from them by force, minus the strict minimum needed to avoid death from starvation.

The Bolsheviks' state communism was thus nothing but state capitalism that in no way improved the situation of the working world, neither economically nor from the point of view of social rights. Even more, during the period of decadence and the crisis of 1920 this capitalism attempted to realize the idea of the militarization of labor and mandatory labor, which would reduce the entire working class to a state of militarization.

It is perfectly natural that the dictatorship of the party and the capitalist activity of the Bolsheviks gave rise to protests and provoked energetic resistance on the part of proletarian and peasant revolutionary circles, seeking, in keeping with the aspirations of the social revolution, to begin the true socialist innovation: the socialization of industry and the land on the basis of self-management.

The Communist authorities responded to these protests and acts of resistance with terror. It began civil war with the left, over the course of which the supporters of communist anarchism, revolutionary syndicalism, and socialist maximalism were partially annihilated, partially tossed in prison or forced to go into hiding and act clandestinely. The entire non-communist revolutionary press was stifled, the organizations wiped out.

The revolutionary peasant masses, who didn't recognize any authority, were treated with even more ferocity by the communist government. It acted with the assistance of military divisions, enslaving the independent and rebellious regions with their artillery.

Having stifled all attempts at socialist innovation, at socialist self-management of workers and peasants, the Bolsheviks, in so doing, disorganized and killed the economic development of the country, plunging it into a state of putrefaction and decomposition.

Economic disorganization reached its culmination in 1920, with the militarization of labor and the introduction of mandatory labor. It was also the culmination of governmental terror, called on to defend the positions of those in authority. Every day the voices of protest from the revolutionary masses grew louder. In southern Russia, the cannons of revolutionary insurgents, peasants and workers, had thundered for three years already. In March 1921 tens of thousands of revolutionary workers and sailors, the sons of Kronstadt, the citadel of the revolution, rose, weapons in hand, to protest definitively against the mutilation of the revolution by the Bolsheviks, against its transformation into a simple basis for capitalism. They categorically demanded the reestablishment of free elections to the soviets; the reestablishment of revolutionary rights and freedoms; the right to organization and press for anarchists and left socialist currents; and, in general, the return to the watchwords and conquests of the workers and peasants in the October Revolution.

The voice of Kronstadt sounded the tocsin across all of revolutionary Russia.

The moment of the catastrophe of Bolshevism seemed imminent. At whatever cost, a way out had to be found. The "communist" authorities hastily mobilized their military forces and launched them from Petrograd (Leningrad) to crush Kronstadt once and for all. A bitter struggle ensued, where thousands of men of Kronstadt perished, pioneers and heroes of the October Revolution. At the same time, the last forces of the revolutionary movement were crushed in the south.

Bolshevism was victorious. Immediately afterwards, it declared the New Economic Policy: NEP.

This was the beginning of the second period of the constructive economic activity of the Bolsheviks in Russia.

The meaning of the NEP was this: while maintaining large-scale industry and the enormous reserve of lands, as well as a keeping a monopoly in foreign trade in government hands, the Bolsheviks set aside for private capital the second half of industry: the right to (internal) trade, that of exploiting human power (the workers), and that of farming for personal profit.

A capital combine, private and state, was thus established, which led to the creation of new classes of exploiters, that of the bourgeoisies of the cites and the countryside, the Nepmen, and the kulaks (rich farmers exploiting the others).

According to the official data of the Commissariat of Finance, in 1925 the rural bourgeoisie already constituted 13% of all peasant farms, concentrating in its hands 50% of all agrarian production. The same bourgeoisie made up 85.4% in the agricultural cooperatives (the kulaks—well-off peasants—30.1%; the seredniaks, middle peasants, 55.3%) leaving just 14.6% poor peasants. It goes without saying that it was the rural bourgeoise that held the leadership posts in the organs of Soviet power in the countryside.

For their part, the Nepmen were a considerable economic and political force in the cities. There, however, the dominant capitalist force was the Bolshevik party itself. This capitalist power held in its hands all of large-scale industry and immense stretches of land.

The inauguration of the NEP was the natural and inevitable consequence of the contradiction produced between the dictatorial policy of the Bolsheviks on one hand and the aspirations of the revolutionary masses for socialist self-management on the other. Having eliminated these masses from all creative functions in socialist construction, the Bolsheviks created for themselves the situation of an isolated group, holding the national economy in their hands by force of governmental power, but were powerless to set it in motion by their own means.

They had to choose: either give the masses the right to socialist initiative and creativity (in the form of their organizations of production) by themselves taking their place in the ranks of the workers, or maintaining the monopoly of power and dictatorship by relying on other social classes. The Bolsheviks chose the second road. With the NEP they established the social base they lacked, having created economically privileged classes with an interest in the preservation of communist power. As for the workers and peasants, they remained in their usual situation, that of laboring classes.

In the field of international policy, Bolshevism manifested the same tendencies and methods of organization that characterized its political activity in Russia. It aspired to subordinate the international workers' movement to its center and, through its intermediary, all the classes of contemporary society.

The easy victory it had achieved over agrarian and industrial capital in Russia, as well as the general revolutionary situation in Europe, at first inspired it to have faith in the imminent collapse of the capitalist system throughout Europe and the United States and filled it with hope for its international hegemony.

The Comintern and the Profintern were created as organs called on to realize the directives of the Central Committee within the international revolutionary movement. The direct duty of these two institutions was the establishment of the hegemony of Bolshevism over the revolutionary movement of Europe, the United States, and other countries.

The tactic of putsches, adopted for several years in Germany and Estonia, that of splits in socialist parties and the workers' movement, and the more recent one of "contact" or "united front," all of these maneuvers were nothing more than manifestations of the general political strategy of the Central Committee of the Bolshevik Party.

But as the Bolsheviks stimulated the development of capitalism in Russia and reinforced the latter, and as contradictions emerged and grew more explicit between their social system and the real interests of the working masses, becoming veritable social antagonisms, the international policy of the Bolsheviks underwent profound modifications.

The center of this policy gradually shifted from the proletarian milieu to that of the international bourgeoisie. Since 1925 the

Bolsheviks have carried out serious negotiations with the latter aimed at their incorporation into the general network of capitalist states. The basis for the discussions is simply the total renunciation of the "sins of October" in the internal and external policies of the Soviet power.

In internal policy this renunciation has already begun. The 14th Congress of the CPUSSR in December 1925 broke the last ties that still attached the Bolsheviks to the October Revolution by crushing the opposition represented by Zinoviev, Kamenev, and Krupskaya and overtly taking the road to the restoration of capitalism in Russia.

At present in Russia, Bolshevism, aside from the bourgeoise of the cities and country, relies on mechanical forces of order:

- On an enormous party that represents a powerful organization based on ultra-military principles, enjoying social privileges and monopolies, deploying a maximum amount of energy and activity;

- On a magnificently organized (in the statist sense) Red Army, armed and disciplined, surpassing all armies of the world in its military qualities;

- On a political police (the GPU) which deploys an espionage system unprecedented in the history of states, and espionage penetrating every pore of the existence of the laboring masses of the USSR.

***

This is the face and the historical path of Bolshevism.

This movement grew out of the political and statist aspirations of the democratic intelligentsia. Seeking to become master of the revolutionary might of the laboring masses, it only half-heartedly paid tribute to their socialist aspirations and revolutionary slogans. Having succeeded through the revolution in establishing itself in its post as master, it returned to its departure point and restored the edifice of class domination on the basis of forced enslavement and exploitation imposed on the workers.

—P. Archinov

Bomb (from the Italian *bomba*, from the Latin *bombus*, fracas) The word bomb originally meant a hollow, ball-shaped projectile filled with powder, provided with a fuse causing it to explode when fire reaches its charge. By extension the word bomb today also serves to designate an exploding apparatus of variable form and composition and that can be either thrown or posed by hand. Bombs date from the sixteenth century but are no longer used in modern artillery, where they have been replaced by shells. Explosives launched by planes and dirigibles are still called bombs, which can be of considerable volume and weight.

There was a time when bombs were the preferred arm of terrorists and anarchist propagandists of the deed. When a tyrannical government prohibits all free protest, either written or spoken, violence is the sole means of protest left to revolutionaries, and they are forced to resort to it—though they are repelled by its use—because they are gagged by a worse form of violence. From which the rise of terrorism and the use of bombs, for example among the Russian nihilists prior to the revolution of 1917. Among the celebrated attacks in which Russian terrorists employed bombs we will cite Grinevitzky's device of March 1, 1881, which mortally struck Tsar Alexander II.

Class Struggle In this sociological problem we find ourselves confronted with two fundamental, opposed theses. The first is the bourgeois thesis. It recognizes the existence of different classes within modern society, as well as their antagonism. It cannot deny these facts. It is the explanation of them that is characteristic. For bourgeois theoreticians, the existence and antagonism of classes—as well as the inequality of men as to abilities, intelligence, et cetera, which they say is their true cause—are normal phenomena and hence, immutable. This is not all. According to them, the existence, the antagonism, and the bitter struggle between classes are far from having the importance attributed to them by the socialist, syndicalist, and anarchist doctrines. Along with class interests, there exist, they say, many others far more important placed high above the latter, that can and must smooth them out, such as national interests, those of society taken as a whole, those of individuals taken separately, et cetera. From this flows their practical considerations, their political ideas, and their justification of the capitalist system. The interest and advantages of the owning class are, according to them, natural and legitimate. The very nature of human societies demands organizers of national, social, and economic life. The bourgeois class is precisely that great organizer. It must live on and have in its possession the means necessary to exercise its functions, which are essential. It must command, guide, and govern. The capitalist class is far from being one of parasites; on the contrary, it is hard-working. It organizes the life of the masses, it ensures their existence and the order and progress of all of society, of which it is an indispensable element. It handles capital, makes expenditures, and even sacrifices. It runs risks. It is thus natural that it should want to be rewarded for its activities, these complicated and difficult activities, heavy with responsibility, must be duly remunerated. If the other classes are unhappy with them, too bad. It is a result of lack of understanding, of selfishness, envy, and demagogy. The interests of the different classes of society can be perfectly reconciled, and this depends strictly on their good will. It is the state that is called on to play a conciliatory role by placing itself above class interests. It is the state that must attenuate and dissipate the antagonisms that emerge between them. The more successful the state is at this, the more justified is its existence and form. It was democracy that, over the past century, claimed it was most appropriate for fulfilling this task. Today it is fascism that, casting aside a disqualified democracy, makes the same claim. This is the bourgeois thesis.

It is vigorously combated by the concept of class struggle par excellence, the Marxist concept. Its formula, established by Marx himself, asserts that all the struggles that have taken place within human societies over the course of history were, at bottom, class struggles. But there is more. Marxism considers the class struggle as the sole, real determinant element of all manifestations of human life. According to it, class interests can invariably be found at the heart of all these manifestations. And not only the social, economic, political, and juridical lives of human society are determined by this primordial element but also all the phenomena of spiritual and intellectual life: religious struggles, national conflicts, the sciences, the arts, literature, et cetera, are, for Marxists, nothing but the different expressions and applications of the instincts, interests, aspirations, or movements of this or that class of society. There are no "national" interests, nor any of "all of society," or "of individuals taken in isolation." There are only, at bottom, the interests of the different classes, in struggle against each other. The rest is only window dressing, a *trompe l'oeil* capable of misleading the profane. Class origins are to be sought in the distant progress of labor techniques and productivity that, having dealt a mortal blow to the primitive clan communities, led to a surplus of products, to inequality, and, consequently, to divisions into classes, some sharing the surplus of products, or surplus value, the others deprived of them.

The appearance of classes, as well as that of their struggles, varies over the course of history, but the basis of these struggles always remains the same: the classes monopolizing surplus value seek to preserve it forever and at whatever cost, to subjugate and dominate those deprived of it, while the latter strive to shake off the yoke, free themselves, do away with surplus value, and, finally, classes themselves. The domination of a given class in society is always more or less fleeting, corresponding to a given historical era, to a certain state of development of the "productive forces." The antagonisms and the class struggle flow from the given "relations of production."

Thus, the classes of a society are not immutable, and in our era the feudal class had to cede its place to that of the bourgeoisie. Subsequent development led to the birth of a new class, that of the proletariat, whose interests are opposed to those of the bourgeoisie and is in struggle with the latter. In conformity with Marxist doctrine, the proletarian class is called on to overturn the bourgeoisie, to free itself, and to restore a society without either class domination or struggle.

Their practical considerations, political theses, and entire strategy for class struggle is a result of the Marxists' theoretical understanding. According to them, the bourgeoisie, which at a given moment of history played a progressive role, gradually lost it as the economy developed, ending up a regressive force. It is currently in a state of decay, a parasitic class. The current state of economic development demands another form of social organization and other organizers. This new form of organization is "the proletarian state" and the organizer is the proletarian class. The capitalist class will disappear in the same way as the feudal class. The state is in no way a conciliator placed above classes. On the contrary, it is the most qualified interest in the hands of the owning classes. It is with the aid of the state—independent of its form—that the bourgeoisie oppresses and exploits the proletarian class. The state is thus nothing but an instrument of class domination. In order to suppress this domination, to defeat the bourgeoisie, the proletariat must smash the bourgeois state and organize the proletarian state. The proletariat, having no interest in exploiting anyone at all, the state, in its hands, will serve, not as an instrument of exploitation, but strictly as a means of dominating the resistant bourgeoisie, of definitively defeating it, of suppressing it, and of completing the task of the total reorganization of modern society: the suppression of classes and class domination and the restoration of a free and egalitarian social organization. This is the Marxist thesis.

It must be added that in general the socialist doctrine includes other currents opposed in some ways to the strictly Marxist theory. While basing themselves on the fundamental principles of the struggle of the exploited classes, these currents are nevertheless opposed to reducing the entire historic process to this sole factor, viewing human history more broadly. They accept the great importance of other historic factors outside that of the class struggle, taking into account other forces and elements of human evolution. And what is of greater importance, they understand the very notion of class struggle more broadly than do the Marxists. They have a different appreciation of the role of the peasant class and of exploited intellectuals. This is why they have a different notion of the "dictatorship of the proletariat" (after its victory over the capitalist class) and the "proletarian state." This is why the supporters of these currents speak of the "exploited and oppressed classes," of the "laboring classes" rather than the "class of proletarians," and "working class." What is more, these currents are in disagreement with "orthodox Marxism," not only in relation to the theory of class struggle, but also on other points of a philosophical and sociological order. They make a greater case for psychological, ethical, and other movements, formulating objections to the doctrine of historical materialism.

Let us add that Marxist concepts—and socialist ones in general—are not in agreement concerning how the exploited classes should carry out their struggle, some ("reformist" right-wing socialism, Menshevism) calling for the gradual and slow conquest of political power within the bourgeois state, and others (left-wing "revolutionary" socialism, Bolshevism) insisting on the sudden and violent method.

**

What is the anarchist point of view vis-à-vis the above doctrines?

Let it first be said that the sociological notion of class has not yet been defined scientifically. As we know, the manuscript of the third volume of Marx's *Capital* stops precisely at the beginning of the analysis of this notion. As for the other works of this thinker (and of Engels), the word "class" is used in quite different senses, often being confused with notions like "caste," "body," or "profession." As a result, one would seek in vain not only a scientific definition, but even a more or less precise notion of social class. Other social authors, be they bourgeois, socialist, or other (Adam Smith, Voltaire, Guizot, Turgot, Mignet, Saint Simon, Considérant, Louis Blanc, Spencer, Proudhon, Charles Gide, Kropotkin, Jules Guesde, Jaurès, Kautsky, and Lenin, to cite only the best known), all use the word class in varying and imprecise ways. [Pitirim] Sorokin, a young Russian sociologist, who in 1920 began the publication (in Russian) of an important work in eight volumes (*System of Sociology*), attempted, in the second volume (the last one to appear, as far as I know) a precise definition of social class. This definition is closely tied to his entirely personal, sociological edifice. It can only be understood if we consider the entire edifice and it should be subjected, before being generally accepted, to examination and criticism.

It is in part due to this imprecision concerning the fundamental notion that there exist disagreements and divergences in opinion on the related problems. Several bourgeois writers severely criticize this lack of clarity, mocking all those who speak of "class" and "class struggle" and "class consciousness," et cetera, without being able to define the term. These bourgeois are wrong. First, because they too operate under a number of undefined notions (it suffices to note that of right), which in no way prevents them from making use of these, either theoretically or practically. Then—as is almost always the case in the social realm—because while not yet being scientifically defined, the notions "class," "class struggle," et cetera are sufficiently clear intuitively and respond to undeniable and known historical and social phenomena. Generally, the word "class" is understood to mean a social group characterized by certain properties related to ownership, profession, and the extent of rights at one's disposal. The enormous difference between the groups owning everything, having all rights and advantages from the professional point of view (including the right not to have one), and those who, having neither property nor right have only killing labor for themselves and are exploited by the former, is a certain and demonstrated historical fact.

The anomaly of this fact from all points of view and, consequently, the historical need for social reform, are truths accepted by every sentient being. The resistance of the fortunate classes to this reform, which is historically necessary, is an undeniable fact. The struggle of the disadvantaged and exploited classes, who have an interest in this reform, against the privileged and exploiting classes, is a fact that plays an increasingly preponderant role in the social events of the past centuries. This struggle fills modern history with its din. Its successes, along with those of the technical conquests of our time, mark the steps of human progress. Only the blind do not see this.

As we have already said, the lack of precision in all that has everything having to do with the notion "class" is cause of division among socialists in general as well as Marxists. It is the same imprecision that in part explains the disagreements between socialists and anarchists. And this is what also causes some division among anarchists themselves.

Let us linger for a moment over this final point.

The normal interests characterizing and guiding men living in our time are of three kinds: class interests, largely humanitarian interests, and individual interests. A problem that greatly concerns anarchist circles is this: is the anarchist concept one of class, or is it humanitarian or is it an individual theory? There are anarchist currents that respond as follows:

1. The anarchist idea is largely and strictly humanitarian. It has nothing to do with the doctrine of class or class struggle. Consequently, it must cast aside anything related to it, the latter being a strictly Marxists doctrine. Anarchism should only concern itself with the problems concerning humanity as such, without any class distinctions. The class struggle is not in its domain.

2. Anarchism is a strictly individual idea. The individual is the sole reality. The problems that concern it will resolve all the rest. Classes, humanity, even society are nothing but abstractions, fictions which a true anarchist has no reason to concern himself with.

It would take us far beyond the framework of this study if we were to criticize these points of view in depth. We will limit ourselves to saying that a doctrine that would not take into account the salient social fact of the human history, class struggle, or rather, the struggle of exploited classes for their emancipation as the progressive force of our time, that such a doctrine would be nothing but an abstraction, a fiction without any value, neither social, nor humanitarian, nor individual. It could only be a doctrine of the blind, unable to demonstrate to us how all of humanity, or the individuals that make it up, could have arrived at the greatest possible amount of happiness on earth outside the salutary struggle of the millions and millions of the oppressed.

We will hasten to say that within the ranks of the international anarchist movement these two currents form a tiny minority. The overwhelming majority of anarchists—especially those calling themselves communist anarchists—resolve the problem in quite another fashion. They declare that anarchism is essentially an idea capable of reconciling, of theoretically and practically satisfying the three seemingly contradictory varieties of interests: those of the exploited, laboring classes; those of humanity; and those of the individual. These anarchists affirm that there is no reason to oppose these three kinds of interests. On the contrary, it is necessary to attempt to bring them together, to unite them. Unfortunately, the lack of precision of which we spoke does not yet allow the resolution of this problem with the needed finesse. One of the most pressing tasks of anarchism is that of bringing as much precision as possible to the synthesis of these three elements: class struggle, humanitarian movement, and the individual principle. This would be the surest way of putting an end to the dispersion of anarchists, of bringing about their unification. The precondition for the accomplishment of this task is the most precise definition possible of the notions "class" and "class struggle." It is only in this way that we can arrive at a clearer and more complete formula that will once and for all reconcile, in a harmonious and all-encompassing proposition, the three elements in question and lay out their respective roles. Class struggle as a method; humanitarian social organization as a result of the victory and of the emancipation of the oppressed classes, as well as material basis for all social and individual progress; and the freedom, the unlimited flourishing of the individual as the great goal of every social revolution.

Naturally a task of this kind can only be undertaken in a work especially dedicated to this subject.

Here it remains for us to state that the crushing majority of anarchists have the class as their principle and recognize the revolutionary struggle of the exploited classes as the sole road for social progress in our time.

The question arises, what separates the anarchists from the socialists in general and the Marxists in this realm? What separates them, in the first instance, are several theoretical considerations, then the practical considerations that flow from the profoundly different foundations of the two ideas, socialist and anarchist, notably, the ways they each conceive the forms, tactics, and strategy of the struggle of the laboring classes.

As concerns the theoretical, or rather historical side of the problem, the anarchist view is close to that of the anti-Marxist socialists who were spoken of above. Like the socialists, the anarchists are opposed to reducing the entire historical process to the sole factor of the class struggle. They view human history more broadly, admitting the great importance of other historical factors. They object to the doctrine of so-called historical materialism, et cetera (see above the characteristics of socialist currents opposed to "orthodox" Marxism). There is, however, one reservation that must be made: while the socialists (and the Marxists among themselves) disagree about the reformist or revolutionary roads of the social struggle, all anarchists are supporters of the revolutionary idea, with the exception, perhaps, of the Tolstoian tendency, which views revolution in quite a particular way.

It should be added that the opinion of the anarchists on the origin and development of classes, as well as on the past "progressive" role of the bourgeoisie, differs from the Marxist idea.

But what is most typical of the difference between the socialist and anarchist views regarding the class struggle is the practical side of the question.

While socialists of all tendencies see the class struggle as a political one, which logically leads them to the formation of a political party called upon to conquer political power and to organize, with the aid of this power, the new "proletarian state"—an essentially political and authoritarian organism exercising the "dictatorship of the proletariat"—the anarchists assert that the class struggle is an apolitical and essentially social struggle, having nothing in common either with parties or political power, or with the state, authority, dictatorship, et cetera.

The anarchists affirm that the political road (party, power, state, authority, dictatorship) and the political struggle (understood in this sense) are contrary to the class struggle. They claim that the latter is deformed, mutilated, destroyed, and reduced to total impotence by political methods. They cite the case of Bolshevism in Russia, whose saga, in their eyes, confirms their point of view. They declare that the class struggle, that every class action seeking to achieve real victory must be led by the interested party—the laboring classes themselves—organizing and acting themselves, directly, in the strictly social, economic, and class realms, without having any recourse to political parties or their political programs for power, the state, dictatorship, et cetera. They think that the truly victorious revolution will be that which will only be negatively political, i.e., which will kill all politics, all political parties, all political programs, all power, all authority, all states, all dictatorships, and that, from the positive point of view, will strive to establish the new society on an apolitical, social and economic basis.

Logically, anarchism rejects the political party, the state, authority, and dictatorship. It considers the so-called "proletarian state" or the famous "dictatorship of the proletariat" to be nonsensical, considering that every state and every dictatorship can only be exploitative bourgeois institutions, and that every political method is equally a bourgeois process.

This is why anarchists claim that their theory and ideology are the only ones that truly depend on the real class struggle as the immediate lever for the salutary social revolution.

***

This difference in fundamental concepts logically leads to that of all the notions derived from them. For socialists, class consciousness consists in the exploited realizing that he belongs to a great family, to the class of workers whose interests are opposed to those of the bourgeois class; that consequently he is conscious of the great social task of his class; that he takes active part in the struggle carried out by that class; that he is ready at any moment to sacrifice his personal interests to those of his class, et cetera. And above all, he accepts the "political party of his class," he is "conscious" of the need for political means, and recognizes the principles of the conquest of political power, the establishment of the "proletarian state," and the "dictatorship of the proletariat."

Agreeing on all the other points, the anarchists naturally reject the last one; they affirm precisely the opposite. For them, every one of the exploited who lines up behind the political doctrine lacks class consciousness: he is misled, has lost the true terrain of the class struggle, and lacks a true notion of it. For them, true class consciousness implies the condemnation of political methods and goals. They consider the confusion of *class* with *political party* to be a lack of class consciousness.

Socialists and anarchists agree that justice today is class justice skillfully disguised by the servants of the owning classes. But while the former prepare to substitute for it "justice" organized by the self-proclaimed "workers' state," the latter, considering that every state is fated to be bourgeois and that a "workers' state" is an illusion or a lie, logically conclude from this that this new "justice" will be nothing other than the justice of the new privileged ones, and will be even more skillfully disguised and aimed against the eternally exploited. The famous "justice" exercised today in the Soviet state shows them to be entirely right. They thus think that after the Great Revolution true human justice will be achieved outside any form of state and in forms having nothing in common with political, statist, or juridical forms.

Both socialists and anarchists know full well that the modern army is a class army called on to defend the owning class, but while the socialists foresee after the revolution a new state army (the Red Army in Russia) which, in their opinion, must defend the workers, the anarchists assert that any state army will defend the privileged against the workers. They understand the defense of the revolution in non-statist forms, by the organized forces of the workers, established on other foundations than those of a state army.

We could give many more examples, speaking of class education, class teaching, class science, and so on. After all the preceding, we consider it superfluous to do so.

***

There is an objection often made to anarchists, particularly by authoritarian "communists." If it's not the political party, or the political power, or the workers' state, or the dictatorship of the proletariat that will lead the nation, the class struggle, the social revolution, that will assure their success, their victory, and the solidity of the latter, who will it be? What will be the forces, the elements, and the organizations that will lead this formidable and complicated struggle of the exploited and oppressed classes to total success?

The response of anarchists would not be difficult, especially today.

The forces and elements? But that will naturally be the exploited and oppressed classes themselves.

The organizations? About forty years ago the anarchists responded: the class struggle and its culmination and end point, the revolution, since they must be the work of these classes themselves, they will surely find the appropriate forms of struggle and create the organizations that will answer to the needs of the hour. This prediction has already been partially realized, and so the response can be even more precise. In all countries, workers have created organizations of struggle and combat: the revolutionary unions. While not lacking in defects—as are all human institutions, especially in our time—and without our thinking of reducing all actions, the entire orientation of the struggle and the revolution to them alone, union organizations are the prototype of the class organizations called upon to assume several of the fundamental asks of this struggle, this revolution.

Despite its natural—though excusable and unimportant—weaknesses, and despite momentary retreat as a result of the war and its consequences, it is revolutionary syndicalism that serves as a concrete response to political parties. It *is* the concrete response. It will be neither the political parties nor the anarchist groups that will lead the class struggle, workers' action, and the entire formidable revolution to victory and total success. It will be the masses themselves, the millions and millions of workers of the cities and fields, assembled in their social class organizations and not in political organizations—union and others—that will take them in hand.

A large majority of the anarchists agree with this response. Life, history, and the near future will decide.

—Voline

Direct Action   According to the *Larousse Dictionary*: The resort to force advocated by revolutionary syndicalists in preference to constitutional action aided by the state.

According to us: Individual or collective action exercised against the social adversary through the action of the individual or a group. Direct action is, in general, employed by organized workers or evolved individuals as opposed to parliamentary action, aided by the state or not. Parliamentary or indirect action takes place exclusively on the legal terrain through the intermediary of political groups or their elected representatives. Direct action can be legal or illegal. Those who employ it have no reason to concern themselves about this. It is, in all fields, the means of employing the force of the workers against the force of the bosses. Legality has no part to play in the solution of social conflicts. Force alone settles them.

Nevertheless, direct action is not necessarily violent, though it does not exclude violence. Nor is it necessarily offensive. It can perfectly well be used defensively or preventively against an attack launched by the bosses or on the point of being so. For example, against a partial or total lock-out declared or likely to soon be declared.

A few examples are needed in order to clarify things.

1. The worker who discusses his interests with his boss, either to preserve the advantages already obtained or to have new demands met is carrying out an act of direct action. He is, in fact, placing himself alone, face to face with his employer without resorting to assistance from outside the social conflict.

Whether he obtains satisfaction or not, whether the boss recognizes in good faith the validity of the demands submitted to him and grants or rejects them, it is still direct action. If the boss surrenders, out of momentary powerlessness or calculation—which is frequently the case—or if he resists because he feels strong enough to brave the collective force he senses behind the worker who demands and discusses, there is, on the part of the individual carrying out the struggle in this way, direct action.

If the discussion remains courteous or degenerates into an argument or a brawl, the worker's act remains, whatever the case, a manifestation of direct action. It is class discussion.

What the worker must not lose sight of in this discussion is his class duty. He must never surrender ground to the enemy. He must only conquer advantages while preserving his dignity as a man. He must not sell his conscience or his professional knowledge at any price, even if he is poverty-stricken, by accepting personal advantages in exchange: a post in a position of command or supervision, a secret wage higher than that of his comrades, et cetera.

Arriving at a compromise with the boss or receiving personal satisfaction refused to others means committing an act of treason vis-a-vis his brothers in poverty and labor. It is better to remain silent than to make oneself even the unwitting instrument of the enslavement of one's comrades.

The worker who charges himself with demanding his rights and those of his comrades must have a profound feeling of his class duties. If he doesn't know them, he must learn them before acting.

2. A union can, of course, employ the same method of struggle. It must behave in the same manner as the worker acting alone. It too must neither promise nor give the enemy moral or technical assistance that would reinforce the power of the bosses to the detriment of the workers. A union that would accept that its members, controlled by it or not, enter capitalist directorial or management organisms could no longer, under any circumstances, practice direct action, since the interests of the bosses and the workers, even if unequal, would be intermingled.

Collective class discussion must result in neither compromise nor abandonment. It can assume all the characteristics of individual discussion. Nevertheless, it differs from the latter on one important point: An individual act, which often occurs in an environment contrary to class spirit, generally involves only the firing or the voluntary departure of the offended but powerless worker. On the other hand, collective class discussion, in the event of failure, almost always results in a strike, as long as the working-class forces are alert, connected, and organized for the predicted struggle and have the battles to come in mind.

In all cases, a strike is a serious act. It should only be utilized advisedly and knowingly, after close examination of the situation and the state of the conflict. It is also appropriate to take into account as accurately as possible the results to be attained, the conditions of the struggle to be carried out, and the repercussions in the event of success or failure.

For example, when the decision to strike is taken, everything must be put in motion to make the work stoppage effective, making sure everyone acts with vigor, courage, and method. A victorious strike is a factor in the development, expansion, and attraction of the union organization. On the other hand, a defeat generally diminishes the confidence and combativeness of individuals. It often provokes the desertion of union members. It blunts their ardor and their spirit of solidarity.

3. The worker who, in the course of a conflict, decides, in accordance with his conscience, to carry out a destructive act or one aimed at putting work materials or tools out of commission, or who carries out a violent act against a representative of the enemy class or one of his comrades unaware of his class duties, is also engaging in direct action.

However, such an act must only take place if it is a factor in the success of the action engaged. In the contrary case, if the act is mindless, a simple manifestation of anger, it risks doing a disservice—often a considerable one—to the movement that is under way.

Before employing this mode of action—which might impose itself—the individual must consider the impact of his act and its probable consequences. He should only execute it if he considers it truly useful to the success of the cause he is defending. Allowing oneself unthinkingly to accomplish an act of violence or sabotage is proof of weakness, lack of education, and lack of understanding. It means laying yourself open to the enemy and often justifying adverse violence, even if you are provoked, which is often the case.

4. A union can also decide to employ violence or sabotage. Nevertheless, it cannot impose their execution on those of its members who don't accept these means of struggle or don't wish to employ them themselves.

In this case, each man's conscience alone decides on the carrying out of acts recognized as necessary. It is best if the participants or executors alone are aware of the projects, of the attacks to be carried out, and are the only ones to decide on the means of action. Secrecy is *de rigueur*. Only those who have decided to act for the common good can judge the results. They must not hesitate to condemn any new activity whose result is unfavorable to the common cause. Just as a collectivity does not have the right to oppose necessary acts, individuals must not carry out acts running counter to the sought for result. It is a matter of conscience and of circumstances. What was bad yesterday may be good tomorrow, and vice versa.

5. A man who by whatever means kills a tyrant, a fearsome oppressor, also carries out an act of direct action, even if he is not attacking the regime itself and rarely puts it in peril. He is acting directly against a social enemy who is particularly harmful.

6. A group can be called on to act under the same conditions. In this case it is necessary that the participants accept this method of struggle, as they would do if it was the case of an act of sabotage, of destruction, or collective violence. The same precautions should be taken, and the action should only be undertaken or continued under the conditions laid out in Section 4 above. Such an act or series of acts might sometimes impose itself and become an important and even decisive factor in the success of a revolutionary period.

As can be seen, direct action can present itself in many different ways, according to the circumstances and the ends pursued.

Taking the preceding examples into account, it can be said that it has the following characteristics: individual discussion or collective class discussion; strikes with their many aspects; sabotage; ill treatment of bosses or workers lacking in consciousness; attacks on an oppressor or a group of representatives of authority.

Just as there can be class discussion without a strike, there can be strikes without sabotage, violence, or manhunts. Any one of these manifestations alone characterizes direct action. It is enough that it be employed individually or collectively, from one class against the other, without resorting to forces foreign to the conflict itself.

In a revolutionary period, direct action immediately takes on the character of an insurrectionary general strike. Its goal is that of allowing the working class to seize the means of production and exchange that at all times ensure the continuity of social life. It suppresses the partial or total assistance of the indoctrinated proletariat. On this occasion, direct action necessarily becomes violent, since it is used against an enemy who defends himself by force.

It is the first revolutionary act of a proletariat aiming at the replacement of political authority with social organization after having destroyed individual property and establishing collective property.

It stands in opposition to insurrection, the arm of political parties, all of whom, without exception, have but one desire: seizing and holding on to power.

Direct action is the sole and true social weapon of the proletariat. No other can, however it might be employed, allow it [the proletariat] to free itself of all yokes, of all forms of authority, of all dictatorships, including the most absurd of all, that of the proletariat.

[...]

In summary, there is a notable difference between the bourgeois definition of direct action and the true meaning we give it. While it is understandable that our adversaries want to show direct action to be a disordered act or series of acts, brutal and violent, without reason or motive; to be destructive acts carried out for the pleasure and satisfaction of those executing them, we assert that direct action is ordered, methodical, thought-out, and violent only when needed, and is aimed at concrete noble and humane goals.

—Pierre Besnard

Direct Action It is not only the action by which syndicalism and certain revolutionary schools think they can have their demands met that can be called direct action. There is also, and in parallel to this collective form of direct action, the individual form of the latter. The terrain of this form is man himself. It consists in the inner evolution of the individual, in the violence he exerts upon himself, in his efforts to overcome himself, to elevate himself, and become better in the war he makes on his passions, in his daily victories over ugliness. The results of this direct action are positive. Art, ideas, and books aid the individual in discovering himself; they reveal him to himself. They act directly on his consciousness in order to reform it, to make it grow, and to fortify it.

Emancipation The bourgeoisie give this word a different meaning from ours, which is related to Karl Marx's famous prophecy: "The emancipation of the working class will be the work of the working class itself."

This simple and clear meaning is adopted by all the true emancipators of the proletariat, by those who don't contradict themselves by engaging in electoral politics after having proclaimed the doctrine of the self-emancipation of the proletariat.

All of the anarchists' propaganda aims at this goal: the economic and social liberation of individuals; their individual emancipation.

Every one of them wants the total emancipation of all those who the capitalist system exploits and enslaves. This amounts to saying that they identically lean toward a social emancipation that can only result in a revolution of a kind we have never yet seen, since the Commune of 1871 was defeated and the Russian Revolution resulted in nothing but a dictatorship of the proletariat.

Advocating libertarian education, leading the working masses of the cities, seas, and fields to freely organize and to self-administer through freely arrived at agreements means creating a popular mentality that fits the concept of a free society of emancipated producers. It means training a generation of individuals capable of organizing a free life for free men.

This is how we think the social emancipation of all should be understood. But in order to emancipate others it is essential to first emancipate oneself by ridding oneself of all the prejudices of authority, hierarchy, discipline, et cetera, which have nothing to do with freedom, harmony, and unity for life.

—G. YVETOT[1]

---

1. Georges Yvetot (1868–1942). Anarcho-syndicalist typesetter; anti-militarism and syndicalism were the primary focuses of his activity. His pacifism led him to oppose the war against Germany. See page 12 above for more on Yvetot.

Fascism Fascism is currently the best organized and most active counter-revolutionary force. The word "fascism" is Italian, but the thing is international. Just as hypocrisy is the homage rendered to virtue by vice, fascism is the admission of the extreme danger in which the capitalist regime, seriously threatened by revolution, finds itself. Along with reformist socialism, it is the last cartridge of a bourgeoisie backed against the wall.

Whenever the bourgeoisie thinks it is on the edge of the abyss, on the eve of a revolutionary victory, it casts its own legality aside, destroys its own democracy, and tells all its ideologies, all its "metaphysical whores" (liberty, rights of man, respect for judicial forms, et cetera) to go to the devil. It sets itself to killing, arson, torture, illegally destroying all legal organizations. It dissolves parliament and suppresses or chains the press, even its own democratic press. The dictatorship of capitalists and bankers publicly takes off its clothes and strolls about in its horrifying nudity. The "wall of silver" becomes a "wall of bronze" against which all vague reformist or democratic desires run aground. In a word, *fascism is threatened capitalism defending itself by all means, legal and illegal.* It is a gendarme combined with a bandit. It is unhindered, limitless violence.

Already, in ancient Rome, when patricians and big landowners were threatened with revolt by the plebes, a dictatorship was established as an omnipotent sovereign to put down the exploited class through merciless reprisals. But the dictators of ancient times still had some shame. They limited their extraordinary power with specific time frames (six months, for example). Fascist dictatorship knows no shame: it is limitless in time and space.

Every class struggle results in repression and dictatorship, either hidden or open. Thermidor, Bonaparte, the gunfire under the Restoration and the Monarchy, the bloody days of June 1848, the massacre of the Communards in 1871, and the *lois scélérates*[1] represent, in different periods and to differing degrees, the dictatorship of the dominant classes defending themselves by all means possible.

But like the dictatorship of ancient Rome, the bourgeois dictatorship had until now had a certain respect for forms. Before being exercised it waited for the moment of an open popular uprising, when barricades were raised on the streets. It then declared itself to be in a state of self-defense and declared a state of siege, a *state of exception*.

In our time, fascism is preventive dictatorship, the brutal dismissal of all normal legality. It is government hiding itself behind a gang of *bravi*, of paid assassins. It is the alliance of organized ferocity with hidden, underhanded cowardice. It is the carabinieri parading down the street while surreptitiously giving the assassin waiting in ambush a sign to attack the unsuspecting passerby.

Around the time of the first Russian Revolution of 1905, tsarism had already inaugurated this system of clandestine and illegal defense, assisting and augmenting the formidable legal apparatus. The secret police had its printing presses, its illegal organizations and literature, its agents provocateurs, its *sicarii*. The majesty of the state and its solemn laws descended into the caves of Cartouche and Ali Baba and lowered themselves to the situation of a vulgar criminal. Mussolini invented nothing. He imitated Rasputin, who is in no condition to protect his copyright.

Even in our oh-so-democratic and legalistic republic, at the moment of the general strike of railroad workers, a fascist theory was outlined from the parliamentary tribune: "I will go as far as illegality" to defend the capitalist order, said the then head of state.

Another characteristic of fascism: it erects violence into a system. It has a cult of violence, of violence for its own sake. It is in this way, *among others*, that *reactionary* violence distinguishes itself from *revolutionary* violence. The revolutionary respects human life and only resorts to violence when forced to by the violence of the regime he is fighting. His ideal is the solidarity of all, of all producers, the end of all iniquity, of all exploitation. The revolutionary cannot be a defeatist on the question of human progress. He believes in a

1. Anti-anarchist laws passed in France in 1893–1894 after a wave of anarchist terror attacks.

better future for humanity, of a classless future, and thus without class violence.

Fascism, on the contrary, defending the regime of exploitation and violence, believes, or feigns to believe, that violence is eternal, beneficent, and fortifying (see Joseph de Maistre, de Bonald, Proudhon, Nietzsche, Georges Sorel, Bernhardt, Foch, and other more or less illustrious men of war and reaction). It seeks to render eternal the regime of antagonistic opposed classes and, with them, the rule of violence.

War, with its cult of "beneficent, national, and patriotic" violence was the best preparation for fascism. When we said and wrote that the imperialist world war would mark the return to the barbarism of the Middle Ages, with its *Faustrecht*, the right of the strongest, was the exact truth, which fascism charges itself with justifying with every step.

We don't have the right to leave the subject of fascism without noting that apart from the war it was also reformist socialism that prepared favorable ground for it. Indeed, in disarming the proletariat morally, intellectually, and politically with its propaganda of democratic illusions, it handed the masses over to the fascist gangs who knew in advance they'd encounter no effective resistance.

The reformists confuse the ideal, the final goal of socialism, with the means, the arrival point with the departure point. Yes, our final goal is harmony, solidarity, peace for all time, and fraternity. But do we have the right to forget that we live in a society based on class struggle, armed to its teeth and only preaching non-violence to the weak, the oppressed, and the exploited?

Disarming the proletariat means arming the fascists. Telling proletarians that it is enough to wait for parliamentary majorities means opening the working class to fascist blows.

Even if the proletariat has the majority in parliament the capitalist class will not surrender. It will smash its own parliamentary legality by force. Fascism will become world-wide. With each passing day we see the black stain of fascism spread over a greater number of states. Along with the progress of the proletariat, fascism grows and develops. Hiding this means betraying the working class or being duped by one's own ignorance, by one's "democratic" illusions.

Another feature of fascism: it prefers to address former socialists, entrusting leadership to them. Mussolini is a former socialist militant, as is Millerand. And there are others. Fascism is the meeting place of all crimes, villainies, and treasons.

While taking off its democratic and legalist mask, in order to lead the unconscious masses fascism needs to drape itself in a general interest, which is order. Which is the fatherland. The strongbox is hidden behind the national flag and sacred order.

It can be easily demonstrated that the other counter-revolutionary forces, in supporting and advocating the same slogans, "order" and "fatherland," must inevitably, whether they want to or not, arrive at the same tactics, the same acts as fascism, which plays the role of precursor and model for all defenders of the capitalist and imperialist regime. *The counter-revolution is one and indivisible.*

—CHARLES RAPPOPORT[2]

2. Charles Rappoport (1865–1941) was a Lithuanian Jew who settled in France in the 1890s, where he was a central figure, first among Jewish radicals, and then in the larger French revolutionary movement. An active opponent of World War I, he later was a founding member of the French Communist Party. Though he only left the party in the late 1930s, his place in the *Anarchist Encyclopedia* is perhaps explained by his epitaph, drawn from one of his works: "Socialism without freedom isn't socialism; freedom without socialism isn't freedom."

Flag n. [Drapeau] (from the Latin *drapellum*) The word "flag" originally served to designate the piece of material used to wrap infants and which is now called swaddling clothes. It later became synonymous with rag, an old piece of cloth or linen: "A merchant of old irons and drapeaux." Finally, in our time it designates the piece of cloth placed at the end of a lance that serves to distinguish nations and parties through its colors.

The word matters not at all: the use of a flag is very ancient, since the twelve tribes of Israel already had insignias of different colors bearing particular signs.

If it's not considered a god, a flag can be of some use. It serves as rallying point and can be used as a signal mechanism. In our eyes, this is pretty much its sole use. Unfortunately, our point of view isn't shared and flags are something other than they should be, than what they are: vulgar rags paraded at the end of a stick. [...]

The vast majority of men see in the flag the symbol of their parties, their nations, and their dogmas and make such an idol of it that they render it special honors, sometimes having themselves killed for it. This would only be a demi-evil if they didn't force all their like to give themselves over to their ridiculous practices.

The cult of the flag exists everywhere. It is a divinity before which people bow and render public homage. Some have a passionate veneration and devotion for it.

The flag has its churches and its priests. Every nation has its flag, and in France there is one per regiment that, aside from the regiment's number, bears the slogan "Honor and Fatherland" and the names of the four greatest victories inscribed in the annals of the corps. The flag is generally placed in the regiment's hall of honor and, when it is taken out—probably so it can get some fresh air—it is carried by an officer, lieutenant or second lieutenant, and surrounded by its guard, made up of a non-com and four privates first class, chosen by the colonel.

When you see a regiment and its flag you should take another route if you don't intend to pay it the homage it is owed, for there is no question but that among the mass of imbeciles and bounders there will be someone stupid enough to knock your hat off your head. Do not show lack of respect for the flag if you want to preserve your freedom, for any insult to that rag will lead to your standing before the judge. It is a god, like all other gods, and one must believe in it. It represents the bloody past, and its glory is having caused thousands of young men full of strength and life to die beneath its folds.

Before 1789, the French flag was white. A decree of June 30, 1790 prohibited standards of that color and put in its place the tricolor: blue, white, and red. At present in France the white flag symbolizes the monarchy or, in time of war, serves to indicate that a truce is being requested and negotiations are desired.

Every political party or philosophical sect also has its flag, its emblems, its standard. The red flag that "by virtue of a decree of the Constituent Assembly, should be deployed whenever martial law is proclaimed and preparations are being made to break up an assembly by force of arms," later became the symbol of "the Revolution." The socialists adopted it as well as the authoritarian communists. Both prostituted it politically, and if in the past the people fought around it, today it is no longer anything but a rag like the others that is idolized and which serves to mislead and enslave the people.

The red flag, like the tricolor, has its fanatics, and before it the same movements, the same mummeries are executed, and the profane are equally threatened by the popular herd when, on certain occasions, they refuse to participate in the adoration of the new god.

The anarchists also have a flag. It is black. The anarchists are the only ones who see in it not a symbol, but a rag that serves to rally all comrades over the course of a stroll or a demonstration. They would just as well replace this flag with a placard or some other utensil, but a flag borne on high is more practical and is seen from a greater distance. It sometimes happens that they defend it, not that they think that a meter of old fabric is worth fighting for or costing the lives of comrades, but because it's never their flag that is attacked, but their ideas. Though not having a cult of the flag, the anarchists are nevertheless the bravest and the first to attack and defend themselves when they are physically and morally brutalized by the forces of reaction. They judge everything at its correct value and they're not religious devotees who expend their energy adoring images, statues, or flags.

Guillotine n. Instrument of punishment used in France for capital executions.

The invention of the guillotine is erroneously attributed to the physician Guillotin, a member of the Constituent Assembly who on October 10, 1789, proposed subjecting all those sentenced to death to the same punishment and requested that a simple and rapid machine be substituted for the executioner. He provided no description of this machine.

The guillotine had already been in use since the early 16th century in certain parts of the South of France and Italy. It was only around the end of 1791 that the order was given to a famous surgeon of the time, Dr. Antoine Louis, to construct a machine for the cutting off of heads. He adapted the machine used in the South of France, which was called the *mannaja*, and began his experiments.

On April 19, 1792, Dr. Louis wrote to minister Rolland: "The experiments on Dr. Schmitt's machine were carried out at Bicêtre on three corpses, which it so cleanly decapitated that we were amazed by the force and celerity of its action." We should add that it was a piano maker, named Schmitt, who had provided the updated model of the guillotine. The first execution took place in Paris on April 25, 1792.

Since then, how many poor devils have placed their head beneath the blade? We won't address the question of the brutal need for executions during revolutionary periods. We know—and we regret—that revolutions aren't made without the spilling of blood. Revolution is a violent manifestation of evolution and it is up to those who arbitrarily own all social riches not to push the oppressed to violence.

But in periods of calm the death penalty is an unspeakable iniquity, and not only from the anarchist viewpoint, but simply from the human viewpoint.

[...]

Some seem to glorify the guillotine, claiming that cutting off a head with a machine is less barbaric than cutting it with an axe. But this is not only a visual matter, which we don't even care to discuss, for we aim higher. We say that no one has the right to dispose of the life of another. That it is not up to an individual, whoever he might be, to order the death of one of his kind, and if a crime is horrible a punishment that finds its expression in another crime is no less horrible. All peoples would do well to think of abolishing in their respective countries the death penalty, which is shameful for a humanity that boasts of being civilized.

Heresy n. (from the Greek *hairesis*, from *harein*: to choose) Doctrine condemned by the Catholic Church.

As soon as it held a certain amount of power thanks to its recognition by kings and emperors, the Roman Church forgot all the persecutions of which its founders were victim.

And no sooner was it armed with its fearsome influence over monarchs and lords than it waged merciless and bloody war on those who did not bow before its commands. The fifteen centuries during which it ruled as unquestioned master of Europe were nothing but a long train of the crimes it perpetrated and committed in the name of religion. It carried out veritable massacres of entire populations. The best-known are:

—The Massacre of the Albigensians (thirteenth century)

—The wars of the Reformation

—Saint-Bartholomew's Day Massacre (1572)

—The Dragonnades of the Cevennes

—The Massacre of the Innocents

The Council of Verona (1183) ordered the Lombard bishops to mete out justice against those heretics who refused to convert. Shortly thereafter, a secret tribunal was established, the "Inquisition," for the seeking and punishment of heretics. Until last century this tribunal sent to the stake—after inflicting horrific tortures—people suspected of heresy. In 1766 a young man of nineteen, Chevalier de la Barre, was decapitated, then burned for having failed to salute a procession and for being suspected of mutilating a cross.

Over the past fifty years the Church has lost much of its influence and, apart from Spain, where it continues to spread terror, it is almost completely disarmed against heresy. Which is a great good.

Everything that constituted a step toward progress was considered to be a heresy by the Church. In 1633 did we not see the Italian mathematician Galileo, as a result of having written a book in which he explained that the sun and not the earth is the center of the planetary system, that the earth revolves around the sun like the other planets, which reflected its light; did we not see this seventy-year-old man forced to abjure his alleged heresy on bended knee? And did he not die blind due to the nine years of captivity the Inquisition inflicted on him?

The Church, at the Council of Trent (1545–1563) created a Congregation of the Index, whose object was the examination of published books and their condemnation if they were judged dangerous. Up till the nineteenth century its condemnation resulted in the burning of the book. This Congregation still exists, though fortunately its decisions are inoperative.

As can be seen, heresies always contained a large part of truth.

What is more, the definition given by bourgeois dictionaries would be enough to affirm the revolutionary character of heresy. A "false or absurd opinion," says the *Larousse Dictionary*.

Is this not how all the privileged have qualified the opinions of thinkers who concluded there was a need for revolt and the total reorganization of society?

Anarchism is thus considered a heresy by all political parties, because it demonstrates the harmfulness and duplicity of all the so-called social doctrines of politicians of all colors.

But it is a heresy that will one day prevail and will end by destroying the commandments of all religious and political churches.

Iconoclast   Means breaker of images (the word "image" in antiquity applied to all painted or sculpted figures). It particularly designates those persons or sects opposed to the adoration of images and that pursue their destruction. Because of this, iconoclasm is part of the history of those religions that admitted and practiced the cult of images.

Around the first quarter of the 8th Century a religious sect was founded whose objective was the smashing of all images of saints and the banning of their cult. This sect of "iconoclasts" was at first approved by the Council of Constantinople in 754.

Approving these acts meant making largely impossible the task of the Roman Church, which has a whole army of more or less miraculous saints to propose to the veneration of the faithful. So the Council of Trent (787) and those that followed pitilessly condemned the sect, which disappeared at the beginning of the following century. Later the Albigensians, the Hussites, the *Vaudois,* and the Calvinists took up the practices of the iconoclasts, for they didn't recognize the "sanctity" of the apostles.

Extending the meaning of the word, giving it a fuller significance, the anarchists call themselves iconoclasts. The *Compagnon* Percheron, in the song "La Ronde des briseurs d'images" [The Round of the Smasher of Images], very precisely explained the why of such an affirmation. Wanting to destroy not only the images of saints, but those of all false gods, of all idols, of all prejudices; bowing before no moral or material authority, the anarchists want to destroy the old society that rules over us from top to bottom. This is why with all their disrespect for established things they are so attached to smashing all the images (state, religion, politics, property, bosses, fatherlands, et cetera) that still today fool the people and that allow slavery to last.

Recognizing the high moral import, the great beneficial value of the lives of certain men devoted to science, philosophy, and the revolution, the anarchists sometimes cite the works of these precursors as an example and a teaching. But not wanting to see any kind of pre-destination in any man they rise up against any attempt, whatever its source, to turn some into legendary personalities. And they smash all the images of all the secular or revolutionary gods that some who yearn for something to adore—and this for not very reputable ends—propose that the crowd venerate.

Illegalism   It serves no purpose to hide this, but whether we recognize it or not, there are anarchists who resolve their economic question extra legally, i.e., by methods implying attacks on property, by the regular or occasional use of different forms of violence or ruse, or by the practice of crafts or professions disavowed by the police and the courts.

It is in vain that [some] communist-anarchist doctrinaires—but not all of them—want to disassociate themselves from illegalists, to thunder against "individual expropriation," which nevertheless goes all the way back to anarchism's heroic period, the era of people like Pini,[1] Schouppe,[2] Ortiz,[3] and Jacob.[4] It is in vain that the doctrinaires of individualist anarchism, like Tucker, combat anarchist "outlawry": there were and there always will be theoreticians of anarchist illegalism, especially in Latin countries.

Before investigating what these "theoreticians," who are above all comrades who seek to explain to us and themselves the illegalist anarchist turn of mind, have to say, it is appropriate to note that the practice of illegalism is not to be preached or propagated: it offers fearsome hazards. It does not liberate anyone economically from any point of view. Only under exceptional circumstances does it not hinder the flourishing of individual life. It requires an exceptional temperament for illegalism not to drag one down to being reduced to the level of social waste.

1. Vittorio Pini (1859–1903). Militant anarchist and illegalist, founder of the group Gli Intransigenti di Londra e Parigi. Died in the penal colony of Cayenne.

2. Placide Schouppe (1858–?). Belgian born illegalist. Escaped from the penal colony in Cayenne, to which he was shipped at the same time as Pini.

3. Léon Ortiz (1868–?). Illegalist sentenced at the show trial of anarchists known as the Trial of the Thirty in 1894. He later turned on his comrades and disappeared after serving a prison sentence.

4. Alexandre Jacob (1879–1954). A leading figure of the illegalist movement, his defense speech delivered at his trial in 1905, "Why I Stole" is a classic text of the movement.

These reservations having been made and proclaimed to the sound of trumpets, does it follow that the comrade who procures his daily bread by resorting to a craft stigmatized by custom, forbidden by the law, and punished by "justice" should not be treated as a comrade by those who accept being exploited by a boss?

All things considered, every anarchist, socially adapted or not, is an illegalist, because he rejects the law. He is an illegalist and a delinquent every time he enunces and propagates opinions contrary to the laws of the human environment in which he evolves.

Between the intellectual illegalist and the economic illegalist there is only a question of species.

The illegalist anarchist claims he is every bit as much a comrade as the small shopkeeper, the town hall secretary, or the dancing master, professions that modify the economic living conditions of the current social environment no more than his does. A lawyer, a doctor, and a schoolteacher can send articles to an anarchist newspaper and give talks to small anarchist educational groups, but they nonetheless remain supporters of and supported by the archist system, which handed the monopoly over to them, allowing them to exercise their profession, and whose rules and regulations they are obliged to submit to if they want to continue in their profession.

The law protects the exploited and the exploiter, the dominated and the dominator in their shared social relations, and as long as he submits to them the anarchist is as well protected in his person and his property as the archist. As long as they obey the injunctions of "the social contract" the law makes no distinction between them. Whether they want to or not, those anarchists who submit, the small artisans, workers, functionaries, and employees, have public authority, tribunals, social conventions, and official educators on their side. This is the reward for their submission. When they force an archist employer to pay half-wages to an anarchist wage-earner victim of a work accident, the forces of social preservation care little that the wage earner is inwardly hostile to the system of wage labor, and the victim profits from this unconcern.

On the contrary, the rebel, the man who rebels against the social contract—the illegalist anarchist—has the entire social organization against him when he sets out to cut corners in order to "live his life."

He runs an enormous risk, and it is only fair that this risk be rewarded by immediate results, if results there are.

Every anarchist, submissive or not, considers those who share his ideas and who refuse to accept military servitude are comrades. There's no explanation for why that attitude should change when it's a question of refusing to allow oneself to be exploited.

It is easy to understand that there are anarchists who do not want to contribute to the economic life of a country that doesn't grant them the possibility of expressing themselves by the pen or the spoken word, that limits their faculties of realization and association in any domain at all. Taking all this into consideration, those anarchists who consent to participate in the functioning of societies where they can't live as they wish are the ones who are inconsequent. If that's what they want to be, that's their affair, but let them not object to "economic rebels."

Those who rebel against economic servitude find themselves obliged, out of the instinct for self-preservation, from need, and by the will to live to appropriate a parcel of the property of others. Not only is this instinct primordial but, as the illegalists assert, it is legitimate when compared to capitalist accumulation, which the individual capitalist does not need in order to exist, accumulation that is a superfluity.

Now, who is that "other" who the reasoning, conscious illegalist will attack, this anarchist who exercises an illegal profession? It won't be those crushed by the current economic state of affairs. Nor will it be those who benefit, without resorting to the exploitation of others, from their "means of production." The "others" are those who want majorities to dominate or oppress minorities; they are the partisans of the domination or dictatorship of one class or caste over another; who are the props of the state, of the monopolies and privileges they favor and maintain. That "other" is in reality the enemy of every anarchist, his irreconcilable enemy. The moment he economically attacks him the anarchist no longer sees in him, no longer wants to see in him, anything but an instrument of the archist regime.

Given these explanations, it is impossible to consider the illegalist anarchist to be in the wrong when he considers himself to have been betrayed when anarchists who preferred to follow a less dangerous road than the one he took abandon or turn their backs on him.

The illegalist replies to the revolutionary anarchist who condemns him for seeking his immediate economic well-being that he—the revolutionary—does the same thing. The economic revolutionary expects his personal economic situation to be improved by the revolution; if not, he wouldn't be a revolutionary. The revolution will give him what he hopes for or it won't, just as an illegal operation either provides the person who carried it out what he counted on or it doesn't. It's simply a question of the date. And even when the economic question doesn't enter into play one only makes a revolution because one expects to benefit by it personally, or to receive a religious, political, intellectual, or perhaps ethical advantage. Every revolutionary is an egoist.

As for the objections of those who enjoy their work, who exercise a profession to their liking, it is enough to oppose to them this remark Elisée Reclus' one day made to me in Brussels when we were discussing this very question: "I enjoy my work and I don't recognize the right to judge those who don't want to do a job that they don't like."

The anarchist whose illegalism attacks the state or recognized exploiters has never turned workers from anarchism. I was in Amiens during the trial of Jacob, who railed against the Church, the chateaux, and colonial officers. Thanks to the intelligent explanations in the weekly *Germinal* the workers of Amiens demonstrated sympathy for Jacob, recently freed from a penal colony, and for the idea of individual expropriation. Even if he is non-anarchist the illegalist who attacks a banker or a big factory owner, a manufacturer, or a treasury, et cetera is sympathetic in the eyes of the exploited, who consider the employees who persist in defending the coin and cash of their private or state exploiter to be in a way lackeys or informants. I've noticed this on hundreds of occasions.

Even though I don't have in my possession the necessary statistics, reading revolutionary newspapers indicates that the number of those imprisoned or killed, rightly or wrongly, for acts of revolutionary agitation (including propaganda of the deed) is far greater than the number of those killed or imprisoned for acts of illegalism. The theoreticians of anarchism, communism, revolutionary or insurrectionary socialism bear a large responsibility for these condemnations, for they have never surrounded propaganda in favor of the revolutionary act

5. Elisée Reclus (1830–1905). Anarchist and geographer.

with the same reservations which serious "explainers" surround the illegalist act.

In a society where the system of repression takes on the character of revenge, of a vengeance that the supporters of the social order pursue and exercise on and against those who threaten the positions they occupy, and that pursues the degradation of individual dignity, it is clear that the man in prison will inspire more sympathy in an anarchist then those who deprive him of his freedom or keep him behind bars. Not to mention that it is often among these "irregulars," these outlaws against an environment based on the exploitation and oppression of the producer, that we find a courage, a contempt for brutal authority and its representatives, and a tenacious force for resistance against a system of individual repression and degradation that one would seek in vain among "regulars" or those who restrict themselves to professions tolerated by the police.

We have the profound conviction that in a humanity or a social environment where the occasion to utilize individual energies will be present at the departure point of every personal evolution and where these occasions will abound all along life's road; where the most irregular will find the capacity for a multitude of experiences and ease of movement, the most undisciplined characters, the most inflexible minds will succeed in fully and joyfully developing without this being to the detriment of any other human.

—EMILE ARMAND

Individualism: Along with their partisanship and insufficiencies, I love the very stupidities of dictionaries, so I went through the small and great *Larousse Dictionaries* looking for the definition of the word *individualism*. In both dictionaries I found entries written by the same author: "A *system of the isolating of individuals in society.*" But in the great *Larousse*, the author specifies: "Social Philosophy. *Subordinating the good of others to one's own good, living as much as possible for oneself is to be an individualist.*" He adds a few superficial notes in order to show that he has read Spencer and Nietzsche.

In the first place, all of this proves that certain men are allowed to teach the French language, which they are ignorant of, since this (anonymous) author doesn't know that there are—absolutely—no synonyms, which leads him to give the word *individualism* the definition that applies to a certain *egoism*, taking this word in its strictest, most unfavorable, pejorative sense.

This proves that certain men are capable of reading philosophical works without understanding them. Unless we are dealing here with bad faith. Anything is possible. In any event, bad faith is nothing but a consequence of stupidity. Like the word *anarchy*, the word *individualism* is a victim of this. Scribbling watchdogs malevolently employ the word *egoism* for *individualism,* and provide only a skimpy, restrictive, and petty conception of individualism.

We will attempt here to restore the true meaning of the word.

If the meaning of the word isn't vitiated, *individualism* is a system that has the *individual* as its basis, its subject, and its object. Listen to the individualists and you will see that the three aspects of this definition are correct. Individualism is thus a system based on the individual, which has the individual as its end, and the individual as agent.

Let us put that phrase in the plural and think it through. We want humanity's happiness. But humanity is not a real entity: only the individuals who make it up are real entities. Thus, when I say I want humanity's happiness I am implicitly saying that I want happiness for individuals. The individual is thus my object. I say *individual*, I don't say *me*.

This could be countered by saying that viewed in this way all systems are individualist. This would be true if individualism were nothing but that. But in individualism the individual is not only the object, he is also the subject. But before dealing with the individual subject, let us finish with the individual as object.

I believe that everything having to do with the crowd is ephemeral, superficial, illusory, and vain. If I were a talented orator it would be easy for me to have a crowd of three thousand people adopt my ably presented opinion. These three thousand people would applaud me "like one man."

At that moment, it is possible to have this crowd commit colossal acts, either heroic or odious. But it would have done nothing that was lasting, because once the enthusiasm passed and the crowd dispersed, the individuals regain control of themselves or are once again conquered by their cowardice. Thus, if I want to do something lasting I must aim not at the crowd but rather, among these three thousand beings, at the few humans capable of becoming individuals. Individualism thus applies itself to seeking out, discovering, and perfecting individuals.

Let us pass now to the individual agent or subject. It's hardly necessary to say after what has preceded, that it is not crowds, or societies, but individuals who, each one working with the consciousness of his means and responsibilities, aims not at the entire society but at individuals for the realization of the greatest sum of happiness and the greatest sum of means.

It can be seen that the final goal is the happiness of all through the happiness of each.

—RAOUL ODIN[1]

---

1. Raoul Odin (1874–1941). A prosperous optician in Paris and individualist anarchist, he left France to found an anarchist colony in Costa Rica. It failed, and he remained in Central America until his death, dying in Panama.

Individualism (Individualist Anarchism)   Individualist anarchism includes several tendencies, from "expropriating" anarchist individualism (Bono, Renzo Navatore,[1] et cetera) to quietist anarchist individualism (Han Ryner[2]). Nevertheless, all schools of anarchist individualism are in agreement on this fundamental point: they consider the individual unit to be the cell of every social totality or group, of every association; they deny the need of a state as regulator or moderator of the relations between men and the agreements they make among themselves; they reject any social and unilateral contract; they defend sexual freedom; they place the realization of their various aspirations (in so far as it is possible for them to conquer them) in the present and not the future.

Today what is called "anarchist individualism" is a synthesis of the ideas of the Americans Josiah Warren and Benjamin R. Tucker, the Germans Max Stirner and John Henry Mackay, the Frenchmen E. Armand and Pierre Chardon, et cetera, to cite only the most representative names of the individualist anarchist movement. Economically speaking, Josiah Warren, Benjamin R. Tucker, and Clarence Lee Swartz (the latter labeling himself a "mutualist") are clearly influenced by Proudhon and recognize this.

The study of this synthesis allows us to rapidly lay out the principal demands formulated by most anarchist individualists.

- Regulating of their relations (intellectual, economic, ethic, recreational, et cetera) by means of contracts signed without resorting to any form of state. These contracts can be terminated at will.

- Inalienable possession of the means of production by the producer, either an association or an isolated individual, as long as it is

1. Renzo Novatore (1890–1932). Italian individualist anarchist activist and theoretician.

2. Han Ryner, born Henri Ner (1861–1938), was an individualist philosopher who write for every important anarchist journal in France.

113

the association or the isolated individual that makes a claim to it by his own means and at his own risk and peril.

- The product to the producer—association or isolate—and total freedom to make use of it as he wishes without going through an imposed administrative network or a central organ.

- Free issuing of exchange monies that are legal tender solely among those who want to use it.

- Full and entire right to voluntary association in all fields.

- The guarantee of the non-interference of any individual or central power in the private life of individuals or the private functioning of associations.

- Full freedom of competition between individuals and associations, with guaranteed equilibrium at the departure point, in such a way that the producer does not fall into the ranks of manual labor and the consumer not be forced to accept a product of inferior quality.

- The guarantee of non-intervention in the functioning of associations of a sentimental or sexual order, whatever their modalities, as long as people adhere to them or depart from them of their own will.

- Full and entire right to expression, distribution, and publication of ideas and opinions, written and spoken, publicly and privately.

- The autonomy, integrity, and inviolability of the human person, of the social unit, and of the male and female individual, as the basis, the raison d'être and the end of relations between countrymen, wherever they live and whatever their race.

In general, anarchist individualists count far more on education and example than on any other factor to have their demands met.

In general, anarchist individualists want each to "receive according to his effort"—cerebral and physical, mental and sentimental, psychic and muscular (i.e., the capacity for different manifestations of the individual organism)—but they consider "non-societarian" communist anarchists to be individualists, that is, those who view communism as a question of local, temporary, relative, and private association.

It goes without saying that those anarchist individualists sympathetic to "making do however it's done" and illegalism accept these methods of last resort only as they relate to a society where the social contract is imposed. Where there exists neither domination of the environment or the individual over the human unit or vice versa, nor exploitation of the human unit by the individual or the environment or vice versa—the absolute ability to live in isolation or in association without external control or constraint—neither making do nor illegalism have any reason to be or exist.

I will be told that in an environment so constituted work tools and the engines of production are conceived and built exclusively to favor or intensify multitudinist production and have herd production predominate over individual production. This being so, it is not possible for the producer to completely enjoy or dispose as he wills (which come to the same thing) of the product of his labor and the fruits of his efforts. I do not contest this. But the civilization we suffer under is not an "anarchist civilization," and it has never occurred to me to contest the difficulty of the realization of a large-scale individualist milieu in the current social environment. I thus conclude that in today's social surroundings the individualist feels maladapted. Since he is persuaded that the tendency towards greater liberty can only emerge if "being" is not hemmed in by "assets," he feels himself to be in a situation of self-defense, open or hidden resistance against any societarian organization that imposes on the producer the renunciation of the enjoyment or the free and total disposal of the fruits of his labor.

The individualist also does not intend to have the herd solve his economic question for him: he wants to resolve it himself, by himself, for himself. Those systems that replace the economic exploitation of man by man by the economic exploitation of the human unit by the collectivity inspire no confidence in him. It is exploitation that must be destroyed, and not the method that must be modified.

The individualist is a man concerned in the first instance with the sculpting of his own personality. He views life, his life, as a work of art, that is, like a statue, a painting, or a poem that he never finishes polishing, carving, or retouching, whatever the perfection or state of the sketches or outlines already obtained or completed. The individualist is not [only] a worker, a simple executor, but also an artist, a creator. An individualist society is only conceivable on condition that all its constituents from all points of view and in all domains be both artists and artisans, never manual laborers or automata, which is the opposite of the current herd mentality.

For an individualist to grow, to prosper, to develop, to flourish, he needs fresh air, the fields and flowers of the earth, the stars of the heavens, intellectual commerce, the active frequenting of those women and men who, like him, want to mold for themselves an original personality. In order for his interior being to be formed and achieve awareness he needs to assimilate all kinds of external interests, he needs to roam freely wherever he wills, gathering the nectar from the flowers he encounters along his route that will serve in the making of the honeyed perfume of his personal life. Nothing that in any way touches on the individual is foreign to him. He finds pleasure in seeing the number of his comrades increase, and so he makes propaganda. Is it not likely that, among the newcomers to the ideas that are dear to him he should meet comrades with whom he will begin anew tomorrow such and such an experiment that failed yesterday due to the lack of ability or affinities of the associates with whom he had joined?

It is impossible to analyze the different tendencies of anarchist individualism unless all these remarks are considered.

As for the reproach made against anarchist individualists that they behave like "bourgeois anarchists," those who say this forget that the bourgeois remains always and despite it all a pillar of his society, bourgeois society, where he occupies his social rank thanks to the system of authority and exploitation. Even when he avoids society's prejudices and conventions, he does so trembling hypocritically, the valet of social mores, publicly praising the social chains he smashes in private.

—EMILE ARMAND

Justice (from the Latin *justicia*)   Justice is the sentiment of the equality or the equivalence between two human actions, symbolized by the scale. Spiritualists claim that the sentiment of justice is innate and was placed in us by a superior being. This cannot be demonstrated in any way. Even if the sentiment of justice might be innate in human beings, it is not so in humanity. It was gradually formed within human societies. It is unlikely that animals possess it, aside from those that live in a society, like ants, bees, and termites. In civilized man, the sentiment of justice clearly appears in simple matters: "Every task deserves a wage." But when the case is complex this sentiment is obscured by a variety of considerations: prejudices, mystiques, and above all interests and passions.

Man lives within a narrow circle of ideas he received from his environment. He can abstract himself from them with difficulty, especially when he has no interest in doing so. This is why the wealthy do not in general believe that they benefit from an injustice, even when they do no work to acquire their fortunes. Self-interest dominates the human soul and the sentiment of justice abstains from shouting too loudly when it is not in harmony with self-interest. People speak of immanent justice and think that injustices will be repaired simply by force of circumstance and time. This is false. There is no immanent justice. Things, since they are lacking in consciousness, can be neither just nor unjust. As for men, they care little for repairing past injustices; only their present interests concern them. When an injustice is repaired it is completely exceptional.

By extension, the name "justice" is given to the state apparatus supposed to render it. The function of this apparatus, tribunals, magistrates, et cetera, is the application of the law.

The ideal of the law is said to be the expression of justice. This ideal is far from being realized. In the first case, in its essence the law cannot be just, because it is general, and the cases when it is applied

117

are individual and therefore much more complex. This is why legal right and natural right are placed in opposition to each other. It is also because of the complexity of individual cases that jurists have been able to say: *Summum jus summum injuria* (the greater the law the greater the injustice). In practice, laws express the interests of the strong and not at all the general interest. Leaders make them against the led; men against women. The apparatus of justice is above all a machine for the crushing of the disinherited of this world. Rarely do the rich sit on the bench of the accused. The clientele of judges is made up of poor folk, guilty of having wanted to appropriate what was not destined for them

The idea of justice, along with that of liberty, presided over the constitution of democratic states. It is in its name that revolutions were made, but until now justice has always been defeated; the strong and the clever have never done anything but reorganize injustice in their favor. Nevertheless, it seems the era of falsehood that was democracy must come to an end. The rising employer class, repudiating its elders, will reject the romantic notions of liberty and justice as outdated. Taking over the idea of class struggle for its own use, it will maintain its privileges and exploit the masses, not by virtue of fallacious laws, but by a brute force that it will avow with no beating about the bush. This is the mystique of fascism, and it is on the road to success in various countries, asking only to extend its reach over the entire world. The victory of this philosophy of force would be disastrous for humanity: it will bring barbarism in its train. The sentiment of justice is a conquest of evolution. Outside it there is nothing but war, i.e., insecurity and misfortune.

—Doctoresse Pelletier[1]

1. Madeleine Pelletier (1864–1939). Parisian born, by age thirteen she was a convinced feminist and at twenty-five was a doctor for the city of Paris. She joined a Masonic lodge, advocating free thought and feminism. She ran as a candidate for the Chamber of Deputies as a Socialist (though this was illegal for women, who had neither the right to vote nor hold office), joined the Communist Party after the split in the Socialist Party, and ended as an anarchist advocating neo-Malthusianism. In 1939 she was convicted for performing abortions.

Kabbalah (from the Hebrew for reception, tradition)   What is the kabbalah, which so many occultists claimed and still claim to be disciples of, the knowledge of that can only be attained, it is asserted, after lengthy initiation, and which can only be spoken of with fingers on lips?

The kabbalah is a Jewish theosophy born about two hundred years before the common era and that circulated secretly until the fifteenth century, the era when Christian erudition began to take an interest in it.

For certain of its enthusiasts the kabbalah is viewed as a divine tradition, transmitted to Adam (!) and was transmitted by others to Moses (!!). The question of origin aside, the Kabbalah has had an enormous influence on Judaism in particular and the human spirit in general. Stripped of all the mystery it was formerly surrounded in, it remains an extremely profound and original theosophical and philosophical system.

The kabbalah is a philosophy of a pantheistic order. One of the first of the Kabbalistic books, the *Sefer Yesirah* (Book of Creation) shows us, allegorically veiled, all beings, both spiritual and corporal, both the angels and the raw elements of nature, emerging gradually from the incomprehensible unity that is the beginning and the end of existence. The name *sefirots* is given to these degrees, these immutable forms of being, of which there are ten: the spirit of God, the air, water, fire, the four cardinal points, and the two poles. God constructed his time, which is the universe, with these elements. In conclusion, in this first book, which explains creation, the Kabbalah considers Unity to be raised above all else and is seen as the substance and form of things. What is more, the principle of emanation is openly substituted for that of creation.

It is in the *Zohar* (Light), a book that appears to have been written much later than the *Sefer Yesirah*, that the kabbalists deposited their most secret thoughts, their system in all its mystical originality.

God's nature is defined as in the *Sefer Yesirah*: it is the substance, the immanent cause, the principle—both active and passive—of all that is. There is only one being and that is He, for everything we take to be independent is simply the varied expression of His unique existence. From within this indivisible unity there emerges the *sefirots*. The first three of them—the absolutely unique being, eternal reason or the word, and the consciousness reason has of itself—form an indivisible trinity represented in the form of three heads combined into one. The seven other *sefirots*: intelligence, grace, and justice, combine to give beauty; the triumph, the glory, and the foundation unite to form the ideal or celestial man, eternal mediator between God and the rest of nature. After having engendered his own attributes God proceeds to the generation of other beings. All emerge from his breast and participate in his being, but at varying degrees, according to the distance between the effects and the causes.

Matter is the final link in this chain, of which the ideal man, or the original Adam, is the first.

The most remarkable part of the system is that concerning the human soul and man as a whole. According to the Kabbalah, man is nature's most accomplished work. Through his soul he is the image of the ideal man; through his body he represents, in part, the universe and deserves the name of microcosm. From this flows the mystical correspondence's that the authors of the *Zohar* seek to establish between the different parts of our human organization and those of the external world.

Spiritual man, the image of the divine trinity, is formed by the bringing together of three principles: 1—that of a spirit, center of intellectual and contemplative life; 2—that of a soul, seat of the will and feelings; and 3—that of a cruder spirit immediately in contact with the body, the principle of instincts and sensations. The *Zohar* recognizes a fourth element of an extraordinary nature, the external form of man, conceived as an existence apart from and prior to that of the body.

In reducing the essence of things to that of thought the kabbalists arrived at the theory of ideas, which in turn led them to the concept of preexistence and reminiscence.

Despite the idealist pantheism that is the basis of their theosophy, the authors of the *Zohar* accept that human freedom is a mystery. In order to reconcile this mystery with the inevitable fate of souls (the return to the divine source), they adopt the concept of metempsychosis.

This too brief explanation demonstrates that the *Kabbalah* offers nothing more mysterious than most Oriental systems, principally those that appeared around the time of the birth of Christianity.

Philo, Avicenna, Raymond Lulle, Pico de la Mirandola, Paracelsus, Reuchlin, and the two Van Hemlonts, were kabbalists.

Freemasonry and the Illuminati of the eighteenth century were clearly influenced by the *Kabbalah*. We find ideas dear to the kabbalists in Spinoza, Hegel, and Nietzsche, and in Monism.

—EMILE ARMAND

Leader   English word (from *to lead*) passed into common usage. One of those words that is universally used.

In the English parliament the leader is the member of the body who assembles around him the men of the same party and opinion, who pursue the realization of the same program. We naturally distinguish the leader of the government from that of the opposition. The leader is the most visible personality of his party.

By extension, we call "leader" the main article of a newspaper. Also, the horse that leads a race, gallops at the head of the others.

In a party one must be careful not to take the leader for the most serious, the most cultivated, or the most intelligent man. He is often nothing but the most changeable, the lowest, the most ignorant. His "superiority" resides in his ability to raise himself to the leading position by the usual political means, i.e., intrigue and a lack of conscience. Being a repetitive loudmouth or having a tireless flexibility are enough to make a man the leader of his party. Rare are those who impose themselves through their talents or their convictions, and in the youngest and most enthusiastic movements—like socialism—the Jaurèses and Lenins are exceptions.

Almost all the political leaders of our era were and are nothing but incorrigible blabbermouths and outright scoundrels. And from palinodes to betrayals they have led the masses to discouragement when they haven't delivered them through their double game to the blows of their adversaries.

—A. LAPEYRE[1]

---

1. Aristide Lapeyre (1899–1974). Anti-militarist, freethinker, and anarchist militant, he served time in prison for "incitement to murder" for his anarchist writings, and was a vocal supporter of Faure's line of "the anarchist synthesis," which viewed communist anarchists, anarcho-syndicalists, and individualists as having common interests.

Morality (Its illusory bases; its current falsehood) Morality was mixed in with religion in the primordial intellectual confusionism. The good is what God commands; evil is what God prohibits.

God sometimes commands acts of general utility: "Who gives to the poor lends to the lord."

But most often, what God orders agrees with the interests of the mighty. He tells the Hindu woman to burn herself alive on the pyre that consumes the corpse of her husband. God orders military murders. The Crusaders set out to the cry of "God Wills It." The German Kaiser wrote on bombshells "*Gott mit uns!*" (God is with us!).

The progress of reason caused God to be put in doubt. It was realized that God's existence cannot be demonstrated. When people attempt to do so they can only come up with sophistries. What then should be the basis of morality?

It is established on the categorical imperative, which itself has a mysterious cause. "Duty, whence your origin?"

In reality, we see the so-called categorical imperative constantly transgressed, and it varies with the latitude. Doubtless certain savages have a categorical imperative that orders them to kill their elderly parents in order not to have to feed them. The categorical imperative, more familiarly the voice of conscience, is nothing but the suggestion of the environment in which one has been raised, which is why all consciences are not the same.

It's a waste of one's time and energy to seek a basis for morality: it has none. Morality is an assemblage of more or less important, more or less stable conventions.

However conventional, morality is not nonexistent. What would become of us if men, instead of living off labor decided to demand their subsistence from theft and murder? Civilization and humanity would disappear. Nevertheless, it is impossible not to see the falsehood that is morality in current society. There is little merit for the rich man in being honest and virtuous. But what is one to think of a morality that orders the poor man to allow himself to die of hunger rather than steal? Morality's primordial function seems to be the protection of property. The categorical imperative is a psychic gendarme.

Since the war, we have witnessed a profound overturning of moral values.

For the first time, the war included cultivated bourgeois participants who were not professional soldiers. The war of 1870 was carried out under the regime of paid replacements; that of 1914 under mandatory military service.

Of course, a number of sons of the bourgeoise succeeded in either being rejected or shirking, but there were bourgeois in the trenches. There they learned that one can kill without the earth opening up. They concluded from this that the morality they'd been taught in college had no real value.

The second cause for the collapse of morality was monetary inflation followed by the fall of the franc.

The bourgeoisie lived according to the ideas of [Benjamin] Franklin, the theoretician of morality and bourgeois life. They believed in honest and steady labor, in intellectual culture acquired through effort and productive of honors and money. They believed in saving. They thought that whoever led a serious, hard-working, and orderly life could not but succeed. The fall of the franc caused savings held in banks to melt away. The bourgeoisie concluded from this that it had lived according to false principles.

Today it can be said that commercial honesty has disappeared. Age-old houses whose success was founded on the renown of their merchandise ("a good reputation is worth more than a gold belt") today sell articles of poor quality. Reputation is mocked and profitably replaced by noisy publicity campaigns. What does it matter that customers are unhappy if advertising brings in new ones by the thousands? Wealth is no longer as it once was the crowning accomplishment of a long life: it can be made in just a few years.

Quality no longer corresponds to price: the most popular hotels serve their customers inedible food. External luxury attracts snobs and nothing more. Deception in commerce is so widespread that the vocabulary has been softened. We no longer say we were robbed by a dishonest merchant, but we were taken in by someone who knows how to get things done.

Literature has been totally commercialized: books are praised in the same way as coffee or chocolate. On the cover, which serves to attract the purchaser, it occasionally occurs that something entirely other than what is inside the book is announced.

With great publicity, titled and decorated scientists launch products that they know full well will not do what they promise. Their scientific situation, which inspires confidence, is a coin whose value increases with their level of celebrity and confidence. After a certain amount of time people realize that the machine doesn't work right or that the medicine doesn't cure, but who cares? Their fortune will have been made. Another scientist, every bit as honorable, will propose another product.

In the press, blackmail and hidden publicity are par for the course. The most general idea serves as a cover for mercantile interests. The dry regime of the Americans is combated, and alcoholism is made fashionable in order to sell wine and alcohol. The writer and the orator are paid by those concerned.

As a result, we see alcoholism all the rage among the bourgeoisie. People who want to be modern have a bar at home. A man in a suit stumbles out of a café and we find that normal. Pederasty and pimping enter the mores of the so-called "well brought up" youth. The young writer, in order to make a name, lends himself to the homosexual passions of a rich or powerful man. Students are kept by prostitutes.

Fidelity to opinions is considered a mark of intellectual weakness. People don't have ideas they can sustain (they have none), but the one that brings in money. Once the idea is no longer profitable, they change it.

It can be objected that it is only the bourgeoisie that is corrupted to such an extent and that the war, which afflicted the governing classes with gangrene, did not touch the proletariat. This is not totally true. Crimes, notably family crimes and crimes of passion have increased greatly since men learned to kill during the war. In truth, these crimes are the act of all classes of both sexes. People kill the mistress or the lover who has abandoned them, the rival, the annoying mother-in-law, the elderly father who stubbornly goes on living. ... The acquittal of criminals of passion enters the minds of the killers while they plan. This acquittal is put up with and we rid ourselves of the man upon whom vengeance is sought, or the woman who is in your way.

The proletariat is less involved in this than the bourgeoisie, but it is above all because they don't think. Their ignorance and their daily labor limit their horizon. With just a few slight differences they live the same rudimentary life they did before the war.

Of course, Catholics don't fail to blame irreligion for the bankruptcy of morality. This is a great error. It is precisely the corrupted class, the bourgeoisie, that is returning to Catholicism, or at least pretends to return to it in order to increase the forces of reaction.

In truth, religion and morality have only a limited influence on life's practices. In order for religion to exert an influence a strong faith is needed, which no one any longer feels in his heart. As for morality, its so-called categorical imperative is in fact not very categorical. *Video Meliora proboque deteriora sequor* (I see the good and prove it, and yet I do evil).

Is morality necessary? No. Or at least not as much as is believed. A rationally organized society would render morality useless, for morality has no other goal than that of palliating a wicked social organization and abusing its victims.

The adage "who gives to the poor lends to the Lord" has no meaning in a society where there are no more poor. The devotion of a parent to a friend struck with illness is of no use if well-built hospitals treat the ill. Taking in abandoned babies is not necessary if society takes care of them. Even moral assistance, the act of being compassionate towards the sorrows of others, of encouraging a depressed person, would no longer have an object. A rational society will know the psychologist, a benevolent professional who will be the doctor of the soul.

The morality of the future will be nothing but an urbanity, a mode of conduct in relations with one's kind, promulgated in such a way that relations can be a source of pleasure and not unpleasantness. Do not lie pointlessly. Do not crush your companions with a superiority that rightly or wrongly we confer on ourselves. Put up with the faults of others as long as they don't render our lives impossible. Do not make everything center around you; believe that others exist too and that they have their personality, just as you have yours.

These precepts do not come from either God or a noumenal beyond. They are relative and conventional, but are no less necessary. They are rules for a good life which human society, like all societies, needs in order to function normally. But in general, the less necessary the morality, the better the society will be.

—Doctoresse Pelletier

Nation (from Latin *natio*) The agglomeration of individuals living under the same laws in a country limited by borders, having common interests, a common language, and more or less common rights constitute a nation.

It sometimes occurs that the word "people" is employed in place of "nation," but it seems more logical to reserve the use of people for multitudes united by a community of origins and ideas and to qualify as a nation peoples legally constituted as a political and sovereign state.

Every nation has its customs and morals, and often various religions. The prerogatives attached to the various branches of national activity constitute a national right that coordinates individual and collective action for the general interest. Among nations, some are bellicose, powerful, and civilized, or barbarous, savage, prosperous, commercial, industrial, agricultural, and rich or poor. Thus, from nations are born the rivalries, competition, alliances, and wars that constitute the saddest scourges that could afflict humanity.

In theory, and in eras of social ignorance concerning the reality of the law, everyone is part of the people and sovereign; in practice, the only ones who are sovereign in the national collectivity are those who possess wealth, which they are able to do either directly or by the interposition of representatives who more or less successfully defend their interests. Rationally, in our time the nation represents a humanitarian circumscription determined by a certain community of ideas concerning the special right of every one of them. As a result, the mores, customs, and institutions vary in every nation. What is truth in one is error in another. With this diversity of individual and collective methods it is impossible to achieve real harmony in social relations.

Nations are constructed on the ignorance of real rights, of social rights. When the idol that summarizes the ideas dominating the nation falls, the nation declines and more or less rapidly dies.

Nations are in a way the incarnations of the personal God, and their mores are inspired by the ideas connected to the cult of the Creator. They will fade away to the extent right passes from the national domain to that of humanity. When society will have substituted itself for the divinity humanity right will have a real moral value, i.e., one common to each and every one of us, and the truth will be the same everywhere, as will error. It is from this moment, that is, that of the knowledge of truth, of the application of equal justice for all, that right will have an uncontested because uncontestable authority. We have not reached this point, but social necessity will lead nations to form just one society made up of all peoples. In our era of social ignorance, the need for harmony is making itself empirically felt. Nevertheless, every nation calls itself autonomous, believes in its independence, and attributes to itself an omnipotent sovereignty in the practice of social justice it proposes.

This is the state of affairs because all national attributes rest on the idea of the rights that the ruling and owning classes have of the power they claim to hold, coming either from God or the sovereign people. These types of sovereignty rest on no proof, simply on faith and illusion. All arrive at the despotism of one person or a few, and in no way at the application of justice.

But these two types of sovereignty, which are called theocracy and democracy, lead to disorder, the second directly, as is the current case, with the despotism of finance, but the first leads there as well by allowing the second to take the lead.

As a result of the application of these sovereignties, we are far from the justice that social need demands to be realized, and that will give birth to the sovereignty of reason, the only one possible in order to have lasting order.

Without our being on the eve of the fusion of existing sovereignties applied nationally, everyone more or less empirically understands the need for a social renewal that will place nations under the dependence of humanitarian right.

The historical mission of nations, the great moral benefit peoples have as their goal is the creation of a new social order where man will be truly free. The sovereignty of force, which is the only one humanity (and subsequently each nation) knew and knows, will necessarily be succeeded by the sovereignty of reason. In our time what is happening to nations is what is happening to individuals. Every man is necessarily sovereign through his reason during the epoch of social doubt, just as peoples were and still are concerning the rights of each, which they will be until the knowledge of right has substituted humanity for nations, and real and logical right for individual force.

In summary, the existence of nations implies that of social ignorance, and social ignorance of the truth of the reality of a right common to all has as its inevitable consequence the necessary application of force for the maintaining of order, so that, to echo Proudhon, the decrees and ordinances that issue from one nation do not offer the same guarantees to all nations.

Hypocritically or openly, two sovereign nations in contact can only be economically in a state of open or disguised war, in a way similar to that, as Colins says, of two families that live in isolation while being neighbors. The brotherhood, the solidarity between these two families can only be illusory and never real. Without the recognition of a right superior to all nations, no real peace can exist between them.

We approve the idea of a League of Nations, just as we approve all pacts that having as their aim the fusing of individual interests with general ones, even if only sentimentally.

For the moment, a new Tower of Babel can be glimpsed on the horizon. Even so, it is a happy symptom to see the great of the earth as well as the exploited of labor take an interest in the interpenetration of a sovereign *right* between nations.

It leaps to the eyes and the mind that when there will be only one law for all peoples, for all families, for all men; from the moment when the need for justice will finally impose its application, the real right that is its expression will force nations to disappear and fuse into Humanity and form just one rational society. Within the universal fatherland nations will then be what departments and provinces are today within every nation, where all will equally share in freedom, in well-being through labor, and finally, in real justice in conformity with acts, both individual as well as social.

—ELIE SOUBEYRAN[1]

1. Soubeyran's name does not figure in any of the reference books on anarchism. He wrote articles for the *Revue Socialiste* in the first decade of the 20th century, and later for the anarchisant *L'En Dehors*.

Organization (The point of view of anarchism) Organization is nothing but the practice of cooperation and solidarity; it is the natural, necessary condition for social life; it is an ineluctable fact that imposes itself on all, as much in human society in general as on every group of people with a common goal to achieve.

Man neither wants to nor can live in isolation. He cannot even truly become man and satisfy his material and moral needs except in society and with the cooperation of his kind. It is thus inevitable that all those who do not organize freely, either because they can't or because they don't feel it to be a pressing need, are forced to submit to organizations established by other individuals, normally constituted in governing classes or groups, with the goal of exploiting the labor of others to their advantage.

The millennial oppression of the masses by a small number of the privileged has always been the consequence of the inability of the majority of individuals to come to an accord, to organize themselves on the basis of a community of interests and sentiments with other workers in order to produce, to enjoy, and, eventually, to defend themselves against exploiters and oppressors. Anarchism remedies this situation with its fundamental principle of free organization, created and maintained by the free will of its associates with no form of authority, i.e., without any individual having the right to impose his will on others. It is thus natural that anarchists seek to apply to their private life and the life of their party this same principle upon which, according to them, all of human society should be founded.

Certain polemics lead one to suppose that there are anarchists refractory to all forms of organization, but in reality, the numerous discussions we have on this subject, even when they are obscured by questions of definitions or envenomed by questions of persons, at bottom concern only the mode and not the principle of organization. And so it is that comrades who are in words most opposed to organization organize like the others and often better than the others when they seriously desire to accomplish something. I repeat, the real question is the application.

I am convinced that a more general, a better organized, more consistent organization than that realized until now by anarchists, even if it wouldn't succeed in eliminating all the errors and insufficiencies that are perhaps inevitable in a movement like ours, which is ahead of the times and that struggles against the lack of understanding, indifference, and often the hostility of the greater number, would at the very least be an important element of strength and success, a powerful means of asserting our ideas.

I think it is particularly necessary and urgent that anarchists organize in order to influence the march of the masses in their struggle for improvements and emancipation. The greatest force for social transformation today is the workers' movement (the union movement), and to a large extent the course events will take and the goal of the imminent revolution will depend on its leadership. Through their organizations, which were founded to defend their interests, the workers acquire consciousness of the oppression before which they bend and the antagonism that separates them from their bosses. Thanks to these organizations they are beginning to aspire to a better life, to grow accustomed to collective struggle and solidarity, and can succeed in conquering all the improvements compatible with the capitalist and statist regime. After this, it's ether revolution or reaction.

Anarchists must recognize the usefulness and importance of the union movement, must facilitate its development and make it one of the levers of their activities, striving to achieve the cooperation of syndicalism and other forces of progress in a social revolution that entails the suppression of classes, total freedom, equality, peace, and solidarity among all human beings. But it would be a dangerous illusion to believe, as many do, that the workers' movement will succeed at such a revolution on its own by virtue of its mere nature. To the contrary, in all movements founded on material and immediate interests (and a broad workers' movement cannot be established on any other foundation) the ferment, the impulse, and the concerted action of men of ideas who fight and sacrifice for the coming ideal is needed. Without this lever, every movement inevitably tends to adapt to circumstances and engenders a conservative spirit and a fear of change among those who succeed in obtaining better conditions. Often new privileged classes are created that attempt to prop up and consolidate the conditions they'd wanted to bring down.

From which the urgent necessity for separate anarchist organizations that fight both inside and outside the unions for the complete realization of anarchism and seek to sterilize the seeds of corruption and reaction.

But it is obvious that in order to reach their goal, anarchist organizations must, in their constitution and functioning, be in harmony with the principles of anarchy. They must thus not be imbued with an authoritarian spirit, must know how to reconcile the free activity of individuals with the need and pleasure of cooperation; must serve to develop the consciousness and capacity for initiative of their members and be a means of education in the milieu in which they operate and a moral and material preparation for the desired future.

It seems to me that it is a false idea (and in any case unrealizable) to unite all anarchists in a "general union," that is, *one* active revolutionary group.

We anarchists can say we are all of the same party if by the word party we mean all of those who are *on the same side*, who have the same general aspirations, who, in one way or another, fight for the same end against common adversaries and enemies. But that does not mean that it is possible—and perhaps it isn't even desirable—that all unite in one association.

The environments and the conditions of struggle are far too different, the possible means of action available to each and all are too numerous, as are the differences in temperament and personal incompatibilities for a General Union, seriously realized, not to become an obstacle to individual activities, and even a cause for bitter internecine struggles, rather than a means of coordination and for combining the efforts of all.

For example, how would it be possible to organize in the same way and with the same personnel a public association made for propaganda and agitation among the masses and a secret society forced by the political conditions under which it operates to hide its goals, methods, and agents from the enemy? How could the same tactic be adopted by educationists persuaded that all that is needed is the propaganda and the example of a few in order to gradually transform individuals and consequently society; and revolutionaries convinced that it is necessary to bring down through violence a status quo that is only propped up by violence, and who believe in creating, against the violence of the oppressors, the necessary conditions for the free exercise of propaganda and the practical application of the victory of the ideal? And how to maintain the unity of people who occasionally for personal reasons neither love nor esteem each other and who might, even so, be good and useful anarchist militants?

In my opinion, an anarchist organization should be established on the following bases: full autonomy, full independence, and consequently, full responsibility for groups and individuals. Freele agreed upon accords between those who deem it useful to unite to cooperate in a common labor and the moral duty to keep one's commitments and to do nothing in contradiction with the accepted program. The practical forms and the instruments likely to give the organization a real life can be adapted on these foundations: groups, federations of groups, federations of federations, meetings, congresses, and committees responsible for correspondence or other functions. But all of this must be done freely in such a way as not to hinder the ideas and initiative of individuals and only in order to give more scope to actions that would be impossible or more or less ineffective if isolated.

In this way, the congresses in an anarchist organization, though suffering as representative bodies from all the imperfections we know all too well from experience, are exempt from any form of authoritarianism because they do not rule or impose their own deliberations on others. They serve to maintain and expand personal relationships between the most active comrades, to summarize and provoke the study of programs for the paths and means of action, to make known to everyone the situation of the various regions and the most urgent activities in each of them, and to formulate the various opinions current among the anarchists and statistically compile them. Their decisions are not mandatory rulings, but suggestions, counsels, proposals to be submitted to all the interested parties. They are only mandatory and applicable for those who accept them and only up to the point they accept them. The administrative organs they name—correspondence commissions, et cetera—have no directorial power and only take initiatives for the account of those who solicit and approve these initiatives. They do not have the authority to impose their own views, which they can of course maintain and spread as groups of comrades, but which they cannot present as the official opinion of the organization. They publish the resolutions of congresses and the proposals that the groups and individuals communicate to them. They are useful for anyone who wants to make use of them to facilitate relations between the groups and for cooperation between those in agreement on various initiatives. But everyone is free to correspond directly with whomever they wish or to make use of other groups named by specific groups. In an anarchist organization, each member can profess any opinion and employ any tactic not in contradiction with the accepted principles and that does not harm the activities of others. In every case, a given organization only lasts as long as the reasons for union are stronger than those for dissolution. In the contrary case, it dissolves and makes way for other, more homogeneous groups. Of course, the durability, the permanence of an organization, is a condition in the long struggle we have before us, and it is also natural that every institution instinctively desires to last indefinitely. But the durability of a libertarian organization must be the consequence of the spiritual affinity of its members and the capacity of its constitution to adapt to changes in circumstances. When it is no longer capable of fulfilling a useful mission, it is best that it dies.

Certain comrades will perhaps find that an organization such as the one I imagine and such as has already been more or less fully realized at different times, is not of much use. I understand them. These comrades are obsessed with the success of the Bolsheviks and they would like, as the Bolsheviks did, to unite anarchists in a kind of disciplined army which, under the ideological and practical leadership of a few leaders, would march compactly to attack the existing regimes and which, material victory obtained, would lead the constituting of the new society. And perhaps it's true that with this system, if the anarchists lend themselves to it and the leaders are men of genius, our material strength would become greater. But with what results? Wouldn't anarchism become what socialism and communism have become in Russia? These comrades are impatient of success. We are as well, but in order to live and emerge victorious, we must not renounce our reasons for living and distort the character of the eventual victory. We want to fight and win, but as anarchists and for anarchy.

—ERRICO MALATESTA[1]

---

1. Errico Malatesta (1853–1932). Friend of Bakunin and Kropotkin, this Italian-born revolutionary spent much of his time in exile in countries round the world and was one of the most important voices of the anarchist movement.

Police (from Latin *politia*, administration of a city.)   Organism that has as its end the executing of laws, decrees, and ordinances issued by the legislative power aimed at safeguarding the security of property, persons, or the state.

Every law, every rule obviously supposes a sanction. Every sanction necessitates a mechanism of constraint. As far back as we go in the evolution of societies this concern on the part of legislators can be seen: ensuring the tranquility of the state and the security of its citizens, i.e., order, through a number of measures, prohibitions, and prescriptions. When order is based on faith, on belief in a supreme magistrate, each believer, that is, each citizen, participates in the state police and the legislator, who is at the same time the prince, can easily oversee the execution of the law without the special, distinct organism that is the 20th century police.

In ancient Greece "the police were intermingled with the totality of institutions that constituted the city, and ancient writers meant by a well-policed state one in which the laws in general ensured internal peace."

Under the Romans it was in the time of Augustus that the police became a specific institution, made necessary by the extent of the vast state that contained peoples with unharmonious beliefs in one or several "gods." It also quickly became a frightfully tyrannical political police force. The *proefectus urbis*, having the *curatores urbis* under his orders, scattered lower agents about Rome and the provinces, charged with reporting on anything offensive to Augustus's power. This police force disappeared with the "barbarian" invasions and only reappeared several centuries later with the great movement for the liberation of communes. In purchasing the right to administer the cities in which they lived, the bourgeois also took security measures on behalf of their persons and their property. They had belfries constructed from which the bells sounded the tocsin when highway robbers or armed bandits approached.

All night an armed police body, the watch, roamed the streets preventing thefts and murders and, the singers of the time tell us, "frightening lovers." A guard service watched the city gates, which were closed at sunset. Every city had its police, its regulations, and its organization. This police force was often opposed by the police established by mistrustful craft bodies. Soon, police forces were established by craft bodies, mayors, municipal magistrates, consuls, and municipal officials and, in seigneurial fiefdoms, by judges delegated by the lord.

An edict of 1669 established a special magistrate in Paris who, under the name provost lieutenant for the police, and later lieutenant general of police, had all the security branches under his orders, including forty-eight policed superintendents and twenty inspectors. For the first time justice and the police were two distinct organisms. We find (in the *Larousse Encyclopedia*) in the preamble to this edict an amiable definition of the responsibilities of the police: "The police consist in ensuring the repose of the public and individuals, in purging the city of whatever might cause disorders, in procuring abundance and allowing all to live in accordance with his condition." With this in mind police lieutenants were created in all the main cities of the kingdom and later wherever a royal seat existed. [...]

Compeltely reorganized by the Revolution, which left it more or less in its current state, the police were saluted in the following way in articles 16 and 17 of the Code of Crimes and Punishments of 3 Brumaire year IV: "The police are established for the maintenance of public order, liberty, property, and individual security. Its principal characteristic is vigilance. Society considered as a mass is the object of its solicitude."

But the revolutionaries of 1789 had other illusions. In reality, the police continued the old tradition of the lieutenancies of the *ancien régime*. Set up to directly exercise authority in the name of established authority, it specialized in the exercise of oppression to such an extent that oppression alone was its raison d'être. Charged with watching over the execution of the laws, with pursuing all transgressions, it has become the very expression of tyranny. Necessarily escaping any real control, it is above all laws, an organism of denunciation, provocation, and putridness.

Policemen are recruited among the least educated, least conscious, least susceptible to understanding. Poverty, ignorance, and idleness are the recruiting agents of the police. When these individuals are granted a little bit of authority—that conferred by a spiked collar on the landowner's dog—they forget their class of origin and social ignominy and become the firmest supporters of the regime of the day. Déclassé, sexless, and brainless, on calm days they are "Plain folks who spend their time strolling."

Garbed in the costume specific to domestics, butlers, coachmen, doormen, bishops, judges, and soldiers, they chase off the streets the paperboys and street merchants who don't obey the law that guarantees registered, rented commerce with its gilded mirrors and storefronts; they pursue wild and poorly groomed dogs; they pace in front of prefectures; they beat drunks in their filthy and flea-ridden station houses. On May Day, on dark days of strikes when the plebe cries out its hunger to the tune of an undisciplined "Internationale," armed with clubs and sabers they beat women and children and kick in the heads of the elderly. When night extends its cloak over the alleyways, walking two by two they are holy and majestic order. And when the wicked attack a late-night pedestrian, in order to avoid being bothered the Cop-Representative of Order drags his feet and reaches the battlefield when there is nothing there but the dead and the wounded in order to write his report. They are sometimes stupid, often nasty, but everyone knows them.

There is a class of policeman that sports the bourgeois mode of attire. Only the naive think that they are in any way secret. In their stride, their gaze, and the undefinable tone of villainy that immediately classifies them as "dangerous animals" or "wolf traps." If not skillfully, at least shamelessly, they pull the string that springs the trap that catches either the poor rabbits of crime or confused idiots. Rodents and large birds of prey fear their nets no more than would bears. Living off the thief, the murderer, the whore, and the pimp, who make their existence necessary, if they didn't already exist the police would invent theft, crime, prostitution, and pimping.

The political police are recruited from among the category of plainclothes officers, far and away the lowest, vilest of them all—men whose methods are squealing and provocation. Their sole and unique goal is protecting those in power from spoken or written criticism and individual or social action. Certain of being covered in all circumstances by the masters of the day, there are no ignominies they refuse. Sidling up to a possible enemy, gaining his trust, becoming his friend in order to surprise his thoughts and acts and then denouncing him and selling him. Or mouthing the ideas of our pals in a group they've penetrated, pushing them to act, obtaining for them the means of doing so and then, when they're irremediably compromised, selling them out in order to earn some money or a stripe. What difference the suffering, the despair, even the death of those who greeted him like a brother? The cop is only doing his job. What a sad profession!

But is it at least of some use? The evil it does, the ugliness it spreads, are they compensated for by some good, some joy, some beauty? Under the tutelary eye of the police, can noble sentiments and fertile joys flourish?

Independently of the necessary conditioning that's an outgrowth of the profession, the police claim a) to protect property; b) to protect persons; c) to ensure order.

Let us see if that is really the case.

Protecting property: In our policed societies, all wealth—land, the subsoil, instruments of labor, products of labor—all are the thing, the good, the property of a few. The others, far and away the greater number, own nothing. Those who own all social wealth are precisely those who have never participated in its production, and those who own nothing are those who have produced all that wealth. The police thus do not defend the producers against the hoarders, the profiteers—not in the least. The law sanctions the fact of this dispossession of the large number of producers by the small number of profiteers, and the police keep an eye on the execution of the law. That is, the role of the police, under the pretext of defending property, is that of defending the robbers against the protests and revolts of the robbed.

The police useful? Socially useful? Who could dare say so?

Protecting persons: First off, who protects persons from the whims of the police? In order to protect the property they stole from the producers, some exploiters slowly kill nine tenths of humanity through lack of hygiene, rest, healthy food, spacious lodgings, and fresh air. For their profits these exploiters unleash wars where they cause the suffering and death of millions of producers. Do the police prevent killing by privation or war? Does it defend those millions of producers, of persons against the exploiters who kill them? Of course not! When the victims rebel against their executioners, the police strike the victims, imprison them, kill them. The police defend the persons of a few exploiters against the just revolt of millions of despoiled producers.

Can it be said that the police are socially useful in the protecting of persons? Of course not!

Guaranteeing order! What order? Is it the social harmony we dream of, where all humans, fraternally united, will assist each other in creating a life ever more beautiful, ever more joyous? No, no. The order protected by the police is the current state of affairs. This wealth of a few, built on the poverty of all the others, this permanence of insecurity and pain, this is the order the police protect. It considers any improvement, any modification in this horrific order to be disorder, and it cracks down harshly against the "disorderly."

Inseparable from the current order, the police force is an institution that must disappear along with this order. Theft disappears with private property, crime with self-interest, and disorder with the state.

—A. Lapeyre

Reformism, Reformist "Reformism" is the doctrine of those who, while saying they are in favor of a social transformation whose objective is establishing society on principles and foundations opposed to those that currently exist, propose to arrive at this result by a more or less considerable series of important partial reforms realized within the framework of legality.

"Reformist" is the name that serves to designate a person, group, organization, or party that considers the whole of these successive and legal reforms as the best, if not the only means of transforming the social milieu, or, to state it more precisely, for substituting the collectivist or communist world for the capitalist world.

Those political parties who say they are the "vanguard" and proclaim themselves revolutionary are all more or less reformist. The more reformist they are, the less revolutionary they are, and—the logical consequence of this—the less revolutionary they are, the more reformist they are. [...]

The anarchists are frequently accused of professing the doctrine of "all or nothing." There is some truth to this accusation, but only some, for it is true that the libertarians will not declare themselves satisfied and won't be so until they will have forever smashed all the social obstacles that oppose themselves to their motto: "Well-being for each and for all; liberty for all and for each." From this point of view, it is perfectly true they will fight until not even one stone remains on another of the authoritarian fortress that must be totally destroyed, so that no vestige of it remains. If it is thus that the doctrine of "all or nothing" is conceived, then it is true: I don't deny that such is the libertarian doctrine. But it doesn't at all follow from this that the anarchists don't take account of the blows that can be delivered, in the efforts that can be accomplished in pursuing the goal of attacking the fortress that they intend to bring down. And even less does it follow that they don't appreciate the value of these efforts and blows that have as a goal, and could have as a result, the weakening of the solidity and the diminution of the force of resistance of this fortress. Anarchists are reasonable people with a practical sense. They want 100 and that's the end goal. But if they can only have 10 they pocket this down payment and demand the rest. They see that the improvements obtained through reforms are only agreed to by the capitalist and bourgeois rulers on condition that they don't fundamentally infringe upon the authority of the rulers and the profits of the capitalists. They know from experience that after having been backed against a wall for a greater or lesser time—and buying time is a maneuver in which the leaders excel—the privileged class ends up granting that which it is in no condition to refuse. They aren't ignorant of the fact that when a reform touches upon the very bases of the authoritarian mechanism, the state and capitalism, it runs up against the desperate resistance of the established powers, and that resistance can only be smashed by a revolutionary impulse. Those in power only place a cost on the means directly employed by the proletariat working for its emancipation, and they are certain that in no case, in no conjuncture, will the latter truly free itself without having recourse to the sole instrument for its liberation: the triumphant social revolution. [...]

—Sébastien Faure

Resistance The quality of a body reacting to the action of another body (*Larousse Dictionary*). This is not the appropriate point of view here for the word resistance. Instead, we will discuss it in the sense of personal or collective resistance to everything that oppresses, depresses, pressures, and exploits the individual. It is in this way that, in the world of the exploited, the collective action of the resistance of factory and construction site workers, and of workers of the countryside and the ports, is manifested in the collective action called the strike. Resistance in all its forms is only of interest from our point of view if it is the conscious manifestation of one human or social force asserting itself against another human or social force. This is the way we view all popular movements, every spirit of revolt of the people against tyranny, from wherever it might emanate, against all tyranny as well as all entities in the name of which it is exercised: God, truths, fatherland, honor, universal suffrage, labor, property, the Church, the state, law, dictatorship, justice, the general interest, peace, right, civilization, humanity, progress, et cetera. For all these big words in the mouths of priests and politicians are nothing but deceit, lies, cheating, and brainwashing. Their hold must be resisted. Resistance, along with reflection, is the beginning of wisdom and the critical spirit, of the spirit of revolt. The mindset of resistance against all that seems beautiful and good and noble but that too often hides the opposite denotes an individual with character and free and healthy mind, and sometimes a man of action. United with other individuals, this individual force is multiplied and developed in the masses who for their part do not think enough, not being defended and supported by a large enough power of resistance. Honest individuals arising from among them, of whom we spoke above, can at times exert so great an influence over crowds that through a contagious force of sincerity and faith they manage to explode sparks of truth that engender not only resistance, but revolt, according to the motives, the place, and the circumstances.

From which the need to incite in every thing and every place the victims' resistance to the scourges created by an evil social organization: the high cost of living, outrageous exploitation, revolting authority, scandalous social inequalities, legalized fraud and theft protected by the law, the magistracy, and the police. Finally, resistance to all social evils is indispensable and must be permanent among the wronged popular masses, crushed and sacrificed by all the profiteers of the bourgeois regime.

For the salvation of all, resistance should be a way of understanding our role in a society based entirely on social iniquity. It is rendering a service to our fellows to lead them to resistance. They then learn from experience that the only way to win is by always balking against social scourges, against their causes and their effects. The workers have the right to everything for the simple reason that they have nothing. Against this state of affairs, resistance is a duty for all producers in need.

It was in this spirit that around the middle of the nineteenth century the workers, who had not yet conquered union rights, were able to cleverly get around the law and turned their mutual assistance societies into clandestine resistance societies where their corporate interests were discussed. The police hunted them down and they were constantly threatened with prison. "Resistance societies" was the right word for these workers' groups. The workers had come to see that it was only through resistance that the exploiters of the time, who took the workers for ambulant materiel, could be shown they were thinking beings.

Resistance societies are the ancestors of our corporative unions, whose slogan is "Emancipation will be the work of the workers themselves," and their unwavering goal, "Well-being and freedom through the suppression of bosses and wage labor."

Time has gone by and ideas have evolved, but though resistance is still honored the goal has not been reached. Our resistance societies are undergoing horrible crises.

Syndicalist militants don't have to hide in the mountains or the frosts, like plotting bandits, or to isolate themselves at sea like the shipwrecked to discuss their corporate interests, as they did in the last century. But they do have to evade obstacles posed by events on the straight road that leads to the goal. It is governmental corruption, politics and its harmful effects, the vanity of some, and the ambition of others that allowed syndicalism to go off the rails, despite the resistance of some. What is to be done in the face of this if not maintaining the pure logic and the incorruptible sincerity that constituted the power of the CGT that preceded the cataclysm of 1914.

Do not despair. Believe in the future and don't fight division by increasing it. Know in all circumstances how to resist any attempts at splitting our unions. If they are honest and not mere weathervanes, the place for militants with revolutionary convictions who are not politicians is not always in places where people think like them but, on the contrary, where there are minds to be enlightened, initiatives to be encouraged, virtues to be persevered in, and courage to be made to blossom in united actions for the total emancipation of the exploited. In a word, in unions, in cooperatives, everywhere we must be, outside of any politics, resisters against everything that corrupts, leads to deviations, and disunites. With patience, will, and character, militants young and old will see real syndicalism reborn, filled with enthusiasm for direct action, for perpetual and fertile resistance!

—G. YVETOT

Revolution [...] History has registered many acts called "revolution." It was not unreasonable to call them such, given the more or less great upheaval they engendered at the time and in the places they erupted. The same or similar acts, if they occurred in our time, would pass for simple and hardly profound reforms suffered by the current social order.

The error of past revolutions.

Experience has proved that these events, lacking in real depth and positive results, were nothing but passing crises provoked by a momentary fever state, and that the fever having gone down and the crisis having ended, the previous state of affairs was more or less quickly reestablished without it having been seriously transformed. In the past, many were the popular revolts, insurrections, and uprisings directed against the principles and institutions ruling the existing order. But nearly all these movements showed themselves to be powerless to achieve their goal, because these popular revolts, insurrections, and uprisings attacked the apparent effects and neglected the then unknown cause of these effects. As a result, the cause not having been done away with the effects quickly reappeared, which was inevitable.

In our time, in order to be considered a revolution it is indispensable that such an event should attack not only the evil a revolution intends to remedy or vanquish, but the very cause of this evil. If past revolutions, up to and including the most important of them (the French Revolution of 1789 and the Russian Revolution of 1917, to cite but these two), arrived only imperfectly and partially at their expected results. This is because they stopped half-way and did not pursue to the end the goals they assigned themselves. It was inevitable that this be the case, because with the evil manifesting itself in broad daylight, while the cause of this evil remained in the shadows, people thought—perhaps in good faith—that they'd put an end to the infection, when in fact the locus of the infection having remained intact, it was quickly reborn.

In France, the revolutionaries of 1789 thought that by replacing the monarchy with a republic and substituting the Rights of Man and the Citizen for the duties of the subject their job would be done. Since then the insufficiency of such a result has made itself ever more clearly and strongly felt. In Russia, the revolutionaries of 1917 thought that by replacing the dictatorship of the Romanovs and the nobility with that of the peasants and workers they would establish on the ruins of a social regime of political despotism and economic exploitation a state managed—at least in appearance—by the proletariat of the cities and countryside and that, concentrating all political and economic might in the hands of this so-called "proletarian" power, they would endow the Russian people with a social regime that would put an end to the scandals, abuses, inequalities, and iniquities of tsarism. But sixteen years after the revolutionary days of October 1917, the worker and peasant masses of Russia are still bent beneath the yoke and subject to an exploitation in no way less harsh than before.

The error into which all past revolutions fell is that of having limited their efforts to a partial objective, when it was indispensable to expand them to a total objective. Some were exclusively moral, others were specifically political or uniquely economic. In a social organization where all institutions, proceeding either from the moral, political, or economic orders, are indissolubly bound together, everyone neglected to smash the ties that unite them, bind them, and arrange them into a homogenous and compact whole. The result of this error was that, weakened at certain points, the existing social order found it needed to strengthen itself at other points so that the equilibrium indispensable to the life of every society, broken more or less cleanly by the revolutionary upheaval for a greater or lesser amount of time, could be reestablished.

The "social" revolution.

Applying the preceding remarks to today it can be seen that any revolution that brings down a part of the social structure while leaving the rest standing will be only a half-revolution, a failed revolution.

It is not without reason that in this article the word "revolution" is accompanied by the adjective "social." The object of this adjective is to precisely qualify the revolution that is in preparation, that is on the way. Responding to the needs of the hour, inspired by the needs, aspirations, and the will of humanity in the 20th century, flowing from a social state where political, economic, and moral problems overlap to such an extent that they can only be separated for purposes of artificial classification aimed solely at facilitating its study, the revolution that is needed will be social or it will not be at all. This social revolution will have as its goal, and must have as its result, the tearing up of the social contract that presently codifies all the relations that the complexity of individual and collective life imposes on one and all and the writing of an entirely new social contract on a basis totally opposed to that of the current one. To imagine and accept that things could be otherwise would mean demonstrating an unforgiveable lack of experience and an inexcusable naïveté.

When I say that this revolution will and must be social, lacking which it will not be at all, I mean to affirm that it must be at one and the same time political, economic, intellectual, and moral. I maintain that it must not neglect, respect, or spare any part of the social edifice it aims to destroy from top to bottom so that not a single stone remains atop another.

The word "revolution" is debased.

I recall—O! Time of my youth, how distant you already are!—the feeling of terror that the simple word "revolution" caused in the bourgeois world fifty years ago. The word then had a meaning it was impossible to mistake: social revolution, meaning the pure and simple confiscation without indemnification of private fortunes; the suppression of all the privileges that birth, education, influence, wealth, and power unjustly confer on a handful of individuals; destruction of the armament of collective violence, of systematically organized repression from the odious squealing informant to the ignoble executioner, including the cop or gendarme who carries out arrests, the magistrate who condemns, or the guard who imprisons; the abolition of the state and of all the institutions of lies, oppression, brigandage, despoiling, and iniquity that flow from and support it: government, parliamentarism, magistracy, police, and army; the wiping out of juridical, patriotic, familial, religious, intellectual, and moral impostures that paralyze the growth and hinder the free development of the individual; the disappearance of all tyrannies, exploitations, frauds, inequalities, swindles, competitions, hatreds, and the countless degradations that bear the seal of any social environment in which there is a perpetual and fatal conflict between rich and poor, wage payers and wage earners, rulers and subjects, masters and servants, leaders and subordinates. At the time, this was the content of the word revolution.

The word wasn't overused, so weak did those few units in an immense mass who risked speaking or writing it feel at the thought of the immeasurable forces whose violent eruption, whose brutal explosion and tumultuous unleashing it invoked. Those who were bold enough to publicly proffer it were aware that this word was one of those that must not be spoken lightly, because it synthesized an entire world of destruction and upheavals aimed at forever burying poverty and slavery beneath the rubble and at having emerge from these necessary ruins a new life made of well-being, liberty, and harmony. But one also had to see the shiver of horror this terrifying word—"Revolution!"—heavy with catastrophes, gave rise to in the world of the haves. But on the other hand, there was also the profound emotion and the shiver of enthusiasm this magic word caused to enter the hearts of the disinherited!

Such, alas, is no longer the case. All the scribblers who deposit their trash in the newspapers and all the sonorous and empty loudmouths in parliament and at public meetings are lavish with the word "revolution" in their writing and speech, a word that is even so rich in threats against some and in promise for the others. All use it or, more precisely, fraudulently exploit it wherever and whenever. [...]

No political party is revolutionary.
[...]
Given that all political parties, without exception, have as their goal, not the smashing of power, but rather the wresting of it—legally or illegally, peacefully or through violence—from those who hold it in order to exercise it themselves, one can, and logically must affirm that no political party is, properly speaking, revolutionary, and that

whatever they might be, absolutely all political parties are counter-revolutionary, since all are opposed to a revolution that will make tabula rasa of all institutions proceeding from a central power or whose function would be a holdover, even a weakened one, of the authority principle. If a political party has the impudence to call itself revolutionary it is a flagrant imposture.

Only anarchists declare that without a social upheaval destroying capitalism and the state to their roots, i.e., authority over persons, property, and government, there is not and cannot be a true revolution. Only they forthrightly and fearlessly teach this capital lesson, which is why from one end of the world to the other they are bitterly combated and persecuted by all existing governments and all parties whose ambition is the seizing of the state. The verbiage used by a political party or the methods it employs or counsels do not, in themselves, have any consistent or positive meaning: only the goal it proposes, even if unspoken, is what matters. A reactionary priest can use the most violent and subversive terminology, but this wordplay does not prevent him from remaining reactionary. Caesar can hide his despotism beneath the cloak of order, peace, and liberty, but he nevertheless remains Caesar. A dictatorial party can exalt the use of revolutionary methods for the conquest of power, it is no less a party of dictatorship and, consequently, of despotism and counterrevolution. The language employed and the methods of action used or advocated are often nothing but fictions; the goal pursued is the sole reality that counts. Centuries ago, a Latin poet exclaimed, in expressing this opinion: "*Sunt verba et voces; proetereaque nihil*" (They are words and voices and nothing more). This quotation applies strictly and rigorously to socialist and communist declamations, which distort the current meaning of the word "revolution" and belie the fundamental idea this word expresses today.

That idea is that at the hour ringing on history's clock, in the countries where capitalism and the state have reached the current state of their evolutionary course, *there is only true revolution, in the precise and complete sense of the term, when there is a top to bottom upheaval, when tabula rasa is made of all current principles and their application, when a totally new starting point is adopted, when people operate on a basis and with a practice not only different, but, even more, diametrically opposed.* I have demonstrated in the most irrefragable fashion (see the entry for "Anarchy") that the social structure rests on the authority principle and the institutions that flow from it. The idea of social revolution thus necessarily entails:

1- The total abandonment and the definitive collapse of any social architecture having the authority principle as its foundation;

2- The adoption and the putting into practice of methods diametrically opposed to it: the principle and methods of liberty.

The anarchists have the unshakable conviction that the future belongs to them and will justify their doctrine. They are certain that sooner or later, after having exhausted with great difficulty all the methods and forms of social organization that proceed from the authority principle, humans will ultimately reject them with horror and, confident and resolute, will give the methods and forms of organization engendered by the diametrically opposed principle a trial run. Then and only then will the idea of social revolution, as they conceive it, triumph and grow in the realm of reality. Then and only then, the "everything belongs to a few" of the capitalist period having made way for the "everything belongs to all" of the libertarian times, and the "everyone obeying a few" of authoritarian epochs having been replaced by the "no one commands and no one obeys: neither masters nor servants" of the anarchist era, all individuals, without distinction as to sex or nationality, will live in the well-being and freedom they will have conquered through the true revolution.

Anarchists take part in all popular uprisings of a revolutionary tendency.
One should refrain from drawing the conclusion from this assertion that anarchists remain and must remain indifferent to attempts at revolution that—and this is all too certain—will precede the setting in motion and triumph of the many and great realizations to be derived from the economic, intellectual, and moral liberation issuing from a social revolution in keeping with their ideas. However optimistic we might be, we do not nourish the hope of covering in one leap the distance that still separates us from this magnificent result. We have no illusions on this subject. We know full well that between

the social order—or rather, the social disorder—we live under and the social order we want to establish there is a world of ideas, sentiments, traditions, and habits that must be completely transformed, and we are not unaware that so formidable a transformation cannot be quickly accomplished. There is thus no doubt that humanity will only reach the goal I specified above by incremental steps. It is certain that a number of small and medium-sized combats will be delivered before what Pottier's "Internationale" calls "the final combat" will be engaged. There is no doubt that victory will be the crowning event of a series of happy encounters and more or less crushing defeats.

So be it! The anarchists will not wait for the final battle to begin before acting. They will take part in the skirmishes that will lead to it. They will involve themselves in all the campaigns, all the agitation, all the broad-based strike movements and popular uprisings directed against the capitalist regime and inspired by the hatred of authority. They will be in the front ranks of the rebels, insurgents, and revolutionaries everywhere. They will be at the combat positions that will demand the greatest amounts of intrepidness and calm; they will be the leaders and authors of the boldest coups de main, the most audacious initiatives, the riskiest actions, the boldest acts, pushing the attack as far as possible.

Let there be no doubt: the anarchists will be among those—for I hope they will not be alone—who, in the most responsible posts and in contact with the most violently unfettered passions, will maintain their presence of mind and will not lose sight of the goal to be reached. I will express here, without exaggeration or romanticism, my most profound thought: I am convinced that whenever insurrectionary ferment will begin and emerge, whenever popular effervescence will take a revolutionary turn, the anarchists will throw themselves into the heart of the melee. First, because they are not unaware that when movements begin one never knows where they will stop, and because, even if they are defeated, drowned in blood, and then suffering fierce repression—the ransom of the fear that will have struck the bowels of the owning and governing class—insurrections of that nature always leave something behind them. The terrain conquered can be measured by the force of the popular flood and the distance covered by the revolutionary wave. And finally, because their temperament and the internal forces that animate them will prevent them from standing by with their arms folded, watching the tragic face to face duel with a present that does not want to succumb and a future, which wants to be born and live. [...]

Theoretically, one can admit the idea of a non-violent revolution.

Nothing is easier to conceive of theoretically than a revolution occurring without brutal combat, without street battles, without bloodshed. And yet, in the minds of almost everyone, the idea of revolution is accompanied by scenes of carnage and killing. As soon as the word "revolution" is spoken it instantaneously and without thinking evokes the appalling picture of pillage, disorder, and murder. It projects in the imagination the abrupt and instinctive impression of a bitter battle in which unquenched hatreds, unsatisfied revenge, and reprisals to be taken are given free rein. Why? Because until now this has been the experience of those events history records under the heading revolutions. Annalists and historians impress upon these events—which have more or less strongly marked past centuries, a dramatic character—a tragic and sometimes horrifying aspect. They speak of their origin and results even when the latter have constituted unquestionable progress less insistently than they do of the passions unleashed in those eras of upheaval and of the outbursts of violence and excess that followed them. Men having maintained the memory of these tragedies, their imagination having preserved the impression of these dramatic tales, and their natural sensibility remaining shocked by these tales of pillage and crime, it is natural that in their minds the idea of violence remain indissolubly attached to that of revolution.

This, though, does not mean the social revolution of which we are speaking will necessarily and ineluctably be violent and that the birth of the new world, whose coming we can sense, is fated to come about in the pain of combat, in the brutality of conflicts, in the tears, blood, excesses, and hatred that accompany violence. For I repeat that one can perfectly well admit, at least in principle, that the social revolution will occur peacefully, and the anarchists will be the first to rejoice in this and would be happier than anyone if such were to be the case. It is enough to know them, to know them well, to be certain of this.

Libertarians are commonly represented as hard, unfeeling, and cruel, and it's not difficult to discern to what end the rulers, who hate us, have drawn a portrait of us so contrary to reality. The truth is that we are profoundly humane, tender, gentle, and merciful, and that if we hate slavery, servility, ugliness, deceit, injustice, and inequality, we do not hate individuals. I have often said (and I affirm that it is true): "I can look deep in my heart, and I will nowhere find there a hated name."

Severe in regard to institutions, our philosophy is extremely indulgent as it relates to individuals, because experience proves every day that the individual thinks, feels, wills, and acts in function of the situation he occupies, the profession he exercises, the hereditary influences that impel him, the education he received, and the mentality and customs of the environment in which he was born, grew up in, and lives in (I do not take into account here the few exceptions that only confirm the rule). It must be known that if we keep ourselves at a distance from electoral competitions it's not only because politics—or what is currently called politics—are dirty and dishonest and because parliaments are lairs of corruption and duplicity, but rather because we are men and nothing but men and we know that subject as we are to failings, errors, and cowardice, and exposed like the common run of mortals to the bite of greed and ambition, if we were to commit the sin of soliciting and had the misfortune of conquering power, we would be every bit as powerless as anyone else to do good and could not conduct ourselves better or differently from them.

If the revolution is violent the masters alone will be responsible.

I indicated above what anarchists expect of the social revolution, what they ask and demand of it: that revolution close out the calamitous regime of authority and open the beneficent era of liberty. For them, this is all that counts.

If this result can be the fruit of persuasion, kindness, and accord between capitalists and proletarians, between governors and governed, no one's joy would be comparable to theirs. But if it is absolutely indispensable to appeal to violence to achieve this goal libertarians will not hesitate to resort to it. Well then! Who does it depend upon whether the social transformation will be peaceful or violent? I have no hesitation in saying that this does not depend on the working class, but on the capitalist class; not on peoples, but on governments.

Let us suppose that the ruling class finally opens its eyes and in the bright light of events realizes that these events are made to inspire in them the salutary fear that is said to be the beginning of wisdom. Let us suppose that the most intelligent and best-informed bourgeois end up becoming conscious of the grave danger hanging over their heads. Let us suppose that the most intelligent of these representatives and spokesmen for big capital, alarmed by a situation that from one end of the world to another grows worse with each passing day, come to think that the catastrophe is imminent. Let us suppose that they arrive at grouping all that follows from this in a somber tableau that will not fail to impress them: the anger of the laboring masses odiously starved by the lack of work; the disquiet of the other workers who have until then been spared unemployment but who live in the distressing uncertainty of the morrow; the touching fear of the people who hear rolling over their heads the sinister rumbling of the thunder that will fall on them in the form of a war whose horror will be beyond imagining; the growing discontent of the enormous mass of taxpayers upon whom the ever more crushing weight of taxation falls; the malaise and anger felt in both the petit and middle bourgeoisie by the general paralysis of affairs, the gradual decrease in the stock market, the banking debacle, and the devaluation of coinage. Let us suppose that the great capitalists who currently reign over humanity and preside over its destiny finally have a clear vision of the grave dangers that all these worries, irritations, discontents, fears, angers, and latent revolts cause their wealth and, worse still, their persons to risk. However improbable these suppositions might be in practice, can we not admit the possibility and foresee that, surrendering to the fear of seeing their property and lives taken from them by the revolution, the owners of capital and power will deem it prudent and wise to renounce the profits of capital and the advantages of power rather than run the risk of being dispossessed of them by revolutionary violence?

The field of hypotheses is immeasurable; let us not halt along this path. Let us wander further into the domain of conjectures. We just attributed intelligence to the powerful and the fortunate. Let us also be generous and grant them fairness, indulgence, and kindness as well. Let's say they are fair. Comparing the opulent idleness into which they have settled to the life of labor and privation to which the largest part of the population finds themselves condemned, let us suppose that the fortunate few are finally struck by this shocking inequality. If they reflect just a little bit they will discover, not without a certain shame mixed with a little remorse, that their idleness and opulence are built on the activity and indigence of the workers. Their hearts are moved and the sense of justice is awakened in them. They attempt to relieve the unfortunate surrounding them. But they quickly discover that their charitable efforts do not and cannot succeed in even feebly stifling the lamentations and cries of distress emitted from the too large and too deep abyss of human suffering. Unable to escape this distressing fact, their hearts, first penetrated with love and justice, open themselves to pity and finally incline to kindness. On the one hand, the spirit of justice that lies within them led them to recognize that it is monstrous that some enjoy a superfluity while others are deprived of the necessary, that the right to life is inalienable and that life demands that everyone eat his fill, be properly dressed, comfortably lodged, properly cultivated, and endowed with a sufficient share of affection and tenderness. The feeling of kindness, which is the complement of fairness and which gradually fills their hearts, then leads them to see all men as brothers, all women as sisters, all the elderly as their parents, and all little ones as their children, resulting in their fulfilling the duties of solidarity entailed in the bonds uniting the members of a family. In doing so they elevate themselves to the highest morality. This ascension enlightens them concerning the profound immorality of a social organization that grants everything to some and refuses everything to others, that allows a handful of the well-to-do to confiscate for their benefit the advantages conferred by power and fortune, while weighing the rest down with the burden of servitude and spoliation.

The day is finally rising when, listening to the counsels—better, the orders—of their justice-loving consciences and surrendering to the appeals of kindness, whose sweetness moves what is deepest in them, they solemnly and with a common accord are abandoning the wealth they own and the authority with which they are invested. The abdication of the intelligent was dictated by the fear of seeing themselves, their wealth, and their power swept away by the irresistible gust of the revolutionary storm. The abdication by the good was dictated by justice and benevolence. The result is the same: a social transformation accomplished without brutal and bloody force; it is the peaceful revolution being gently realized, without violence, since, with everything they have demanded having been benevolently granted, the discontented will not have to employ violence to conquer it.

Unfortunately, hypotheses opening out into such magnificent perspectives are nothing but gratuitous conjectures that do not resist the tests of experience and reason for two minutes. Experience testifies to their unlikeliness and reason proclaims their inadmissibility. I only allowed myself to formulate these suppositions with the goal of making clear—as is only fair—that the responsibility for violence in the event of a revolution falls strictly on those upon whom it depends whether the latter be violent or peaceful. If the defenders of capital agree to restore to the community the land, the means of production, transport, and exchange they seized through plunder, conquest, theft, fraud, the exploitation of the labor of others, the methodical robbery of savings, speculation, and a thousand other forms of despoilment, it will not be necessary to resort to violence to wrest it from them. If the rulers and all those who are their servants, supporters, and partisans resign themselves to voluntarily abandoning the posts they occupy; if they renounce the functions they fulfill; if they cease to maintain their grip on the authority they hold there will be no need to call for violent methods to dispossess them of any of this.

The delicate and controversial problem of the use of violence in the period of transformation, i.e., of social revolution, is thus posed in the simplest and most precise terms, and its posing establishes in the most unarguable fashion that its solution is found, not as we are led to believe, in the hands of the proletariat who call for the well-being and liberty to which they have a right, but in the hands of the owning and governing bourgeoise which can freely grant or refuse the exercise of this right to well-being and liberty. Is this clear? Is it understood that if instead of occurring without bloodshed—which is desirable but which seems to me impossible—the social revolution is accompanied by violence, the real responsibility for this violence can be imputed to those who, through their lack of lucidity and altruism, will have rendered recourse to the latter necessary?

The social revolution demands serious preparation.

Every revolution must be the object of more or less lengthy methodical preparation. The greater the task to be accomplished, the higher the revolutionary stakes, the more care and time the preparation demands. It is the duty of the conspirators who hatch a plot to foresee as much and as correctly as possible all that might occur. It is possible for them to accomplish this because a plot ordinarily is limited to a small number of conspirators, the principal ones taking on the role of leaders, making the decisions, arrangements, and measures that will ensure success. The day, the hour, the watchwords, the places of concentration, the distribution of forces and positions, the movements to be executed, the precautions to be taken, the modifications to be foreseen, the maneuvers to thwart, the resistances to be broken, the complicities to be assured, and the assistance to obtain. All of these details are the object for the promoters and potential beneficiaries of the plot, of careful study arriving at a plan that must, as much as possible, regulate all, predict all, and leave nothing to chance and the unpredicted. This is why the essential condition for the success of every conspiracy is scrupulously guarded secrecy and the passive obedience of the troops engaged in the plot.

A revolution, and even more, the social revolution we are analyzing in this article, is completely different. In the first case, it is impossible in general and in its grand lines to maintain the secrecy of the preparation for revolutionary action. Secondly, it is impossible to demand passive obedience and blind submission from the insurgent masses, neither of which is even desirable. Can written and spoken propaganda, which are indispensable in inculcating the spirit of revolt in the masses if they are to commit to decisive action when the time comes, be cloaked in secrecy? Is it possible to organize in mystery the apprenticeship of the multitude and its training in what is called "revolutionary gymnastics?" Can it be a question of fixing in advance a date, a precise hour, a determined place of concentration, a *ne varietur* plan, coordinated coups de main, surprise attacks, improvised maneuvers, spontaneous movements, et cetera, when we are dealing with a revolution which, to attain its goal, must take on the aspect of a popular uprising from the beginning and maintain it to the end?

I do not envision the revolution as a chaotic, disordered movement, beginning on a whim and continuing in the same way; I understand it even less as occurring without a well thought out plan. A plan discussed, conceived, and laid out in advance is useful and necessary. But this plan must contain only the essential lines; it must remain elastic and flexible; it must have great mobility, leaving the door open to initiative; it must be able to easily and rapidly adapt to changes and modifications counseled and demanded by the changing circumstances and conditions of the struggle, for though excellent in some cases, this or that revolutionary strategy can be harmful in others.

The hour of the social revolution cannot be fixed in advance by a divine or prophet. It is like a bill with no set duration that the proletariat will draw on the capitalist and ruling bourgeoisie and for which it will demand payment. This bill will only be presented when the bearer and beneficiary of the bill has the ability, in case of non-payment, to seize, expel, and expropriate capital and the state, the associated and joint debtors. But if it is within the power of no man to assign a precise due date to this bill, it is nonetheless necessary to foresee this date and be able to demand payment on this letter of exchange. This is how I see the preparation for the revolution.

This preparation implies the assembling of three necessary elements: education, organization, and action, and it is only fitting to give equal importance to each of these three elements separately and as a unit, because the fate of the social revolution—its victory or defeat—will be conditioned by the weakness or vigor of each of these elements and by the weakness or the strength of them as a whole. [...]

It should not be forgotten for a moment that the social revolution must be anarchist under penalty of being a failed revolution. That consequently the education must be anarchist, the organization must be anarchist, and the action anarchist as well, and this immediately, for we are now in the midst of the period of preparation and this preparatory labor consists in hastening the blossoming of the revolutionary phase properly speaking and in ensuring for anarchism, from the moment of its advent, the greatest vitality and the best conditions for development. [...]

The transitional period—Dictatorship.

In the socialist and communist parties, they endlessly discuss, or rather split hairs, over what these parties call the transitional period. What the theoreticians and leaders of these two currents of authoritarian socialism mean by this is the indeterminate time span during which the revolution, as they conceive it, being a *fait accompli*, will have to deal with the question of both repelling any attempt at an offensive return which the combined forces of capital and the state will not fail to deliver, while also proceeding to the establishment, development, and stabilization of the new social organization. For them the transitional period begins at the moment when the insurrectionary movement has triumphed, extending this until the time when the new regime, having rid itself of its internal and external enemies, will buckle down and establish a socialist or communist social environment. These two fractions, which love the notion of the socialist state, go so far as to advocate for the immediate morrow of the triumph of their revolution a regime that will be a ferocious and absolute dictatorship that they have the effrontery to baptize "the dictatorship of the proletariat." They have the hypocritical impudence to assert that this dictatorship is indispensable for the safeguarding of the revolution and the defense of revolutionary conquests. What's important to know is the nature of the merchandise that travels beneath this flag.

Well, this merchandise is nothing but flea-bitten, shoddy goods, and the revolution whose conquests the beneficiaries of the dictatorship claim to defend is nothing but a pitiful counterfeit of the social revolution. What is this cheap junk? What do these revolutionary conquests consist in? Let us coldly examine the latter and the former from the revolutionary point of view that is ours, a point of view whose exactitude no revolutionary can contest.

Thanks to many convergent circumstances which have discredited the established authorities, have brought to light the maleficence and absurdity of the capitalist regime, provoked exceptional ferment among the popular masses, and laid bare the incompetence of the leaders; which have, in short, created and publicly revealed a catastrophic situation, a mighty insurrection has broken out. Its natural breadth and extent has quickly attained the proportions of a formidable revolution. The rebels have driven out military and civil government, the armed forces have been routed, and the revolutionaries have remained masters of the battlefield. In this magnificent outburst of anger and revolt, all proletarian forces have united and forced the masters of the day and their defenders to flee. Attacked on all sides, besieged, the fortress from which just yesterday were issued all the decisions to resist and all the orders for massacre, was forced to capitulate. Seized with panic, terrorized, and confused, those who occupied it dispersed in a headlong, every-man-for-himself flight and, taken prisoner and held as hostages, deprived of weapons, those who hadn't the chance to take advantage of the general debacle were reduced to impotence.

In its just rage, the revolutionary masses are resolved to set fire to the four corners of that accursed fortress, the center and seat of all political, economic, and moral authorities. When that citadel, now the prey of avenging flames, will have been totally destroyed, when nothing will remain of it, the long-blocked road will be liberated. Then the proletariat, finally master of its destiny, in an irresistible burst of enthusiasm, confident in the close union that gained it its deliverance, remaining solidly united and acting in solidarity, responding to pressing needs will rapidly organize the egalitarian and fraternal life glimpsed by anarchists and for which they, by their active, persistent, and passionate propaganda, prepared hearts and minds.

But this radiant prospect does not at all please the leaders the political parties have endowed themselves with. Did these gentlemen write so many articles, give so many speeches, and construct philosophies and systems of a solidity they declared scientific that they said could stand up against all tests; did they push themselves into parliaments and establish themselves in the most advantageous positions; did they acquire so brilliant a notoriety; in short, did they work so hard, take so much trouble, impose such heavy sacrifices on themselves; did they so tirelessly work to free the workers from the influence of the evil shepherds of the bourgeoise and place them under their own guidance; did they do all this so that with one blow the dream of domination that has haunted them for so long should collapse? So that they draw no personal profit from victory they so fervently prepared and whose hour they waited for so impatiently?

Are we going to ignore the wise (or cowardly) advice they so generously offered in the darkest times to the flock of the faithful they recruited and who not too long ago followed them blindly and obeyed them passively in application of the discipline they sententiously declared to be the primary force of parties, in the same way professional soldiers affirm it to be that of armies?

No and no again! This is not possible.

Leaders and sub-leaders quickly assemble in order to: think things over, to study the situation, and decide on the necessary measures. They are careful never to admit to each other the ambitions eating away at them. They hide as best they can the thirst for domination that devours them. All those who in the preceding years specialized in agriculture, in foreign affairs, in finance, in internal administration, in public education, in justice, in war, in the navy or aviation, in public works and the postal service, in the fine arts, in commerce and industry, hygiene and health, in labor or in any other branch of national life assert their competencies, attract their colleagues' attention to the services they are capable of rendering. Each insists on the gravity of the circumstances, on the urgency and need to meet immediate demands, to reestablish order, to reassure the comrades, to inspire confidence in all. They outdo each other in oratorical feats. Each of them thinks the moment has arrived to assume the most crushing responsibilities and, hand on heart, with trembling voice, eyes gleaming with the flame of the purest devotion, every specialist declares himself ready to sacrifice his repose, his health, and even his existence to defend, from the post that will be imposed on him by his friends' trust, the sacred interests of that revolution that the admirable people signed with their blood.

In addition, they are all penetrated with the profound sentiment of their superiority that the habit of speaking and acting as leaders who are listened to and obeyed introduced and gradually developed in their personalities. More, they are so convinced that the masses are incapable of leading themselves, of discerning the road to be followed, of adopting reasonable decisions and sensibly conforming their conduct to it, that they imperceptibly arrive at convincing each other that it is their duty to constitute themselves as a kind of provisional government, invested with the most extensive powers.

This proposal is adopted unanimously. The provisional government, called "of revolutionary defense," is established, beginning with a distribution of posts and powers meant to satisfy ambition and greed. Now, without wasting a minute, it's a matter of informing everyone of the great news. The night sufficed for the accomplishment of so many tasks. The next day the walls of the capital are covered with posters lyrically announcing that the most intelligent, the most conscientious, the most honest, the most competent men, those who, thanks to a life dedicated to the defense of the humble, to the education and the training of the laboring classes with the aim of establishing a society of men free and equal, deserve the people's trust, agreed to the request of the most powerful revolutionary organizations that they assume the weighty responsibilities and crushing charges of power.

This proclamation doesn't fail to assert that their power will be gentle toward the good, that is, those who contributed to the victory and collaborated in the efforts of the government, but that it will employ the severest sanctions against the wicked, that is, all those who will attempt to combat, to hinder or compromise the revolutionary conquests. Finally, it expressly declares that the provisional government will strictly limit its duration to that of the transitional period.

Airplanes, automobiles, and speedy trains launched in all directions, along with the feverishly employed telegraph, telephone, and radio spread this information to even the most modest provincial towns.

But it is at precisely this moment that the fate of the victorious revolution is at risk. If the insurgent populace does not immediately react, if it doesn't there and then have the feeling that this provisional government signifies the stifling of the revolution, if it doesn't immediately have the conviction that in arming itself with unlimited power this government will transform itself into a dictatorship and that this dictatorship means the confiscation of the revolutionary conquests for the exclusive benefit of the dictators and their party, the victory of the rebels finds itself ipso facto nullified. If the indignation of the truly revolutionary elements isn't expressed at that very instant by a repeat of the popular insurrectionary uprising, if this uprising does not achieve the power of a tidal wave smashing the new authority, the revolution is mortally wounded and will soon expire, murdered by the perfidy, pride, and spirit of domination of the very people who proclaim themselves its defenders.

The least respite granted the new masters allows them to reestablish the functioning of the levers of command that were taken from their predecessors and to seize and again set into motion the entire governmental mechanism. This means the installation of their people at the head of all the leading services; their surrounding themselves with a mass of bureaucrats and an army of functionaries; the reviving of the magistracy, the army and the police that the revolution had drawn and quartered, basing their power on the self-interested assistance of some, the servility of others, and the indifference of the majority.

Once established, the dictatorship becomes increasingly intolerant and repressive. It equals the most abhorred regimes in abuse of power, arbitrariness, and ferocity. The profiteers of the dictatorship—masters like any others, and sometimes worse—will never recognize their uselessness, and even less their maleficence. They will never admit that "the transitional period" has reached its end and that having accomplished the mission they assigned themselves their role is no longer necessary. They never think that the moment has come to abdicate, to abandon the power to which their despotism, their vanity, and their appetites, desperately cling. And a new revolution is needed to get them to let go.

The program of the political parties that style themselves socialist or communist consists in expropriating the capitalist class politically and economically and driving the bourgeoisie from government while setting themselves up in their place: this is what they mean by the political expropriation of the capitalist class. Seizing the riches of all kinds that class owns and, having carried out this confiscation, nationalizing property, declaring it the property of the nation, and entrusting its management to the state, their state: this is what they mean by the economic expropriation of the bourgeoisie. This is their revolution!

Such a concept of the revolution leads naturally to the so-called transitional period. If one accepts that in order to reduce the duration of this transitional period to a minimum a strong government, an intransigent authority is indispensable, one is naturally led down the slope that leads to the notion of dictatorship.

But this concept of the revolution is not ours. It corresponds to the idea of a politico-economic revolution, but not to our idea of what will be, what must be, under pain of a fiasco, the social revolution, our social revolution, outside of which history will henceforth record no true revolution.

Our revolution.

The social revolution that libertarians have in sight and to whose preparation they dedicate the best of themselves will, as I have said, be preceded by a more or less lengthy gestation period, and it will only break out when the following conditions are all met. Above all, it is necessary that a series of events and a confluence of circumstances create a revolutionary situation. I will not be so imprudent as to predict what this confluence of circumstances and series of events will consist of. It is possible that it will be a wide scale strike movement pulling into its orbit an ever-greater number of corporations and strikers effectively attaining the proportion of an insurrectionary and expropriating general strike, bringing a multitude of workers onto the streets. It is possible that it will be the threat of a general mobilization against a particularly unpopular, imminent war. It is possible that it will be an economic crisis provoking, from stratum to stratum, a general unease, a profound disquiet, and an increasingly bitter discontent. It is possible that it will be a too openly unjust fiscal regime, or a great administrative or judicial scandal, or a parliamentary decision shocking public sentiment, or an abuse of governmental power disgusting the popular conscience. All of these circumstances are capable of setting the fire and, in the blink of an eye, causing an immense and raging flame if the spark falls on material saturated with flammable products.

It will then be necessary that the general situation be so grave and inextricable, that it so profoundly implicates the social regime in its responsibility, that it so clearly demonstrates the inability of the government to reestablish equilibrium, to remedy the ill, to forestall catastrophe, that the people will end up losing all confidence in those who govern.

Finally, the situation being revolutionary, it will be necessary that there exist in the popular masses a sufficiently pronounced spirit of revolt and revolutionary ferment for a conscious minority, active, enlightened and in contact with the masses, to be able to raise the latter, as yeast does the dough.

Let us add these essential considerations:

a. An increasingly marked rupture in the political, economic, and moral equilibrium of the capitalist regime;

b. An active and persistent propaganda, stimulating the revolutionary education of the workers;

c. A solid, powerful organization capable of uniting, at the hour fixed by the gravity of circumstances, all the forces of revolt constituted by the many and energetic groups;

d. A proletariat driven to decisive action by a series of troubles, agitations, strikes, riots, and insurrections.

These conditions assembled, one can be certain that a revolution—breaking out when one of those events occurs that arouses, impels, and enthuses crowds and instinctively drives them to a tumultuous rush against the regime they want to overturn—will not stop half-way. This movement, into which the anarchists will have been the first to leap with the quickness, verve, determination, and bravery that cannot be denied them, and of which they will continue to be the leaders, will be carried on to the bitter end, that is, until victory. [...]

I will briefly summarize my thoughts on this point: during revolutionary periods the libertarians will have to destroy, to impede, and to reconstruct. They will have to do all that depends on them so that these three tasks be undertaken, follow one after the other, and be accomplished in the shortest amount of time. They will dedicate all of their efforts to

1. *Destroying.* Destroying what? I would like to hope that no one will do me the insult of thinking that I mean by this the destruction of buildings, machines, products of various kinds, masterpieces piled up in libraries, artistic treasures that adorn museums, of that fabulous accumulation of artistic treasures owed to the unstinting labor of past and present generations. What then of revolution on the ruins? Our revolution must result in restoring to the human community the magnificent patrimony accumulated through centuries of labor and that tyrants and birds of prey stole from him. It would be folly and a crime to destroy this patrimony, and destroying buildings would mean depriving the population of homes it will need to lodge itself, of beds, furniture, and utensils necessary to it. Destroying machines, smashing those metallic workers whose mission, once the revolution is made, will be that of almost totally abolishing man's arduous efforts while infinitely

multiplying their productive ability, would be monstrously stupid. Destroying the products of all kinds heaped in shops and storerooms while the need for food and clothing can only be met with the assistance of these abundant goods would be inexplicably idiotic. No, all these riches will on the contrary have to be preciously preserved and, as far as possible, carefully sheltered from destruction. But destroying from top to bottom, with no hesitation or restriction, all the abominable institutions that since time immemorial have been the cause of man's unhappiness: property, the state, parliament, the army, the magistracy, the police, religion, imposed morality, all things that were only born and lived thanks to the authority principle, a spreader of lies, errors, absurd beliefs, prejudices, cowardice, deceit, cruelty, injustice, inequality, and hatred that made the earth a planet constantly watered with tears and blood. This is the destruction that must be carried out.

2. *To impede.* To impede what? Impeding, by all means necessary and at whatever the cost, the authority principle, which the social revolution will have as its goal to bring down and to prevent from surviving or being reborn in a new form or under a new name. Woe on any social revolution that fails to go to the end of the road that must be taken. In such a case, it will have labored in vain. None of the revolutions of the past fully attained the goal it proposed because (I've already said this, but there are truths that cannot be repeated too often) they all attacked only a part of the evil that had to be totally killed, and so the evil reappeared in new forms, unsuspected and unforeseen. Victorious, having dozed off in the shade of its laurels, confident in its victory, which it had thought definitive, the revolution awoke imprisoned and defeated. The evil it thought it had killed in fact hadn't been. Seriously wounded, it had bandaged its wounds and imperceptibly returned to life. It was a tree whose branches had been cut and whose trunk had been cut down by the revolution, but that had spared its roots; a fire whose flames had been extinguished by the rebels without their having completely extinguished its source, without drenching its still burning ashes; an evil whose external manifestations the revolutionaries had combated without extracting its internal seed;

a hydra whose six heads the Hercules-people had chopped off but who neglected the seventh. The roots of the tree they'd wanted to bring down not having been extirpated, the tree grew anew. The source of the fire not having been completely extinguished, the smoldering ashes not having been either dispersed or drowned beneath torrents of water, the fire was re-ignited; the evil authority that ate away at the social body only having been combated in its external and visible manifestations and the virus of evil was not torn out, the evil recommenced and produced the same devastation. It's the history of all the revolutions that shook the world and whose results were later wiped out. *The social revolution, in whatever era it might break out, will find fearsome enemies along the way.* These enemies will be all the more dangerous in that to a greater or lesser degree they will involve themselves in the battle (if not in the person of their leaders, at least in that of their militants). The vigilance of the anarchists must not relax for a single moment. If the revolutionary movement is defeated there is nothing to fear from the maneuvers of socialist and communist leaders. But watch out if the revolution carries the day! The activity of anarchists and anarcho-syndicalists, of all those who *sincerely* and wholeheartedly work for the social revolution will be to jealously keep an eye on these leaders, to boldly denounce their plots, to intrepidly combat their chicanery, to incite the mass of rebels against their tricks, and finally, to oppose an impassable barrier to the accomplishment of their criminal designs and in so doing to *impede* any authoritarian relics, i.e., any provisional government, any resurrection of the state. This is what I mean by the term "impede."

3. *To reconstruct.* This word is sufficiently clear and expressive, so I can dispense with long explanations. Reconstructing is the consequence and the follow-up to destroying and impeding. Authority having been destroyed, any restoration of capitalism and the state having been impeded, it is obvious that it is necessary to reconstruct. And this reconstruction should follow destruction as closely as possible. The positive work should so to speak succeed the negative work without interruption. Reconstructing

immediately will be a necessity because no more than individual life can collective life suffer prolonged interruption, the social organism, for the same reasons as the individual organism, having functions to fulfill and needs to meet at every moment. [...]

Conclusion

Still quivering from the just finished battle and crowned with victory, the multitude will not be sparing in its confidence in the brave companions who, through the boldness of their initiatives, the intrepidity of their actions, and the example of their disinterest, will have been the artisans of this victory. Knowing clearly what they want at whatever the cost, and, even more, what they do not want in any way, shape, or form, the anarchists will make the best use of the confidence they showed themselves to be worthy of to oppose a solid, invincible battle front against any attempt at political domination or economic exploitation. Their task will not end there. It will also consist in avoiding deviations and false maneuvers. They will above all set themselves to rendering immediately tangible the advantages a real revolution should place at the disposal of all.

Anarchists will work ardently to inspire and vigorously second the efforts of the laboring masses seeking within themselves and finding in their creative powers, in their natural aptitudes allied to their experience, the higher forms of fraternal production and fair distribution of the wealth of which labor is the sole source. The vigilance of the companions will only be relaxed when all the institutions of brigandage and oppression will have been totally wiped out; it will only slow down when love and the practice of free life will have so thoroughly saturated the new man that any return of authoritarian conspiracies will be struck powerless.

When the working class and peasant masses will have taken their destiny in hand, when in possession of self-leadership, they will have acquired mastery of their movements, thoughts, and feelings, they will not delay in placing in themselves that confidence that leaders have forever made every effort to take from them so as to exploit to their advantage the abused masses' belief in the need for providence and saviors.

Then, thanks to free agreements, thanks to the fraternal accord that the masters will no longer be able to trouble, and finally, thanks to the spirit of solidarity that will naturally emerge from the disappearance of classes and the reconciliation of individual interests, there will arise a social structure more beautiful, more spacious, more airy, and more radiant, where everyone will settle according to their affinities and in which all humans will taste the charms of peace, the sweetness of well-being, the joys of culture, and the incomparable benefits of liberty.

—SÉBASTIEN FAURE

Sabotage   According to the *Larousse Dictionary*, this word deals only with the making of sabots—wooden shoes. For that dictionary, it's nothing but a masculine noun. Learning sabotage means learning the craft of the *sabotier*—the clog maker. It is also the operation of obliquely cutting sleepers on railroad rails in order to attach bearing cushions or rails. Even so, the dictionary also indicates that "Sabotage is the action of executing a task quickly and badly. Printing: dishonest act of the typesetter who knowingly introduces errors in the composition or damages the printing material entrusted to him."

The latter definition of sabotage is not ours. It is not acceptable that a worker does damage to his work or material without reason. When an activity is understood in this way it's because the worker is a bad worker who doesn't love his profession, doesn't have the love of labor that makes—or should make—man proud and free. And in any event, why cite the printshop as an example and the typesetter as the type of a saboteur, when there are so many other professions where the task is more serious and the material more precious? The saboteur of *Larousse* is poor in spirit or a discontented sneak taking revenge.

Thus, in a few lines the *Larousse Dictionary* says all it can about sabotage. In a few words it nevertheless touches on what interests us here. But it is necessary to be clear about the form of direct action that in our theory of revolutionary syndicalism we have propagated under the name sabotage.

It is precisely because the enemies of the organized working class have never ceased distorting the meaning or ridiculing the meaning, the action, and the goal of sabotage that it has seemed indispensable to syndicalist militants to explain it in speech and writing whenever the occasion arises.

According to the *Larousse Dictionary*, sabotage is simply the act of executing a task quickly and badly. A saboteur is nothing but a worker, an employee, a wage earner who, fully aware of what he's doing, quickly and badly executes his task.

Here is something clear and brief.

But the good *Larousse Dictionary* isn't acting unthinkingly when it abstains from digging deeper into the action of sabotage and knowingly failing to develop more fully the value we attribute to it in the daily struggle in support of our demands and in defense of the exploited against the exploiters. We will attempt to fill this gap here.

The following is an excerpt from a pamphlet already old (1908) but still topical on this subject:

Direct action also includes sabotage—What has not been said and written about sabotage? Lately the right-thinking press has set itself to distorting its meaning. Fortunately, writings of syndicalist militants or their declarations before tribunals have reestablished the exact meaning of worker's sabotage, which should not be confused with bosses' sabotage.

The sabotage of the bosses attacks the public by tampering with products, by fraud in wines, butter, milk, flour, et cetera, by the poor quality of material necessary for works of public utility. [...]

Worker sabotage, against which the newspapers have sabotaged the public's judgment, against which judges have sabotaged justice and equity, is completely different.

In the first place, it consists, for the worker, in giving his labor for the price paid: for bad pay, bad work. The worker practices this system quite naturally. It can even be said that there are workers who carry it out unconsciously, instinctively. This is doubtless what explains the poor quality and cheapness of certain products. It's commonly said of poor products sold cheaply that it's work that comes from a prison workshop. [...]

The intelligent sabotage of the worker generally attacks the direct interests of the exploiter. It is legitimate; it is defensive; it is vengeance. The bosses' sabotage attacks only the public interest, since it harms the public's health, security, and life. No confusion is possible.

Sabotage is thus direct action, since it attacks the boss with no intermediary. Sabotage is direct action that can be exercised in moments of relative peace between employers and wage earner, as well as in times of strikes and conflict. (excerpted from *The Syndicalist ABC*)

Here then is a definition of sabotage that corresponds quite well to what the worker understands when it is a matter of protesting or defending himself by the best means within his reach and that, far from being harmful to a collective, protects it at the expense of the interests of the bosses. [...]

We could cite many examples of sabotage. During a strike of registered seamen, the strikers committed an act of intelligent sabotage by printing posters denouncing the villainous sabotage of the Compagnies Maritimes. These posters warned travelers that such and such a boat was dangerous, given the poor condition of the boiler (duly inspected) or machinery; that another ship might suddenly stop in mid-voyage due to the unquestionable fact that the horizontal axis was cracked and was certain to break at any moment, consequently immobilizing the ship in the middle of the ocean. It should also be remarked that the seamen, called saboteurs, warned the passengers of the risk they ran, placing their confidence in the incompetence of the Compagnies Maritimes. The latter, from criminal rapacity, remained silent about dangers they were aware of, but they made the passengers pay—in advance— enormous sums for the trip. Even with this, they only paid the crew after the voyage and never paid out wages in advance. This self-interested calculation is the same for all. These firms never allow their dishonest actions to be considered sabotage. The clientele and users of the transport companies have never protested against this system. As for the state, it never intervenes against the companies: their legal proceedings are reserved for the exploited of these companies when they denounce these crimes. The police forces of provocation and repression are eagerly employed against strikers demanding security, well-being, and respect for their dignity as workers. The state also never fails to intervene with the same old speeches lamenting shipwreck victims and then bailing out the navigation companies, always in deficit. This kind of capitalist and governmental sabotage has never caused as much ink to spill as a simple act of worker sabotage, knowingly distorted by a servile press serving its own interests. The latter always knows how to make an act of sabotage seem criminal, excelling in sabotaging the facts. For contemporary journalism the sabotage of public opinion in service to capitalism is a professional duty. There is sabotage and there is sabotage—this is something that must be said.

It should be not be forgotten that laws and decrees almost always emerge from resounding protests by parliament, public opinion, and the press after a catastrophe. But these laws and decrees are almost always unapplied and un-applicable, so sabotage continues against the lives of miners, railroad employees, seamen, and all those workers who risk death daily in order to earn a living and enrich exploiters of all categories: entrepreneurs and administrators as well as those who profit by doing nothing but amassing dividends and enjoying them all their lives. [...]

It remains to us to define in what form sabotage should be implemented. We all know that to increase our enslavement the employer usually chooses the moment when it is most difficult to resist his encroachments through a partial strike, the sole method employed until now. The results have not always been all that was hoped for. While not neglecting the means of struggle that is the strike, it is necessary to employ other methods, with or without strikes.

Lacking the power to go on strike, workers who've been attacked have no choice but to submit to the demands of the capitalist.

With sabotage things are completely different. Resistance is possible. The exploited are no longer at the complete mercy of the exploiter; they have the means of asserting their virility and proving to the oppressor that they are men. They have in their hands a defensive weapon that can become an offensive weapon, depending on the circumstances and the use made of it.

What is more, sabotage is not as new as is thought: workers have always practiced it individually, though not methodically. It was not always ineffective. It inspired in those who profit from exploitation a salutary fear that only grew when the power of collective sabotage asserted itself. Workers instinctively slowed down their production when the boss increased his demands. The workers more or less consciously applied the slogan "for bad pay, bad work."

The bosses thought they had parried this defensive tactic of the slaves of the factory and the building site by substituting piece work for daily wages. They realized that their interests, less harmed on the quantity side, became more so on that of quality. When, for example, it was the contrary, that is, when the boss substituted daily wages for piece work, thinking in this way to enslave the worker, the latter, naturally also employed the opposite method to reach the same result. Let it not be said that it was bad workers who acted this way, for we insist that they were the most skilled, the most intelligent, and consequently those most conscious of their value. The bad worker is the eternal saboteur and can never be anything but, and the boss knows this. The former only has any value through the group he is part of, for individually he counts for little. It is in his interest to follow the boldest in order to keep his job and not be employed at disagreeable tasks.

Sabotage can be adapted to all kinds of tasks. It is practiced in all professions and modernizes in step with progress in production. It becomes fearsome with the perfecting of mechanization. We can't say all there is to be said about the application of sabotage, but during the years from 1900 until 1914, France amply demonstrated the awesome power of revolutionary syndicalism, inciting the direct action of the conscious and organized proletariat with the aim of freeing themselves of the exploitation of man by man. The report to the workers' conference of Toulouse (1897) concluded thusly:

"Sabotage can and must be practiced in piecework labor by striving to show less care for the work performed while still producing the quantity required to avoid reducing the wage paid. The boss, thus ensnared, will have the choice of meeting his workers' demands or losing his customers. If he is intelligent he will turn the tools he owns over to the producers who know how best to use them without sabotaging them."

But this would be the beginning of the end for the employers and exploitation. We should not count on it.

Sabotage in the factories, in centralized production, on building sites, and in large-scale enterprises can be exercised with discernment and intelligence against tools and engines without posing the least danger to the public and strictly to the detriment of capitalism. The emotion produced in the bourgeois world is still remembered when the secretary of the railway workers union declared thirty-three years ago that an employee, a trainman, or a railroad mechanic could, with ten centimes worth of a certain ingredient totally paralyze—and for a long time—one or even several locomotives.

We could write an apology here for sabotage and the boycott by citing nothing but our memories.

In France, and particularly in Paris, there were incidents of sabotage that were, in some cases, comic, and in others tragic or that threatened to become so. There were some days and some nights that allowed us to hope for the social revolution, making war impossible.

The agendas of our workers' congresses prior to 1914 presaged victories that in the end were nothing but bitter and cruel disappointments. We prefer not to linger over them in order not to sabotage the new hopes that still animate us, so unshakable are our revolutionary convictions, so immutable is the anarchist ideal in the heart and mind of the sincere and modest man who believes in the future of freedom and harmony between men of good will.

—GEORGES YVETOT

Soldier [soldat] n. (from the Italian *soldato*) *Milit.* Member of the military who receives wages paid regularly by the prince or country he serves. Simple soldier. Unranked soldier: a military man of the third category, since the army is made up of officers, non-commissioned officers, and soldiers.

The more stripes an officer has the further he is from a soldier, having, as he does, more authority and higher wages, with more honor and fewer risks. A soldier is paid a minuscule salary, but he receives shelter, clothing, food, and a bed. All of this for a stupid task—stupid in its exercise, criminal in its intentions, and infamous in its accomplishments and goals.

Not everyone who wants to be a soldier can be one. The infirm, the idiotic, malingerers, and the weak of body and mind are permanently exempt. Majors with few scruples examine, listen to, and palpate the flesh of twenty-year-old men, forced to present themselves at an appointed date and time for what is called their physical [exam]. All conscripts have a very good chance of being considered apt for service, especially if there is need for cannon fodder to defend interests having nothing to do with their own, assuming they aren't capitalists or sons of capitalists. If the poor soldier has the naiveté to believe that he is called upon to fight for an ideal or a more or less acceptable reason, unless he is a cretin he will quickly see that he has been tragically duped. But if he is a solider he is no longer a man: he is a number, a machine made to obey, a machine to kill his fellows. At a given moment he sees before him another man who suffered the same ignoble training. That man, whom he doesn't know, is the enemy. And yet, he resembles him like a brother, is a man like him. No, he's a soldier like him. And the contest is to see who will kill the other one. This is why they were both turned into soldiers. But things aren't as simple as that. This duel exists only as a result of the hazards of war: the circumstances that place a man before another man are extremely rare. In fact, it would perhaps be dangerous if these men weren't the soldiers that those who, from their place of safety, sent them to face each other want them to be. It is possible that these two men will recognize each other as men, both victims of an atrocious machination, and that they will fraternize, as has more often been the case than people think, despite the care shown to stifle such potentially contagious bad examples. And so, war is rarely a duel of man against man. It is, on the contrary, a blind, mass killing spree. It is a ferocious, savage massacre of maddened brutes, of furious beasts. It is madmen in rabid bands dragged along, drunk on hatred and alcohol. It would seem that what is needed in order to be a perfect assassin is to be stupid, ferocious, cowardly, cruel, and above all, unthinking: In a word, to be a good soldier, a hero, gloriously killing or being killed, as is proclaimed by profiteers, who gain advancement, decorations, and benefits from colonial wars and wars between nations.

For us there is only one kind of war that is acceptable, and that is civil war. In this case it is not soldiers who are needed, but men. They are indispensable in order to give birth with forceps to a society pregnant with social transformation. As for the unfortunate children of the people who by chance are soldiers against their will, at such a moment they have the occasion to become men again by assisting their civilian brothers in making the revolution.

Indeed, this is how a revolution succeeds, as social events have proven. The historical acts of every nation and every era that have occurred with the aim of political and social transformation have only occurred in this way. The bourgeoisie, which has everything to lose, wants to preserve everything. To do so it is ready to do anything.

According to the law, everyone in France must serve the fatherland and, if need be, die for it. In the past, professional soldiers changed their fatherland with ease, depending upon who paid them. Leaders did the best they could, and got value for the money they devoted to training and paying the soldiers they replaced with others when some vanished, changed camp, or were killed. The leader or lord got what he paid for. He made use of them according to his means for God, the fatherland, the king … and himself.

All of this has been changed since the French Revolution. And then the real thing arrived among the soldiers: Napoleon, the flat-haired Corsican. He placed under his boot the people who had taken the Bastille and overturned the monarchy. He led with the saber soldiers in rags whom he allowed to see the world and who he stuffed with glory and blood. It is to the triumphant soldier of the Imperial epic we owe the dreadful prosperity of militarism and the renown of the soldier.

Since then, wars have assumed a large role in the world. It is a far-flung and good business proposition that the world's peoples have paid for. There's no need to speak of this here. We have just had our fill of it. From 1914 to 1918 the World War was a horrific hecatomb of soldiers. The next one won't be satisfied with soldiers; it will want everything that lives.

If one means by soldier someone who embraces the defense of something or someone—the soldiers of the idea—it can be said that draft resisters, deserters, and those opposed to the profession of soldier are tough and valiant soldiers, given the risks they at all times run of physical and moral suffering in order to avoid the execrable obligation of military service.

What can be said of the admirable energy of conscientious objectors who refuse to bow before what is ordered of them by usage and law, by what the interested parties call "duty." Those who consciously, energetically, stoically refuse to touch a weapon are true heroes. They are soldiers of the idea.

These soldiers of the resistance against evil, these men of conviction, these heroes, these martyrs, are men!

They want to kill no one; they want to kill war.

—GEORGES YVETOT

State The adventure of what has occurred over the course of human history to the reality as well as the idea of the state would be the most amusing thing imaginable, if it hadn't taken a tragic turn.

We live in a state. We are, it is said, served by the state. We pay—we know this well!—a tribute to the state. We constantly—every one of us could say something about this!—have to deal with the state. Every one of us could claim to know perfectly well what the state is.

Nevertheless, whoever would suppose that the state is something fully real and definable would be crudely wrong.

Every attempt to define the state precisely, scientifically, and clearly has failed, at least up to the present.

There is a science solely dedicated to the study of the state, but the object of this science—the state—cannot be found.

The definitions of the state found in dictionaries are of no real value.

It is not surprising that the great legal and statist specialists find themselves forced to say that at bottom, the state is a fiction. That all the supposedly distinctive signs of the state, even sovereignty, are applicable to other phenomena and can in no way serve to establish the specific reality of the sate (L. Pertajitsky, Cruet, and M. Bourquin, among others).

Let us immediately make an important deduction: there exists a form of coexistence among humans that does not much differ from certain other "organized collectivities" (for example, the Church, the nation, political and caste groups, and others), but that nevertheless has obtained a special designation over the course of the centuries: the state, to which superior and exceptional qualities are attributed. It is claimed that this social organization stands above all others, that its power is unarguable, sacred, and general. It is imposed on everyone. Absolute and blind obedience is owed it. In this way a fiction, a fetish, was created. This is our first observation.

Let us move on to the second, which is no less interesting.

If you think that the origins of the state are known you are again in error. On this subject we have only more or less likely or unlikely hypotheses. Bourgeois statists, socialist and communist statists, anti-statists, all represent the origins of the state differently. Nothing, or almost nothing, is established precisely, scientifically, clearly. This is our second observation.

The third, the problem of the historic role of the state, is the object of interminable discussions between statists of different tendencies as well as between anti-statists. Here, too, nothing has been established definitively.

Placed before these facts, everyone should ask himself: What, then, is the reason I am forced to obey and submit to an institution that is perhaps nothing but a fiction whose origins are unknown and whose historic role is arguable? Why do they want me to recognize and venerate a fiction?

Is it not amusing to see people take a fiction for reality for centuries and recognize, respect, and serve something that doesn't even exist?

As we have already said, this would be amusing, even very amusing if, alas, the thing hadn't taken a tragic turn.

For the fiction has cost, continues to cost, and will in the future cost much blood.

What is more, it is always for fictions (God! The Church! The State! et cetera) that man has fought and still fights. Reality, everything that is not fiction, escapes him. Ghosts drag him along, lead him, absorb him. Is this not tragic?

And people say that we anarchists are utopians, dreamers!

A thousand times no! Those who believe in fictions are certainly dreamers and utopians. As for us, destroyers of ghosts, we are realists. Yes indeed! We anarchists who, it is said, sail on clouds, are the very definition of the firmly grounded.

***

Well then, as realists, what do we have to say about the state? How do we explain the power of this ghost, its formidable influence, its "reality" for millions of people?

There is abundant anarchist literature on the state. This is understandable, for the negation of the state, the struggle against the state, to a degree equal to that against capitalism, is the cornerstone of anarchism. The works of Proudhon, Bakunin, Kropotkin, Elysée Reclus, Malatesta, Jean Grave, Sébastien Faure, Pouget, Stirner, Rocker, and many other lesser known libertarians deal with the problem in depth. It would be superfluous to cite them here. The reader seeking to obtain a more or less complete education regarding the state need only consult the sources themselves. What is needed here is a brief and clear summary of our point of view.

First, let us come to an agreement on one point: given the absence of a precise and solid definition of the state we will include under this term a system of mutual relations—actions and reactions—between a number of more or less important individuals; a system whose scope, influence, and efficacity are limited geographically, politically, economically, and socially, and whose reality is only intuitively understood by the individuals within it.

What, according to the anarchists, is the essence of this system? This is what we will see.

1. *The origins of the state*—As was already said, they are, alas, wrapped in darkness. It seems impossible to establish and reconstitute them.

Nevertheless, there exist several historically accepted points with which we are in perfect agreement, notably: first, the advent of the state signifies the decisive end point of primitive communism, of the state of economic and social equality in which peoples lived at the dawn of their history; second, a struggle between the primitive community and the triumphantly advancing state took place over the centuries and ended with the total victory of the latter; third, close and organic ties exist between the genesis of private property, exploitation, and the state. All of history proves to us that the state always and everywhere was a social system that definitively established, legalized, and defended inequality, property, and the exploitation of the laboring masses. (The famous so-called "communist" despotisms of ancient Egypt, Peru, and others are not an exception to this, since their "communism" consisted exclusively in a detailed statist regularization of the private lives of the "subjects," but as to privileges, property, exploiting castes, and exploited masses, they all formed the basis of these states.)

It is the final point that interests us here. The fundamental cause that finally brought about the state was the pressing need felt by the nascent dominating, privileged, and exploiting classes to establish a powerful system that would sanction and defend their situation. Wars, conquests, political prerogatives, and material and other means assisted them.

2. *The historic role of the state*—For bourgeois sociologists, the historic role of the state is that of organizing society, establishing order in the relations between individuals and their various groups, and regularizing all of social life. This is why in their eyes the state is not only a useful institution, but one absolutely necessary, the sole institution capable of ensuring order, progress, and the civilization of society. For them, the role of the state was and remains positive and progressive.

This point of view is shared by statist socialists, including the "communists." All of them attribute to the state a positive organizing role over the course of human history, despite the chasm that separates them from bourgeois statists. This chasm consists in the latter considering the state an institution placed above classes and called on precisely to reconcile their antagonisms, while for the socialists the state is nothing but an instrument of class domination and dictatorship. Despite this difference, socialists also claim that from the point of view of general human evolution the advent of the state constituted progress and was a necessity, for it organized the chaotic life of primitive communities and opened new roads for human civilization. In conformity with this vision of the state as an instrument of organization and (under certain conditions) progress, socialists claim that the statist system can still be used today as a progressive factor, notably as an instrument for the liberation of the oppressed and exploited classes. For this to be the case it is necessary that the current bourgeois state be replaced one way or another by a proletarian state that will be the instrument of domination, not of the bourgeoisie over the proletariat, but on the contrary, of the proletariat over bourgeois and capitalist elements.

And so, for the ideologues of the bourgeoise, the historic role of the state is purely positive and progressive.

For socialists, this role was originally progressive and later became regressive, but can again become progressive. The state (like authority) can, in their eyes, be an instrument either of progress or regression, depending on the given historical conditions. In any case, the state, they say, played and can still play a positive role in human history, that of the organization of social life, of the creation of the bases of a better society.

Such a point of view is an outgrowth of the fact that socialists (particularly Marxists) view the life of human societies, of social organization, and social progress in a somewhat mechanical fashion. They don't sufficiently consider the freely creative forces that exist in a potential state within every human collectivity in which every member—every individual—is, so to speak, a charge of creative energy (in one sense or another). Each collectivity is always a formidable collection of varied creative energies; it is these energies that, at bottom, ensure and realize true progress.

Not realizing this, viewing the life and activities of societies mechanically, socialists are incapable of representing human organization, order, evolution, and progress other than through the intervention and constant activity of a powerful mechanical factor: the state.

On the other hand, the anarchist vision is based on a creative spirit and energy unique to every human being and group of men. It absolutely denies the mechanical factor, attributing no value to it at any historical moment in the past, present, or future.

This is the source of anarchists' completely different vision of the historical role of the state.

1. In their opinion the state has never played a progressive, positive role of any kind. Having begun in the form of a free community, laying before human society was the direct road of the later free and creative evolution of the same community. This evolution would certainly have been a thousand times richer, more splendid, more rapid if its normal march hadn't been halted and diverted by the advent of the state. The free activity of creative energies would have brought about an incomparably better and more beautiful social organization than that brought about by the state. The road to this normal progress was clear to all when certain natural causes that no longer exist brought about wars, military, and, later, political authority, property, exploitation, and the state.

The advent of the latter was thus not, in our opinion, a regression. Its role was, from the start, negative and harmful. The state was immediately and indissolubly tied to a mass of factors of stagnation, retreat, and wrong turns.

2. Once established and solidified, especially after having emerged victorious from the battles it had to sustain against the defense of the free communities, the state continued its calamitous activity. It was the state that dragged man down to the lamentable state of narrow-minded beasts of burden, where it currently vegetates. It was the state that mechanized all of human life, stopping or causing its progress to take a detour, hindering its evolution, and damaging the creative blossoming that had been laid out for it. It was the state—that assassin of free, noble thought and creative humanity—that still today claims to guide and take care of its victim, human society. And it is still the state that claims, from the mouth of blind fanatics like Lenin and his misguided followers, to be capable of saving and reviving the humanity it murdered! Yet there are still millions of men ready to believe this masked assassin and to follow him!

We are not among them.

For, aside from any other considerations, we recall the observations of Kropotkin and several other impartial historians who proved that humanity's true eras of progress were precisely those where the disastrous power of the state weakened and that on the contrary the periods when the state flourished were infallibly those when the creative progress of human society languished.

***

Let us return now to the question posed at the beginning of this study: why are we ordered to believe, obey, and submit to an institution that is, regarding its superiority and sovereignty, nothing but a fiction; whose origins are unknown and historic role so negative? How can we explain the power of this phantom, its formidable influence, the "reality" of its sovereignty for millions of people?

The response to this question is not difficult.

Having succeeded in misleading and smashing the primitive community and breaking its resistance, the first dominators—the founders of property, privileged castes, and exploitation—definitively established a system of human coexistence based on the exploitation of the laboring masses by the victors, their aides, and their faithful servants. The so-called state system was, is, and will always be a system of exploitation. In order to loudly and solemnly sanction this system; in order to impose it for good and all on the popular masses; in order to give it the air of being a superior, inevitable, sovereign, and necessary institution, above human free will, these dominating castes, these organized exploiters presented this system as a divine institution, attributing supernatural power to it. Finally, they were able to create so powerful a force to defend it that any struggle against this monster, this leviathan disposing of immense wealth, religiously blessed by priests, armed to the teeth, and supported by the organized forces of the privileged, functionaries, magistrates, and jailers became impossible. It ended up by imposing itself to such a point that its sovereignty was thought mysterious and any idea of another system of social organization disappeared for a long time from the human mind.

This monster was the state. It is only a reality as the most formidable corporation of exploitation and protector of other companies of the same kind (though of lesser importance). As a superior, sovereign, sacred, inviolable, eternal organization within human society it is a fiction, a phantom that was able to impose its fetishes.

Property is exploitation. The state is the sanction of exploitation. It created it, it engenders it. It is born of it, it lives off it. It blesses it, defends it, supports it. ... It never was, cannot be, and never will be anything else. What is more, it is a fearsome, blind, and murderous mechanism that stifles all free creative activity, any human impulse towards a truly human life.

***

After what's just been said the responses to other questions concerning the anarchists' attitude toward the state are obvious.

The state is a fleeting form of human society, destined to disappear sooner or later.

Other forms of social organization—free, liberated from any basis in exploitation, giving creativity a forward impulse—will replace it.

The state being an instrument of exploitation, it can never, under any circumstance or under any condition become an instrument of liberation (which is the fundamental error of the "communists").

The state can never disappear by means of evolution. It must be abolished through violent action, like capitalism.

It is necessary to fight bitterly and immediately against the state at the same time as against capitalism, for they are the two heads of the same monster that must be brought down simultaneously. In killing one the monster still lives, and the other will unquestionably be reborn.

The means of struggle against the state are the same as those in the struggle against capitalism.

The abolition of capitalism alone and the replacement of the bourgeois state by a proletarian state is not just a utopia: it is nonsensical. The state can only be bourgeois and exploitative. It cannot be used in the true emancipating struggle. The laboring masses of the entire world will finally understand this and the Bolshevik experience is there to demonstrate it, palpably and definitively.

The struggle against capital and the state is a simultaneous struggle, a single struggle that must be carried out without let up until the simultaneous and complete demolition of these twin institutions.

It is then and only then that human society, creative life, progress, and civilization will regain their élan.

This is the anarchist point of view.

—Voline

Synthesis (anarchist) We use the term "anarchist synthesis" for a tendency currently emerging within the libertarian movement seeking to reconcile and then "synthesize" the different currents of thought that divide this movement into several more or less hostile fractions. At bottom, it is a matter of *to a certain extent* unifying anarchist theory and the anarchist movement in a harmonious, ordered, finite whole. I say "to a certain extent" because naturally the anarchist idea cannot, should not ever become rigid, immutable, or stagnant. It must remain flexible, vibrant, rich in ideas and varied tendencies. But flexibility should not mean confusion. And what is more, there is an intermediate state between immobility and indecision. It is precisely this intermediate state that the anarchist synthesis seeks to refine, establish, and attain.

It was especially in Russia during the 1917 revolution that the need for such unification, such a synthesis made itself felt. Already materially weak compared to other political and social currents (few militants, poor means of propaganda, et cetera), anarchism was further weakened during the Russian Revolution as a result of internecine disputes that tore it apart. The anarcho-syndicalists refused to come to an agreement with the anarchist communists, and at the same time both argued with the individualists (not to mention the other tendencies). This situation made a painful impression on several comrades of the different tendencies. Persecuted and finally driven out of Great Russia by the Bolshevik government, some of these comrades left to carry on their militant activities in Ukraine, where the political atmosphere was more favorable and where, in agreement with a few Ukrainian comrades, they decided to create a *unified* anarchist movement, recruiting serious and active militants wherever they were found *without any distinction as to tendency*. The movement immediately acquired exceptional breadth and vigor. It lacked just one thing if it was to definitively establish and impose itself: a theoretical basis.

Knowing me to be a determined adversary of disastrous quarrels among the different currents of anarchism; knowing as well that, like them, I felt the need for reconciliation, several comrades sought me out in the small city in central Russia where I was staying and proposed that I go to Ukraine to take part in the creation of a unified movement, that I provide it with a theoretical foundation, and that I expand on the thesis in the libertarian press.

I accepted the proposal. In November 1918 the unified anarchist movement in Ukraine was definitively set in motion. Several groups were formed and sent their delegates to the founding conference that created the anarchist Confederation of Ukraine—Nabat (Tocsin). This conference elaborated and unanimously adopted a "Declaration" proclaiming the fundamental principles of the new organism. It was decided that this brief declaration of principles would be amplified, added to, and commented on in the libertarian press. Stormy events prevented this theoretical work from being done. The Nabat confederation had to engage in uninterrupted and bitter struggles. It was soon "liquidated" by the Bolshevik authorities who were installed in Ukraine. Apart from a few newspaper articles, the Declaration of the first conference of Nabat was and will remain the only presentation of the unifying (or synthesizing) tendency in the Russian anarchist movement.

The three central ideas that, according to the Declaration, should be accepted by all serious anarchists if the movement is to be unified are the following:

1. Definitive acceptance of the syndicalist principle, which establishes the basis for the organization of the social revolution.

2. Definitive acceptance of the (libertarian) communist principle, which establishes the basis for the organization of the new society being formed.

3. Definitive acceptance of the individualist principle, the total emancipation and the happiness of the individual being the true goal of the social revolution and the new society.

In developing these ideas, the Declaration strives to clearly define the notion of the social revolution and to do away with the tendency of certain libertarians to adapt anarchism to the so-called transitional period.

This said, instead of repeating the arguments of the Declaration we prefer to develop for ourselves the theoretical argument of the synthesis.

The first question that must be resolved is the following: Is the existence of different, enemy anarchist currents a positive or negative fact? Does the decomposition of the anarchist idea and movement into several opposed tendencies favor or, on the contrary, hinder the success of the anarchist idea? If it is recognized to be favorable, then any discussion is pointless. If, on the contrary, it is considered detrimental, then all the necessary conclusions must be drawn from this admission.

We respond to this first question as follows: In the beginning, when the anarchist idea was confused and little developed it was natural and useful to analyze it in all its facets, to decompose and closely examine each of its elements, to confront and oppose them to each other. This is what was done. Anarchism was decomposed into several elements (or currents). Its too general and vague body was dissected, which facilitated the thorough examination and study of both the body and its elements. At that time, the dismemberment of the anarchist idea was a positive fact. Differing individuals taking an interest in differing currents of anarchism, the details and the whole gained in depth and precision. But later, once this task was accomplished, after the elements of anarchist thought (communism, individualism, syndicalism) were turned in all directions, it was necessary to reconstitute the organic whole from which they came with these thoroughly worked over elements. After a fundamental analysis it was necessary to (consciously) return to the constructive synthesis.

A bizarre fact: people no longer thought about this need. Those interested in this or that element of anarchism ended up substituting it for the whole. Naturally, they soon found themselves in disagreement and ultimately in conflict with those who treated other parcels of the total truth in the same fashion. As a result, instead of addressing the fusion of the separated elements (which, taken separately, no longer served any useful purpose) into an organic whole, for many long years anarchists undertook the sterile task of resentfully opposing their own current to the others. Everyone considered "his" current, "his" parcel, to be the sole truth and bitterly fought against the partisans of the other currents. There thus began in the libertarian ranks a marching in place characterized by mutual blindness and animosity that continues until today, and that must be considered disastrous for the normal development of the anarchist idea.

Our conclusion is clear. *The dismemberment of the anarchist idea into several currents has fulfilled its role. It is no longer of any use. Nothing can justify it any longer. It is leading the movement into an impasse, is causing it enormous damage, and no longer offers, nor can offer, anything positive.* The first period, where anarchism sought itself, made its ideas clearer, and inevitably broke down into fractions as it did so, is over. It belongs to the past. It is high time to move on.

If the fracturing of anarchism is currently a negative, harmful fact we must seek to put an end to it. It is a question of recovering the entire body, of gluing the separated elements back together, of finding a new, and consciously reconstructing the abandoned, synthesis.

Another question then arises: Is this synthesis possible today? Is it not a utopia? Can it be given a theoretical basis?

We answer "yes," that a synthesis of anarchism (or, if you will, a "synthetic" anarchism) is perfectly possible. It is in no way utopian. Strong reasons of a theoretical nature speak in its favor. Let us briefly note some of the most important reasons in their logical order:

1. If anarchism aspires to live, if it counts on a future triumph, if it seeks to become an organic and permanent element of life, one of its active, fertile, and creative forces, it must seek to be close to life, to its essence, to its ultimate truth. These ideological bases must be in as close accord as possible with the fundamental elements of life. It is clear, in fact, that if the primordial ideas of anarchism were to be in contradiction with the true elements of life and evolution that anarchism could not be vital. But what is life? Can we define and formulate its essence, grasp and fix its characteristic traits? Yes, we can. To be sure, it is not a question of a scientific formula of life, of a formula that does not exist, but rather of a more or less clear and correct definition of its visible,

palpable, and conceivable essence. In this order of ideas life is, above all, *a great synthesis*: an immense and complex whole, one both organic and original, made up of multiple varied elements.

2. *Life is a synthesis.* What then is the essence and the originality of this synthesis? The essence of life is that the greatest variety of these elements, which also find themselves in perpetual movement, at the same time perpetually realize a certain unity, or rather a certain equilibrium. The essence of life, the essence of its sublime synthesis is the unvarying tendency toward equilibrium, toward the unvarying realization of a certain equilibrium in the greatest diversity and in perpetual movement. (Let us note that the idea of an equilibrium of certain elements as being the bio-physical essence of life is confirmed by physico-chemical scientific experiments.)

3. *Life is a synthesis.* Life (the universe, nature) is an equilibrium (a kind of unity) *in diversity and in movement* (or, if you will, *a diversity and a movement in equilibrium*). Consequently, if anarchism wishes to march side by side with life, if it seeks to be one of its organic elements, if it aspires to be in accord with it and reach a real result instead of finding itself in opposition to it, only to finally be rejected, it must also, without renouncing diversity or movement, also and always realize equilibrium, synthesis, and unity.

But it is not enough to assert that anarchism can be synthetic: it *must* be so. The synthesis of anarchism is not only possible, is not only desirable, it is *indispensable*. While preserving the living diversity of its elements, while avoiding stagnation, while accepting movement—the essential conditions of its vitality—anarchism must at the same time seek equilibrium in diversity and movement themselves.

Diversity and movement without equilibrium equal chaos. Equilibrium without diversity or movement is stagnation, death. *Diversity and movement in equilibrium: this is the synthesis of life.* Anarchism must be varied, motile, and, at the same time, balanced, synthetic, and unified. In the contrary case it will not be vital.

4. Finally, let us note that the true foundation of the diversity and movement of life (and thus of the synthesis) is *creation*, i.e., the constant production of new elements, of new combinations, of new movements, of a new equilibrium. Life is creative diversity. Life is equilibrium in uninterrupted creation. Consequently, no anarchist can claim that "his" current is the sole and unvarying truth and that all other tendencies within anarchism are absurdities. On the contrary, it is absurd that an anarchist should allow himself to enter the impasse of a single, petty, "truth," *his own*, and that he in this way forgets the great, real truth of life: the perpetual creation of new forms, of new combinations, of a constantly renewed synthesis.

The synthesis of life is not stationary: it constantly modifies and creates its elements and their mutual relations.

In the realms accessible to it, anarchism seeks to participate in those acts that create life. Consequently, it must, within the limits of its idea, be open-minded, tolerant, and synthetic, while also being in creative movement.

The anarchist must attentively and perspicaciously observe all the serious elements of the libertarian movement and its ideas. Far from plunging into some single element, he must seek the equilibrium and synthesis of all given elements. In addition, he must constantly analyze and control his synthesis by comparing it to the elements of life itself in order to always be in perfect harmony with it. Life does not remain in place: it changes. And consequently, the role and the mutual relations of the various elements of the anarchist synthesis will not always remain the same. At different times it will sometimes be one, sometimes the other of these elements that must be stressed, supported, and put into action.

A few words on the concrete realization of the synthesis.

1. It must never be forgotten that the realization of the revolution and the creation of new forms of life is incumbent not on us anarchists, either in isolation or ideologically grouped, *but on the broad popular masses* who alone will be capable of accomplishing this immense destructive and creative task. Our role in

this realization will be limited to that of a ferment, an element providing assistance, advice, and an example. As for the forms in which this process will be accomplished, we can only approximatively glimpse them. For this reason, it is even more inappropriate for us to argue over details instead of preparing ourselves with a shared enthusiasm for the future.

2. It is no less inappropriate to reduce the immensity of life, of the revolution, of future creation, to petty details and narrow-minded disputes. In the face of the great tasks that await us it is ridiculous and shameful to bother with such small-mindedness. Libertarians must unite on the basis of the anarchist synthesis. They must create a united, integral, and vigorous anarchist movement. As long as they won't have created it they will remain outside of life.

In what concrete forms can we foresee the reconciliation and unification of the anarchist and the creation of a unified libertarian movement?

We must above all stress that we do not present this unification as a "mechanical" assemblage of anarchists of various tendencies in a kind of variegated camp, where each holds on to his intransigent position. Such a unification would be not a synthesis, but chaos. To be sure, a simple, amicable rapprochement of the anarchists of the various tendencies and greater tolerance in their mutual relations (the ceasing of violent polemics, collaboration on anarchist publications, participation in the same active organizations, et cetera) would be a great step forward compared to what currently occurs in libertarian ranks. But we consider this rapprochement and this tolerance to be only *first steps toward the creation of the true anarchist synthesis and of a unified libertarian movement. Our idea of the synthesis and of unification goes much further.* It sets free something more fundamental and organic.

We believe that the unification of anarchists and the libertarian movement must be pursued down two parallel roads, notably:

a. We must immediately begin a theoretical labor seeking to reconcile, combine, and synthesize our various views that at first sight seem heterogeneous. It is necessary to find and formulate within the various currents of anarchism, first, that which does not coincide with the truth of life and that must be rejected, and second, that which should be seen as correct, significant, and accepted. All these correct and valuable elements must then be combined, creating a synthetic whole out of them. (It is above all in this initial preparatory work that the rapprochement of the anarchists of various tendencies and their mutual tolerance can have great importance as a first, decisive step.) And finally, this whole must be accepted by all serious and active militants of anarchism as the basis for the formation of a unified anarchist organism, whose members will thus be in agreement on a series of fundamental theses accepted by all.

We have already cited the concrete example of such an organism: the Nabat confederation in Ukraine. Let us add here what we already said above: that the acceptance by all the members of Nabat of certain shared theses in no way prevented comrades of different tendencies from supporting the ideas dear to them in their activity and propaganda. Some (the syndicalists) were particularly concerned with problems involving the method and organization of revolution; others (the communists) were primarily concerned with the economic basis of the new society; the third group (the individualists) put forth the needs, the real value, and the aspirations of the individual. But the mandatory condition for acceptance in Nabat was the acceptance of all three elements as indispensable parts of the whole and the renunciation of a state of hostility between the tendencies. The militants were thus united "organically," for all accepted a certain set of fundamental theses. This is how we envision the concrete unification of anarchists on the basis of a synthesis of libertarian ideas theoretically established.

b. Simultaneously and in parallel with this theoretical labor, an organization unified on the basis of an anarchism synthetically understood must be created.

To finish, we would like to again stress that we in no way renounce the diversity of ideas and currents within anarchism. But there is diversity and there is diversity. That which exists in our movement today is an evil, is chaos. We consider its continuation a serious error. We believe that the variety of our ideas can only and will only be a progressive and fertile element within a *common* movement, a unified organism constructed on the basis of certain general theses accepted by all its members and aspiring to a synthesis.

It is only in an atmosphere of shared enthusiasm, only in the search for correct theses and their acceptance that our aspirations, our discussions, and even our disputes will have value, will be useful and fertile. (This was precisely the case in Nabat.) As for the disputes and polemics between petty chapels, each preaching "its" truth alone, they can only arrive at the continuation of the current chaos, at incessant internecine quarrels, and the stagnation of the movement.

We must discuss *while striving to find fertile unity* and not imposing one person's own truth against that of others. Only discussions of the first type lead to the truth. As for the other discussion, it leads only to hostility, vain disputes, and failure.

—Voline

Terrorism n. Terror is fear pushed to a high degree, fear of an exceptionally great intensity. We call terrorism that system of government that relies on terror to force the members of a group to obedience. But it is arbitrary to reserve this term for rare periods of history. In reality, fear has always been and remains authority's principal means of action.

"The ancients correctly chose instruments of torture and death as the emblems of supreme power. Without the gendarme, the jailer, and the executioner, a head of state would lose his flaming halo. Force and constraint are the essential attributes that characterize authority. If behind the carnivalesque pomp sovereigns surround themselves with, the prideful haughtiness of their speeches, the profane and sacred mythology that envelops their person; if behind this sumptuous décor people were to glimpse prisons, penal colonies, electric chairs, and hanging ropes they would all become inoperative. To a lesser degree, this is also true of whoever holds a parcel of authority, however tiny. Tax collectors, customs agents, and game wardens are only obeyed in the exercise of their function because of the fear of the punishments that strike the recalcitrant. Governmental power and administrative authority can be reduced to a question of force and rest on fear. Any infraction of the orders of leaders, of the prescriptions of legal codes, of laws issued by parliaments, result in reprisals. The police are the fundamental institution allowing the state to survive" (*En marge de l'action*).[1]

But we recognize that the fear inspired by leaders has its degrees, that a government can be more or less tyrannical, more or less respectful of the lives and independence of individuals. Nevertheless, even if from the historical point of view, one prefers to limit governmental terrorism to certain particularly bloody eras, it must be recognized that official writers demonstrate great partiality in studying these tragic epochs. In France, for example, they recount the crimes of

---

1. *En marge de l'action* is a pamphlet published by L. Barbedette, the author of this entry, in February 1935.

Robespierre and his supporters in great detail, but hardly speak of the murders committed by the royalists at the beginning of the Restoration, or the repression that followed the coup d'état of December 2, 1851, or again of the massacre of the Communards ordered by the government of Thiers.

The White Terror began in Marseille on June 25, 1815, with the murder of 200 people. In Avignon 300 prisoners were massacred; in Nimes 150 people were put to death in less than two months. Royalist bands, like those of Miquelets and Verdets, traversed the Rhone Valley and the Aquitaine basin, setting houses on fire and murdering their political enemies with a refined cruelty, the local authorities doing nothing to stop them, even encouraging the murderers. The violence and murder were quickly organized in a perfectly legal fashion. On the pretext of preventing conspiracies against royal authority the legislative chambers voted draconian measures. "Iron, executioners, and torture are needed," exclaimed Count de la Bourdonnaye. "Death, death alone will put an end to their plots. It will only be by casting a salutary terror in the souls of the rebels that you will forestall their culpable projects." In every department a provost court judged with no appeal the political defendants, and their merciless sentences were carried out within twenty-four hours. The victims were many, and death penalties and banishments freely distributed.

After the coup d'état carried out for the benefit of President Louis-Napoleon on the night Monday–Tuesday, of December 1–2, 1851, a coup organized under the leadership of the Freemason Morny and that, in fact, marked the end of the Second Republic, a reign of terror was established in France. A few courageous people built barricades and were courageously killed. On the 4th, the troops fired wildly on inoffensive women, children, and citizens strolling on the boulevards of Paris. An official report declared that there were 26,800 arrests; in reality, there were many more. A state of siege was declared in thirty-two departments. Mixed commissions, made up of the prefect, the prosecutor, and a general, judged the prisoners, and they showed themselves to be ferocious. The government admitted that it deported 9,581 people to Algeria and 239 to Guyana, but these figures give a feeble idea of the repression exercised by President Louis-Napoleon. Having become emperor, for many years he continued to completely gag his enemies and render any expression of independent thought impossible.

When the troops of the Versailles government entered Paris on Sunday, May 21, 1871, after heroic resistance on the part of the Communards, they committed unspeakable atrocities. MacMahon's soldiers, encouraged by the ignoble Thiers, massacred, with no concern for justice or fairness, whoever seemed to them to be suspect. A mayor of Paris, who was not in the least on the side of the rebels, declared, "I have the profound conviction that they executed more men than there were behind the barricades."

Bourgeois historians, whose partiality is revolting when it comes to the Commune, admit that at least 20,000 unfortunates were executed by the Versaillais. Until 1876 military tribunals sentenced thousands to death, the penal colonies, and deportation. The assassins who presided over these killings would long occupy the highest positions in the state. This is how the Third Republic began, exactly like the Restoration and the Second Empire, by establishing right-wing terrorism.

Today, Terror rules as master over the greater part of Europe, Red Terror in Russia, White Terror in Italy, in Germany, in Austria, in Hungary, et cetera. The establishment of a Marxist dictatorship in Russia provoked in response a violent and lasting fascist reaction in many countries. After an attempt at a Bolshevist revolution, White Terror was established in Hungary with the regent Horthy. In October 1922 Mussolini, aided by the reactionaries, by many Freemasons, and Marxists traitors to the working class, seized power in a coup de force. Implacable toward his enemies, the Duce was hardly any more benevolent towards some of his past allies, the Freemasons, for example. But he lowered his flag before the pope and made himself the protector of Catholicism. Unhappy Poland is being suffocated beneath Pilsudski's boot, whose investment with sovereign power—de facto if not jure—the socialists contributed to in 1926. In Germany, Hitler and his lieutenants are the absolute masters of the country. The leader of the Nazis received enormous sums from the big German industrialists for his propaganda, as well as from foreign capitalists, from Schneider and Creusot, for example. Neither the communists nor the socialists nor Freemasonry nor unions stood up to the new and omnipotent chancellor. They surrendered with a haste and baseness that did them no honor. In reward for their servility Hitler dissolved their organizations and seized their property. Draconian measures were taken against the Jews and all those who think differently from the Nazis. Freedom of the press was abolished, the prisons are overflowing, death sentences for political crimes are frequent, and the concentration camps are filled with suspects upon whom the most refined tortures are inflicted. In Austria the pious chancellor Dollfuss massacred the brave workers who attempted to resist him. Approved by the Pope, supported by Mussolini, he showed himself to be bloodthirsty as soon as he was able to cast off with no danger the mask of gentleness that allowed him to lull those whose destruction he was planning. In Spain, radicals and socialists have equaled and even surpassed the dictator Primo de Rivera in crime. In Portugal too, terrorism reigns, along with the Balkan countries, where the sovereigns have, in any case, always exercised tyrannical authority.

And so it can be seen that when it comes to terrorism, the men of order, the supporters of authority, hold the record. The height of hypocrisy is that, when speaking of terrorism, right-thinking writers speak only of the excesses committed during popular revolutions or attacks carried out by vanguard organizations or individuals. These excesses, these attacks amount to little alongside the countless and monstrous crimes that are perpetrated every day in the name of the law and morality by the henchmen of those in power. Simple ripostes to the unjustified attacks of inhuman leaders, these acts of despair are, alas, easily explained, and the right to self-defense justifies them in many cases. Indeed, whoever resigns himself to servitude deserves contempt.

—L. Barbedette[2]

2. Lucien Barbedette (1890–1942). Anarchist and pacifist philosophy teacher, he contributed to countless anarchist publications. Suffering from poor health, he died at age fifty-two of a heart attack.

Terrorist attacks It is precipitous to assert an opinion willy-nilly, and it is obvious that a terrorist attack has no value in itself, no more than does any other assertion: proof alone has value. An attack has the most varied causes as its basis or reason, and it is almost always connected to extremely diverse causes, currents, and tendencies. By its very nature, its characteristic feature is that a man elevates himself above routine, burns his ships, and practices direct action, which others don't risk. He thus carries out a useful act by removing an obstacle *brevi manu* that no one else dared touch. But the very fact that a man of exceptional caliber is necessary proves that the carrying out of attacks cannot be generalized. It is capable of giving the final push to an already prepared revolt, but it will not inspire the common run of mortals to abandon their routine. Its importance is thus restricted; it is *a* means, but it is not *the* means. It is only *a* means when *all the other* means have already been employed. It is a match that can ignite the biggest fire, but that can also burn itself out without any consequences.

There are many categories of attacks, and there are causes connected to these acts. It has a bit of everything in it, from the simplest act to the wildest act to the most twisted and complicated. Among others, there are:

1. The social attack of great scope: Samson in the Bible. Bakunin said that "he would have liked to die like Samson."

2. Classical tyrannicide: Harmodius and Aristogeiton.

3. An attack resulting from a conspiracy: the death of Julius Caesar.

4. An attack dictated by the Church: (Clément, Ravaillac) or by the conscience of a religious fanatic: Felton, who killed the Duke of Buckingham.

5. The nationalist attack, which has many nuances, from exalted patriotism (by which I mean of genuine quality) from the best there is in this genre (William Tell, C-L Sand, Orsini), to the low-grade nationalism that kills simply to kill a foreigner: the pogrom mentality and fascism, like Oberdank in 1882, the assassins in Sarajevo on June 28, 1914, and the assassin of Jaurès, July 31, 1914.

6. The attack out of generous sentiments, like Charlotte Corday, who killed Marat, considering him a persecutor.

7. The attack out of a vague social sentiment, the first acts of this genre being poor Damiens in 1757, Louvel in 1820.

8. Attacks by conscious republicans and socialists: Alibaud, Darmès, Onévisset, Agesilao, Milano, Karaksov.

9. Attacks with a goal of direct terrorism: the attacks in Russia against Trepov by Vera Zasulich, Mesentsev (Stepniak), Alexander II and III.

10. In all periods there has also been the individual attack of private revenge. This was the case with Emperor Albrecht, who was killed by his nephew Johannes, who has since been called a parricide. There are gradations in this leading up to the more or less unbalanced, like Guiteau who killed President Garfield, or the final attacks of little importance against Louis Philippe (Pierre Lecomte, April 16, 1846; Joseph Henry July 29, 1846).

11. There are also attacks we can call "of contagion," which would perhaps not have occurred had there not been a preceding attack. Thus, when in May 1878 Hoedel fired on Kaiser Wilhelm I and missed, on June 11 Dr. Nobilin fired on him again and wounded him. A few months later Passanante attacked Umberto, the King of Italy with a knife, and in the following months Ostero and Moncasi attacked Alfonso in Spain. This is what is killed "a series."

Looking at the more distant past it is more difficult to clearly separate out attacks and coups de main and assassinations. Thus, of all the Roman emperors I think that none died as a result of a direct attack, but death lay continually in wait for all of them, and a large number died violently. This was also was the case with Tsars, for example the husband of Catherine II, later her son (Tsar Paul), and the King of Sweden in an aristocratic plot, et cetera.

All of this resembles "high treason," which is not considered such when it succeeds. A murder successfully carried out that benefits a party is not called a terrorist attack, as has occurred regularly over the centuries. "A terrorist attack" was (most often) what did not succeed, and the poor martyr was drawn and quartered until his members were torn off, like Damiens in 1757 in the center of Paris. On the other hand, what led to the death of all the dauphins and other Bourbons in the seventeenth and eighteenth centuries was private, petty intrigues and were not called "attacks." It would require someone quite clever to distinguish between terrorist attacks and assassinations in Renaissance Italy, where there was also that amiable sub-variety, assassination by procuration by a paid *bravo* who risked his skin. There were also attacks commanded or inspired by those on high, like Count Wallenstein (Waldstein), killed by his officers under the inspiration of the court of the Emperor Ferdinand in Vienna, the Duke d'Enghien, and Stamboulov, hacked to pieces by *bravi* under the orders of the Russians.

It is on this broad and varied base that what is called the anarchist terror attack took seed. It evolved directly as a consequence of the lack of other means: I am thinking of the gradual shrinking of the real revolution and the spinelessness of the people, who no longer act. There was the Commune, which was crushed, and the revolutionary risings in Spain and Italy as well (1873–1874). Then cases of collective propaganda of the deed are attempted, the revolt that will unleash the revolt, like that of Benevento in 1877, but with no results. So, the people try again, placing their hope in social revolts, as at Montceau-les-Mines, and Decazeville (January 26, 1886), and nothing comes of them except parliamentarism, submission, and persecution. Finally, illegalism develops (Ravachol in the provinces, et cetera) and open action, the fearlessness of many comrades of the time: May 1, 1891 in Clichy—brutality—the people do nothing—finally, Ravachol acts, followed by others.

This was done neither from principle nor in the hope of winning, but because it was inevitable. Of the one or several million individuals who sleep peacefully, there is always some brave person who loses patience and sacrifices himself.

At present, the terrorist attack seems to be submerged in the ambient brutality: it was universalized, officialized, legalized. Reigning fascism and Bolshevism are nothing but usurpations sustained by continual, daily terrorist attacks, become custom beneath the club of the fascist and the pistol of the Chekist.

On the other hand, the generous, liberating terrorist attack has not been generalized; it languishes still, but is rare. The great criminals die in their beds. Here and there communism, nationalism, and the despair of the victims of the treaties of 1919 lead someone to take up arms, but this, too, is rare. In distant countries, like Argentina, there is sometimes someone who metes out justice for generous, libertarian reasons. In Europe people fire in any old direction.

It is thus a return to the dark centuries of the past, when the terrorist attack was confused with general violence and brutality.

"If the anarchists do not manage to create their own method of influence, if they do not wrest a portion of the proletariat from the harmful orientation of the various Marxist tendencies; if fascism and Bolshevism polarize and form a reactionary bloc without having to deal with our firm resistance, what perspectives can we offer the workers tyrannized and softened under the weight of the new dictatorial castes?" (from *El Anarquismo en el Movimiento Obrero* by E. Lopez Corango and D. A., de Santillán).

This is exactly right: in order to react to the immense forces of Bolshevism and fascism, that union of traitorous socialism and capitalism, we must create an anarchist milieu made attractive by its science, its beauty, its generosity, its intelligence, and its learning, and then we will seriously weigh in the balance of events. We must renew our ideas. The terrorist attack seems a small thing alongside these immense needs. Either it will be raised to a serious new height (and there is no trace of such an evolution), or else it will be extinguished as everything is extinguished, like the world that returns to triumphant nationalism presented with a fascist or Bolshevik sauce.

***

It seems to me that terrorist attacks are not a remedy. They push an opened door if they are in accord with the general sentiment, or they are a virtually wasted effort if they are not on accord with this general sentiment.

It is a satisfaction, an *ultimo ratio* that in theory allows the poorer and more oppressed to take from the wealthier the only thing that gold cannot replace, that power cannot restore: life. But objectively it is the exchange of the life of the bravest, most generous, most advanced man against the life of the most scorned and detested individual, and from this point of view it is a deplorable trade: a brave man against scum.

There would be only one key reason that justifies this trade: that the other person, the attacked person, is not only an execrable wretch, but also of rare intellectual force, so that with his loss the enemy truly loses one of its leaders and is disoriented by his death. There are men, great and small, who are harmful. *Sometimes* an attack eliminates them, but all too often the sacrifice is made for an individual who renders himself detested by the life he has lived and does not merit another man's sacrificing himself to exterminate him.

The terrorist attack is thus of infinitely differing quality; it is impossible to codify its functions. I conclude: it is an auxiliary force, an accessory, a sudden improvisation, and no party can count on it. If it does so, the party becomes the terrorist attack incarnate. It becomes decentralized, diluted murder embodied in each individual, as with fascism, where every member is a potential assassin; and with Bolshevism, where people are the soldiers of a doctrine, prepared to kill father and mother for the crime of lèse-Leninism; and with nationalism, where people acquire the quality of pogromist, of someone ready to plunder and torture men of other nations.

We anarchists are at antipodes from this world, and we must truly strive for our pole to become more attractive, more habitable. Force on its own is so stupid that the majority of the world embraces it because it is part of its customs. All in all, fascism is the evil part of every man. Like the man who didn't know he "spoke in prose," the vulgar brute didn't know he was the perfect product of fascism and nationalism. He only felt himself to be a brute, and this is fascism. What a discovery! Everyone partakes in it.

Let us do something different. Let us study and above all be intelligent. The world can't be moved—and this disordered world least of all—by unthinking force, by so-called spontaneous and uncoordinated impulses, by ideas formed by chance or by repeating ancient things thought by others in other times.

—MAX NETTLAU[1]

---

[1]. Max Nettlau (1865–1944). German-born anarchist thinker, and the preeminent historian of the movement of his time. Biographer of Bakunin, author of a multi-volume history of the movement, and archivist extraordinaire.

Theft The right to ownership is a natural right. It was originally held in common and as time passed it became individual. In primitive societies it was held in common, and among savages it still is.

It has a legitimate basis, for it is correlative to the needs imposed by nature: One must eat; one must reproduce; one must have pleasure, in other words, fight against the evil whose antinomy is pleasure.

Necessity is law, from which it flows that the primitive has the right to draw what is essential from his surroundings. Any attack on this natural right is a despoilment, a theft. The shared sentiment of defense created common property in weapons, homes, and food. Even communism in certain animal colonies.

It is the commercial spirit, a function of egoism and ambition that, destroying anonymous communism, created the individual need to own.

Let us consider the individual in the state of society. By definition he has the same rights as in the state of nature or in community. His every day needs are the same, as well as his pleasures. The superfluous sometimes become the necessary. In order to satisfy his needs, man has the right to ownership. This is the consecration of the principle of property.

As a corollary, the principle of property demands the right to acquisition. One must acquire in order to possess.

In nature one simply takes. The plant draws the water it drinks without measuring or discussion, and finds the air and calories it needs wherever it can. Animals do the same. We call it a thief, like the magpie, when it takes maliciously or slyly and hoards as a precaution and through foresight. In organized society we don't take: we traffic, we exchange.

Traffic is a necessity because in organized society every individual, having ensured his right to property, owns legitimately. (So-called human progress prohibits him from purely and simply taking as he would had he remained an individual. It is human law that invents theft as a crime).

So, if humans legitimately own their property, it cannot be seized without injuring them. From this, the notion of theft emerges as a harmful act.

In the state of organization there is another basis for property, the principle of justice.

Every acquisition requires an effort (labor) in proportion to the value of the object and in strict proportion to the need to be satisfied (let us say the "strict" need, for if it is exceeded we touch on traffic, the first step on the way to capitalism).

All forms of labor deserve wages, which is a necessity in order to live in society. Property thus becomes the reward for labor. As a result, depriving the individual of the fruit of his labor means wronging him.

Finally, another principle, one of a moral order, is at the basis of the right of ownership. It is moral to obtain and possess because it is a stimulant, an encouragement to labor, to foresight. It develops human dignity, which is not a vain expression.

It is moral to acquire (it is here a question of a much higher sentiment, one eminently social, the fruit of evolution), because so-called organized society has its unfortunates, its invalids, its infirm, and its lame, and the principle of solidarity imposes upon us the duty to devote a portion of one's acquisitions to the unfortunate. The rights of the unfortunate are categorical, and so charity is an obligation. It constitutes nothing but reparations for damages suffered by the defeated. It is thus also justice, for equilibrium must be reestablished everywhere. Without harmony all is chaos.

Conventional law, superimposed on natural law, consecrates the principle of property by striking out against the seizing of goods to the extent it goes beyond real needs or is not consented to by all the parties to the exchange.

But in this case two agents confront and compete with each other: the robber and the robbed. The definition of theft, as I reminded the reader, is nothing but an artifice, a convention. And a reparatory sanction (moral or penal) is only acceptable if there is a break in the equilibrium between the everyday needs of the one or the other. In applying it we then need to consider the excesses of the two factors, the robber and the robbed. The margin between them is enormous.

Which harms the other more? It is obviously the hoarder, for there is no act more frequent or more spontaneous than that of taking, because it is natural. It is a primordial form of automatic defense, inscribed in the subconscious. By nature and simple logic, man is selfish, greedy, and insatiable.

Our mores are flagrantly iniquitous, even outside intentional and reasoned schemes. Human revolt is an excusable reflex. Its inhibition, either automatic or imposed, is only the product of education.

The principle of legal repression can be dangerous, for it creates in those who escape the law, against the non-pursuable possessor, the illusion that he has the indefinite right to possession.

How many abuses are derived from this!

Collectively, there's the apparent legitimation of all tyrannies, which people attempt to justify by reason of state, majority rights, and the public interest. There's the crushing of defenseless unity. There's blind taxation and the swindles of capitalist sharks; wars of conquest and the systematic despoiling of the weak; colonization and its hypocrisies hidden beneath the word civilization, which in fact is organized theft with horrific poverty among the primitives, who ask only to live for the day; an attack on (the theft of) their freedom by incorporating them into a country for which they have no need, going as far as their leaving their lives on our battlefields. There's the ineptitude, the ignominy of peace treaties, leaving defeated nations groaning with hunger from lack of the natural wealth that's been taken from them. There's commerce itself, i.e., a number of industries creating wealth for the profit of the few and to the detriment of the many.

Individually, the abuses are the same. Nothing stands in the way of seizing hold of what exceeds the necessary, of stocking things up and creating capitalism. Capitalizing is a right, and even something glorious, meritorious: a skill. The most noted crooks are loaded down with honors while populations die of hunger. This spoliation is tolerated around the world: opium grows instead of rice; bundles of merchandise are tossed in the sea without the international conscience being pricked. But capitalizing of this kind is a crime, for it exceeds real needs and ceases to be the just remuneration for labor.

These abuses cannot be done away with, these situations cannot be balanced out solely by written law, which is arbitrary, without reference to human law.

Proudhon's expression is not a pleasantry: property, as it is understood, accepted, and excused, is—more often than not—theft.

But the person who's been robbed can also be in the wrong. Whoever uses and benefits without working is a thief, even when he looks to be the one robbed. There is perhaps no greater fault than that of begging; it is a petty crime when it is inspired by laziness, though we must set aside the weak, the depressed, those with no energy, and the sickly who are irresponsible for their infirmity, which results in their being among the robbed.

All of these general considerations having been laid out, there is an unavoidable conclusion: theft, a harmful act, exists, whatever idea we might have of the right to obtain and own. It is not within the framework of this article to describe the objective modalities figuring in law books, from simple theft to grand robbery, that allow the thief to be taken from one court to another. Pickpocketing, the rolling of drunks, swindling, shoplifting, robbing someone after bumping into them, all of them do honor to the spirit of invention of crooks whose imagination is ever awake. They are of no intrinsic interest to philosophers or economists, if not that they indicate the state of mind of victims: inattentive or stupid, greedy themselves to own outside natural law. The pitiful intelligence of gamblers on the stock exchange, of casino or race track customers, of adorers of the God Chance is the strange counterpart to the great intelligence of street thugs, the good for nothings on the other side of the bar of justice. These two antinomies pullulate in a decadent society where artless probity is a rare pearl, where honesty, which is often breached, can be bought and sold. Let so-called novelists of mores depict its appearance for the museum of social pathology.

I have no further need to depict the therapeutics of theft. It can be seen that such a study would presuppose a total revision of the social state. Theft is the most fully realized form of egoism. It presupposes an ignorance of or a contempt for laws and postulates a transformation of the normal relations between citizens.

Is it necessary to speak of legal sanction and its legitimization? It supposes (I accept this) the possibility of viewing theft as crime and consequently the legitimacy of its discredit in a social state before which we are forced to bow while waiting for a better one. But it is necessary to distinguish between moral sanctions (the application of a punishment) and reparatory sanctions.

A moral sanction presupposes the responsibility of the culprit and society's right to punish.

Here more than anywhere else, it is urgent to weigh matters. Is the distributive justice that we enjoy capable of this? This is doubtful, for the repressive measures employed are still profoundly imbued with the right of force. The texts of the laws are merciless and the room left for the arbitrary is enormous as long as it is suitable to resort to the intervention of a judge, a man himself imbued with the inalienable rights of a wicked-stepmother-society that he is obliged to serve, unless he resigns and passes his weighty task onto another.

The are vast numbers of thieves standing before judges, as there are poor wretches who steal bread and millionaire bankers who ran off with the cash box. Where is the judge who will closely examine the entire life of the defeated man standing before him to balance out what in the incriminated acts results from natural right and what from the truly blameworthy order? And where is the judge who would dare place in the balance the portion of responsibility due to the environment and weigh matters correctly? It seems that we are verging on the utopian in a matter that is actually quite simple.

The sole element to be retained in the matter of crime in the realm of property is purely that of equity and can be expressed in these words: any damage caused, consciously or not, requires reparation. But here again the scale intervenes, and reparation will be inspired as much by the material possibilities of the culprit as the responsibilities of the environment. We have not yet reached this equilibrium, and justice will still for some time cry out: "Catch the crook!"

In these pages, it would be more interesting to carry out a psychological study of the act of theft, whose natural history I would like to briefly describe. This will explain many problems.

Psychologically, the act of taking, the expression of the intention of taking, responds to a series of determinisms whose initial factor is the acquisitive instinct. I have said often enough that this instinct is universal and explained why it exists. In order to fully understand its genesis and its workings it must be viewed in its greatest simplicity. Like the act of a madman or of a tertiary syphilis sufferer who, passing a shop display, plunges his hand into it in full sight of all and pockets the first object he grabs, it is pure automatism. It doesn't even respond to a basic need, other than that of attraction, probably a sensorial one. Everything is viewed in relation to the self. This can be seen in the acts of a baby, barely emerged from limbo, who gathers up everything that presents itself to him with a circular gesture and puts it to his mouth as if to indicate that the mechanical gesture of grabbing is in service to the digestive tract before any other goal.

The child continues to steal. There is no one who is more frequently acquisitive than the child, and his unconscious crime, which will continue into early and later childhood, will, unless corrected, lead him to stand before a judge one day. Nine times out of ten, theft is the crime that leads the child to end up before the competent jurisdiction.

In a child amenable to education crime doesn't go any further in its automatic simplicity. In a great number of cases, it is nothing but the prelude to later adult theft. There is no exception to the rule that we find infantile theft in the antecedents of adult thieves.

(The child steals naturally. Social acquisitions and examples alone teach that stealing is prohibited. People cease to do so before having understood this. Despite this, larceny and pilferage are widespread and, in general, indulgence is professed in their regard.)

But starting with this simple form, theft rises quickly to more or less motivated complexities and up to cases where, being accomplished without a motive, it becomes pathological. We will follow this progression.

There are an infinite variety of determinisms: there are interest, ambition, pride, extreme pleasure, the demoralization of the environment, lesser effort, speculation, and the stock market. There is the bankruptcy of labor, the bankruptcy of dignity and self-respect; there's also that of obligation among leaders who steal and who turn a blind eye. There's the universal scandal of the great fortunes of corsairs who incite envy, which is the mirage poor suckers allow themselves to be taken in by.

Whatever the case, there are always the same steps between simple theft, the circular gesture of a hand guided by the unknown, and complex theft.

Two antagonistic gestures are normal in man: the centripetal and centrifugal movements of the arm; the attractive gesture and the distributive gesture. The hand's attitudes correspond to this, i.e., the closed hand and the open hand.

One offers the open hand, outlining a gesture from oneself toward others. One keeps, one seizes by closing the hand and tracing the gesture that brings back toward oneself. Such is the symbolism of egoism and altruism.

This mechanism, which invalidates the proprietary instinct, is inscribed in our subconscious and betrays a long line of hereditary transmissions.

The primary objective basis for acquisitiveness is thus of an attractive order. It is the obsession with the perceived, seductive object that is, as a result, desired. In psychiatry, the delirium of touching is known, an irresistible obsession that leads to grabbing this or that object or touching this or that object. What can be found find in certain morbid thieves is the erratic, centripetal gesture of seizing, a gesture or, better said, a succession of concentric gestures that I compare to the flight of an eagle tracing circles in space until he "touches" the prey of his desires.

This erratic gesture can be seen in the person who simply likes to ferret through things; it is part of the habits of all of us who like to dig through this or that, a collection, a drawer, a library, et cetera.

Once again, ferreting brings with it the need, the pleasure, the mania for palpating (artomania). One seizes the object mechanically, likes to turn it this way and that. One seems to feel pleasure in it, a charm. Follow closely the gesture of the artomaniac. It does not always conclude with putting the touched object back in its place. The circle increasingly shrinks and you see the palpator unthinkingly, out of distraction or thoughtlessness, pocket it without any precise intention. A number of occasional, semi-morbid thieves will simply be palpators. One must observe this a hundred times in normal people to understand that he could be on the road to theft properly speaking, unless an interested witness observes him and points it out.

Since we are in the realm of a practical psychology fertile in consequences, let us go further and penetrate the domain of sickness.

The gesture of touching, of pocketing, of assembling more or less useful and varied objects can be found in morbid collectors: hoarders, gatherers for the sole pleasure of collecting, of piling up in the attic hundreds of similar, unneeded objects, a need satisfied by having accomplished the act. How many misers are nothing but collectionists (*sylle-gomania*).

Of the same type are hoarders who cannot resist purchasing in order to collect objects of no interest (oniomania).

One can clearly see appear the obsessive gesture of hoarding. This gesture becomes frightening when it concludes with the unthinking pocketing of the touched object, a variety of theft that magistrates and even physicians know little about and that ends in the form of theft I called repetition theft. A recidivist thief is often quickly defamed, when he often possesses an interesting and agreeable mentality. Many recidivists of this kind are banished who are nothing but obsessives to be pitied. In these cases, it is a matter of the habitual and repeated theft of the same object: a bicycle thief will only ever take bikes, which he leaves in a corner after a simulacrum of use and then seeks another bicycle. Hundreds of cases of shoplifting follow the same mechanism.

We now arrive at the perfect, theoretical, stereotypic form of theft, which is kleptomania. Ordinarily recidivate, it coincides with a state of mind pure of any evil intent. It is the very type of perfectly conscious irresistible obsession, which cruelly tortures the obsessive.

From simple pilfering to kleptomania, the cycle is now complete. We have seen all the stages of the centripetal hoarding gesture.

It should be noted that the subjects can stop and remain at one of the above steps, or slide down the slope that will lead them to the syndrome in its perfect form.

Such is the psychological, natural progression of the act of stealing. The reader can easily follow, on one side, the useful, self-interested, reasoned, logical act which from simple desire leads to the crime of theft and, on the other side, the same acquisitive act, useful or not, but stained with morbidity.

Deep down, the internal mechanism remains the same and proceeds from the same subjective elements.

—Dr. Legrain[1]

---

1. Dr. Paul-Maurice Legrain (1860–1939). Legrain was a psychiatrist specializing in problems of alcoholism and an active neo-Malthusian.

Violence (Reflections on) *Georges Sorel is the author of a book bearing the title* Reflections on Violence. *This book's appearance caused considerable uproar. Sorel's work provoked lively curiosity and gave rise to impassioned controversy in those circles that take an interest in the thesis of revolutionary violence or non-violence. The* Revue Anarchiste *of November 1922 published under the signature of our excellent collaborator, Dr. F. Elosu,[1] a remarkable critique of the thesis developed by Georges Sorel, considered the apologist and theoretician of revolutionary violence.*

We reproduce this critique here and follow it with Sébastien Faure's response in the same issue of the Revue Anarchiste. *In doing so, we allow the reader to become familiar with the two aspects of the question.*

First, here is the article by F. Elosu, entitled "Georges Sorel and Violence."

If the dead usually depart quickly, Georges Sorel is an exception to this general rule. The Italian fascists attest to the survival of his teachings, which they lay claim to in justifying their brutal and deadly activities. And so, it is not too late to lay out and attempt to refute what J.-R. Bloch already called, in the January 1913 issue of *L'Effort Libre*, "the beneficent sophisms of Sorel."

The war of 1914, the generator of monstrous crimes, has perhaps modified the opinion of this pre-war vanguard professor and publicist about the "beneficence" of the paradoxes in question. It certainly changes nothing in the sophisms themselves, whose errors remain total, before as well as after the battle. In any event, isn't a sophism by definition an error? And is not the "beneficence" of an error something in the realm of logically absurd ideas?

---

1. Fernand Élosu (1875–1942). Doctor and propagandist for many causes on the margin of anarchism, like population control. He was secretary of the Bayonne branch of the Friends of the Soviet Union at the time of his death from pneumonia.

It is generally thought that the *Reflections on Violence* is the most typical work of the former chief engineer of the civil engineering department, one that earned him the blind hatred of the bourgeoisie, the scorn of parliamentary socialists, the admiration of revolutionary syndicalists, and the sympathy of libertarians. To be sure, one must pay homage to the immense erudition and noble intellectual courage of the former state functionary. But these two elements are not enough to establish the supremacy of an idea. The predominance of a thesis resides in the firmness of its concepts, the logic of its reasoning, the unity and harmony of its deductions, and the precision of its conclusions.

It is a singular irony of fate that force is lacking in the Sorelian studies of violence. This lack of vigor did not escape the author, who admitted it with uncommon modesty: "This is why I quite enjoy taking as subject for discussion a book written by a good author; I orient myself more easily than in those cases where I am abandoned to my own strength."

The absence of a connecting thread is not owed to a failure of method, to a disdainful detachment from the rules of art, as Sorel imagined. Rather it is owed to the creative impotence of a critical rather than a creative mind. Many of his readers were misled in this regard and took a good laborer for a brilliant architect.

The congenital weakness and the arduous development of Sorelian theories was born of the unnatural union of correct observation and a false postulate. After Marx, and with historical materialism, the writer at the *Mouvement Socialiste* follows humanity's centuries-long course, noting in it the perpetual victory of violence. The most varied political institutions: monarchical institutions, aristocracy, oligarchy, Greek democracy, the Roman plebeian tribuneship, and modern republics, in summary, all the forms of the state were successively established, maintained, attacked, destroyed, and restored by means of force or its hypocritical and degenerate daughter, ruse. No one can contradict this assertion, which is glaringly obvious. Thus, a new transformation of society will only be effectuated through violence.

This consequence is erroneous, for Sorel does not see in an eventual evolution a simple surface modification or a change in governmental personnel, but a complete revision, a total renewal of social relations. In the emergence of a solid proletariat, constituted in a clearly distinct class, he discovers one of the most singular social phenomena of history. Logically, a "singular phenomenon" demanded special attention, necessitated a new critique, required original conclusions. Marxism showed itself incapable of this, as did Sorelian neo-Marxism.

Sorel did not doubt the "historic mission" of the worker's world, i.e., its accession to sovereignty, to the leadership of collective life. He considered it a fated process, the fulfillment of an organic function conditioned by the blossoming of capitalism. Having reached its apex, the latter realized its goals and ceded its place to wage labor, until then controlled and enslaved. As a result of this splendid economic progress the bourgeoisie unwittingly prepared the sumptuous bed of its presumptive heir, the proletariat.

Despite this character of necessity, despite pessimism, the negator of apostolic action and paradisiacal utopia, it remained obvious that capitalism would not resign itself to dying peacefully, without being given some assistance. Fate's iron hand had to be guided in its grip by an idealism issued from unarguably efficient forces. This circumstance, that of the indispensable intervention of thought, imposed itself against their will on the purest materialists in history.

Republican democracy did not proceed from this destructive will. An arm forged by the bourgeoisie for its ultimate defense and hidden beneath the cloak of the social, Sorel considered it to be as harmful to the inventor as to the adversary: it unmanned the former and rendered him inferior to his task, while weakening the action of the latter, causing him to be hesitant; for all concerned, it pointlessly delayed the final conflict. What is more, the vulgarity of the lie did harm to its efficacity: the least informed understood the hypocrisy of a so-called collaboration between the omnipotent boss and the worker, eliminated from financial, administrative, and technical management.

In its turn, Sorel harshly critiqued parliamentary socialism, condemning it and allowing for no appeal, while the parliamentary socialists received furious attacks of little consequence. Thus, and above all on the intellectual plane, violence proves its sterility: it turns against its author, whose argument is ruined by the suspicion of jealousy it gives rise to.

The most ferocious anti-parliamentarian would unreservedly and unabashedly subscribe to this assessment by Jaurès:

"The (socialist) leaders who maintain their men in the gentle democratic illusion see the world from another point of view. The current social organization sickens them insofar as it creates obstacles to their ambition. They are less sickened by the existence of classes than by their inability to attain the positions acquired by their elders. The day they sufficiently penetrate the sanctuaries of the state, the salons, and the pleasure palaces, they generally cease to be revolutionaries and learnedly speak of evolution."

No one has forgotten that in the era of Combisme[2] and the Bloc des Gauches, Jaurès could have seized power had he wanted to.

On the other hand, libertarians will fully approve the paragraphs on the revolutionary impotence of parliamentarianism, its inability to ensure the proletariat's accession to sovereignty. Without putting it fully on trial, Sorel denounces the state as the promoter and beneficiary of all forms of violence: the horrors of the Inquisition, the harsh capital executions by the crown, the bloody madness of the Terror. He does not fear accusing collectivist politicians of aspiring to so terrible an inheritance:

"The parliamentary socialists preserve the old cult of the state, and so are ready to commit all the misdeeds of the ancien régime and the Revolution. I only flipped through this book, Jaures's *Socialist History of the French Revolution*, but I saw that one finds mixed in it a philosophy worthy of M. Pantalon[3] and the politics of a guillotine purveyor. I had long thought Jaurès capable of all forms of ferocity against the vanquished."

Sorel's satire of the dictatorship of the proletariat is no less incisive and decisive:

"According to the charlatans of socialism, the best policy for having the state disappear consists in provisionally reinforcing the governmental machine. Gribouille, who throws himself into the river so as not to be drenched by the rain, would have reasoned no differently."[4]

"The dictatorship of labor corresponds to a division of society into masters and slaves."

2. The name given the secularist polices of political leader Émile Combes (1835–1921), primarily touching upon the separation of Church and State.

3. Character in Italian commedia dell'arte, usually a greedy, credulous old man.

4. Gribouille was a 16th century personage of popular lore who was forever escaping from bad situations by throwing himself into worse.

Given this, a conclusion imposes itself: a radical transformation for the benefit of the class of producers cannot be effected by means either of a clumsy and cowardly democracy or by a vague, utopian and, above all, lying socialism.

After the failure of republican and electoral collectivist politics, in the face of the incompatibility of the outdated and obsolete form of the state, given an entirely new arrangement of society, how will the proletariat manage to fulfill its historic mission? By its own action. The emancipation of the workers will be the work of the workers themselves and by the practice of a method—syndicalism—elaborated in the course of the daily existence of the wage earners.

Not a narrow, medieval, corporative, reformist syndicalism, backward in its petty and fallacious concern for the growth of wages, immediately balanced out by a rise in the price of consumer goods or walled in in defense of professional privileges. Rather a broad syndicalism, modern, social, and revolutionary, pursuing an elevated, generous, decisive goal: the suppression of wage labor and employers and their replacement by the free association of producers.

One weapon, one alone, solid and tempered by Sorel: the proletarian general strike. One skillful, effective, tried and true tactic: violence.

What? Violence, the creation and prerogative of the state, identified with it to such an extent as to be its concrete realization; violence, the instrument of the enslavement of men will also be the tool of their liberation and, following the example of M. Prudhomme, is as worthwhile in combating institutions as in defending them![5]

This profound contradiction, this irreducible antinomy, did not escape the metaphysical logic of the former engineer. In order to get around it he took inspiration more from the Pascal of the *Provincials* than the Pascal of the *Pensées*, writing these lines:

"At time the terms force and violence are employed when speaking of the acts of authority, at times when speaking of acts of revolt. It is clear that the two cases result in totally different consequences. It is my opinion that it would be advantageous to adopt a terminology that would avoid any ambiguity, and that it is necessary to reserve the term violence for the second concept. We would thus say that the object of force is the imposing of a certain social order in which a

5. M. Prudhomme is he name of a caricatural bourgeois figure.

minority governs, while violence tends to the destruction of that order. The bourgeoisie has employed force since the beginning of modern times, while the proletariat now reacts against it and the state through violence."

With the best will in the world it is impossible to find in these lines a definition of the two opposed terms, even less a differentiation or a discrimination between them. In dialectics, this mode of reasoning lacking in naiveté and skill constitutes a lovely petition of principle.

We find an equal amount of obscurity when it comes to the proletarian general strike. Its Peter the Hermit knows that is not, like the political general strike, a great mass demonstration somewhere "between a simple threatening stroll and a riot;"[6] that it does not offer "the immense advantage of not putting the precious lives of politicians in peril;" and that it consequently presents the enormous inconvenience of exposing the no less precious lives of the workers to danger. But he doesn't linger over these minor details and presents his proletarian general strike as a myth, that is, a fiction whose plausibility or absurdity is of no practical importance. "We have seen that the general strike must be considered an undivided whole. As a consequence, no detail of execution has any importance in the understanding of socialism. It must even be added that we are always in danger of losing something of this understanding when we attempt to decompose that whole into its parts."

In his metaphysical vertigo, the philosopher of violence considers his entity, the proletarian general strike, as a Bergsonian "intuition." The result of immediate, total, and imperious knowledge, like a revelation, escaping logical analysis, escaping reason! If in the realm of individual sentiment intuition can be taken to be admissible, seductive, and sometimes fertile, it becomes unacceptable, revolting, and disastrous on the plane of collective action. And when it aspires to the frightful power of decreeing the death of others (of many others) without trial or appeal, it borders on bloodthirsty sadism.

What is more, the Sorelian general strike does not possess the value of a myth, for a myth is a tale, a legend, a totally imaginary belief; it is a fable or a construct, either religious or political, with no objective truth, but composed of detailed events, with allegorical characters

6. Élosu is likening Sorel to the leader of the First Crusade, Peter the Hermit.

acting in an unreal landscape and among fantastic flora and fauna, all of them unfurling over the successive and varied phases of a chimerical action. In refusing to analyze and amplify the notion of the proletarian general strike, its virulent promoter strips it of all ideological value and content, of a cabbalistic formula analogous to those employed by magicians for the collapse of walls and the unveiling of treasures.

An armchair militant, Sorel did not make himself incarnate either as a royalist, a republican, or a collectivist democrat. Non-unionized, non-unionizable, he thought himself a syndicalist and "had no difficulty recognizing he was anarchist-leaning from the moral point of view." At heart, [Sorel] lacked an ideal to guide his intellectual life, which explains the stupefying palinodes scattered throughout his *Reflections*. After having, at the beginning of his book, definitively obliterated the noxious institution of the state, this denigrator of dictatorship, including that of the proletariat, at the end weaves immortal crowns for Lenin: "The greatest theoretician of socialism since Marx, and a head of state whose genius recalls that of Peter the great ... he contributed to the reinforcement of Muscovism."

He ingeniously imagined he was honoring a revolutionary, and he praised a master to the skies. In retirement, the former functionary of the Republic took his uniform with him and kept his livery.

This rentier was animated by the warrior spirit and was haunted by Bonaparte's military genius: "In a country as bellicose as France ... every time the people come to blows it's the great Napoleonic battle (that which definitively crushes the defeated) that the strikers hope to see begin."

The strategist of the proletarian general strike neglects to enumerate the armament of the workers in confronting the machine guns, the armored cars, and the flame throwers of the government troops. If he thinks that the army will go over to the proletariat, there will be no more combat, and Napoleon Sorel must renounce his thunderous attacks.

Permanently engaged in paradox, he declared that he did not have too many illusions concerning the post-civil war period. As he wrote concerning the period 1789–1793: "What remained of the Revolution when the epic of the wars against the coalition and the popular *journées* had been suppressed? What remained was not very attractive."

He prophesized: "What remained of Europe? Nothing but the epoch of the Grande Armée. What will remain of the current social movement will be the epic of the strikes."

His martial obsession approaches madness: "It is thus not at all exact to say that the incredible French victories under the Revolution were owed to intelligent bayonets. ... The social war, in appealing to the honor that develops so naturally in every organized army."

It would be cruel to insist on the syndicalist aberrations of a mind that is at times so lucid.

Sorel died not long ago without having precisely answered the question he himself had posed: how will the proletariat fulfill its historic mission as predestined successor of capitalism? Convinced of the effectiveness of the proletarian general strike, he depicted it as a great set piece battle between the workers and the bourgeois, never allowing himself and even forbidding the laying out of a strategic plan or the development of the potential tactical phases. The period following the fierce struggle interested him little or not at all, nor did examining whether or not the bellicose qualities of the victors would suffice for them to organize economic and intellectual production, in keeping with unprecedented modes.

The initial error of Sorelian thought resides in a puerile, false, banal, and bourgeois understanding of the proletarian revolution. Lost in a vast and chaotic historical erudition, impregnated with social pessimism, with a coarse and insidious form of traditional conservatism, isolated in his library, far from the material and sentimental lives of men, the author of the *Reflections* thought that the total transformation and the suppression of classes was realizable with punches, saber blows, bombs, brutality, murder, and ruins. He forgot that violence is the arm of the weak, of autocrats, of dictators, parliamentarians, and oppressive minorities, mighty thanks only to the blindness of the mass of slaves standing up against them; that leniency is the arm of the strong, of the innumerable and productive people, indulgent toward the minuscule handful of despots stripped of their prestige, their ruses unmasked, equaled in their savoir-faire; that true renewal is not a tumultuous and incoherent upheaval, but rather a serene and methodical seizing of possession by labor for labor. The liberating struggle takes place, not on the street, but in awareness, between the false, bloody, and obscure concepts of the past and the sincere, gentle, and radiant hopes of the present. The revolution is not an idea that found bayonets; it's an idea that smashed bayonets.

Authoritarian, war-like, and Caesarian, Sorel never claimed to adhere to the libertarian ideal. He felt, assuming he didn't know, that violence is not anarchist.

—F. Élosu

Violence (anarchist) *And now, Sébastien Faure's response to the preceding article.*

I do not propose to plead in behalf of Sorel. Nor will I serve as defender of the Sorelian thesis, with which, on may important points, I disagree.

Of the long and scholarly attack my friend F. Élosu aimed at the *Reflections on Violence* and its author, I want to retain only the last lines. I do so because on one hand, I have the impression that in Élosu's mind his critical study of Sorelism had as its goal the unreserved condemnation of violence, up to and including revolutionary violence, considered by many to be a painful but inevitable necessity, and because on the other hand, it is the conclusion and the conclusion alone of that study that targets anarchism. I reproduce the final lines:

"[Sorel forgot] that true renewal is not a tumultuous and incoherent upheaval, but rather a serene and methodical seizing of ownership by labor for labor. The liberating struggle takes place, not on the street, but in awareness, between the false, bloody, and obscure concepts of the past and the sincere, gentle, and radiant hopes of the present. The revolution is not an idea that found bayonets; it's an idea that smashed bayonets. Authoritarian, war-like, and Caesarian, Sorel never claimed to adhere to the libertarian ideal. He felt, assuming he didn't know, that violence is not anarchist."

A. *"True renewal is not a tumultuous and incoherent upheaval, but rather a serene and methodical seizing of possession by labor for labor.*

I fear that in order to give his ideas more punch, Élosu exaggerated here the contrast he tends to establish between a tumultuous and incoherent upheaval and the serene and methodical seizing of possession by labor for labor. I know that in order to produce its full effect the form of the contrast must be brutal, impressive, striking, and total. But when it's a question of a debate over ideas it is important that the form be nothing but the clear and precise expression of the idea, with no inflation.

Élosu is right to claim that a tumultuous, incoherent upheaval, i.e., without order or goal, is not a true renewal. But he is wrong to oppose to this hypothetical upheaval, lacking in precise causes and determined end, a seizing of possession that he imagines—so much does he desire it to be so—serene and methodical.

On the basis of what facts does he qualify in advance as incoherent and tumultuous the upheaval that we more commonly call the social revolution? And what authorizes him to foresee a methodical and serene seizing of possession by labor for labor?

The social revolution appears to us to be the culmination and terminus of a more or less lengthy period of education, organization, internal agitation, external effervescence, and preparation and training for mass action: we cannot conceive it any other way. It will in all likelihood be preceded by multiple and multiform clashes provoked by circumstances. It will be inspired by the lessons for which these ever more conscious, ever better organized and methodical clashes will furnish the material. In light of these lessons, the proletariat will acquire an ever more correct and enlightened understanding of the propaganda that must be carried out, of the organization to strengthen, of the dispositions to be taken, and the actions to be realized. As a result, when events will determine the final clash, the decisive battle, what Élosu pejoratively calls the "upheaval"—yes, the upheaval, since it will be a matter of overturning the iniquitous and deadly institutions and reducing to impotence the powers they defend—this upheaval, far from being tumultuous and incoherent, will bring together all the forces for renewal indispensable for the taking of possession by labor for labor.

But is Élosu so innocent as to seriously attribute the character of serenity to this seizing of possession, the hope for which he draws from the generosity of his heart? Does he naively believe that the owners of the land and the sub-soil, of all the means of production will voluntarily despoil themselves or allow themselves to be despoiled without opposing the forces of extermination at their disposal to this expropriation?

Does he think that, recognizing the legitimacy of the demands formulated by the workers and surrendering to the workers' commands, the parasites of capital and the state will give their defenders the order to lower their weapons and will surrender the garrison without a shot being fired?

Élosu is not, cannot be so naïve; he doesn't believe in miracles. And then?

Then? It's either one thing or the other: either wait for the miracle to occur (for the benevolent abdication of the parasites) and, in this case, it would mean indefinitely postponing the necessary hour for the serene and methodical seizing of possession by labor and for labor; or else resolve to employ violence and resort to upheaval.

B. *The liberating struggle takes place, not on the street, but in awareness, between the false, bloody, and obscure concepts of the past and the sincere, gentle, and radiant hopes of the present.*

Again, the contrasts so dear to Élosu: "sincere, gentle, and radiant" hopes of the present against the "false, bloody, and obscure concepts of the past." Again, the opposition: the struggle is in consciences and not on the streets.

A marvelous, seductive force emanates from these antitheses, a force all the more dangerous in that not everything in these contrasts is erroneous.

I would even say that there is a great deal of truth in them.

It is quite exact that the liberating struggle takes place between falsehood and truth, barbarism and indulgence, darkness and light.

All of social progress is summed up in the millennial effort of light to dissipate the darkness, of peace against war, of truth battling lies. Every movement that distances man from his departure point of ignorance, ferocity, and want, and that brings him closer to the magnificent destiny that opens before him of knowledge, solidarity, and well-being, is incontestably progress, a victory, a road to liberation.

Not a single libertarian would fail to recognize the correctness of this point of view. So along with Élosu I would gladly say that the liberating struggle takes place in consciences. But while he adds "not on the streets," I say, "and on the streets."

It is unquestionable that it takes place in consciences, and this is why we increase our propaganda efforts and place the greatest price on educational work. Educating consciences in sincerity, peace, and light is what anarchists have constantly and forever dedicated the best of themselves to.

Well then, consciences are feeling this: they are horrified by the lying, bloody, and obscure concepts of the past; they are thirsty for sincerity, kindness, and light.

What must they do? Should they be content with conceiving deep within themselves hatred of falsehood and war and darkness? Should they limit themselves to nourishing themselves on sincere, gentle, and radiant hopes in the present and go no further?

Is it not their duty, and even more, a necessity for liberated consciences first to assist through education and example in the liberation of other consciences, and then to realize the sincere, gentle, and radiant hopes for themselves and others, to transform them into beneficent and fertile reality?

So how can we conceive the advent of these realties otherwise than through the obliteration of lying, bloody, and obscure concepts?

How can we obliterate these concepts, which have systematically organized force and violence behind them, if it's not by smashing that violence and force?

Does Élosu think that it will suffice to emit ardent vows, to beg, to circulate petitions, to spread by the pen and speech indignant protests against falsehood, war, and ignorance, to vote on motions, to issue formal demands, to wear oneself out in warnings and threats? Does he think that minds that have been set free, however numerous they might become despite the obstacles that desperately delay their education, will only have to oppose the powers of falsehood, blood, and darkness with the weapon of their sincerity and the firmness of their convictions in order to defeat them? Does he not know that these methods, of admitted moral value, have always remained inoperative, and that their bankruptcy is more evident than ever?

So, what now?

Now? One thing or the other is needed:

Either wait for the miracle to occur for the serene and methodical triumph of truth over falsehood and peace over war, of light over darkness, as well as for the serene and methodical seizing of possession by labor for labor. Which signifies indefinitely putting off the necessary triumph of sincerity, kindness, and light.

Or else we resolve ourselves to taking to the streets, employing violence and bringing down by force the lying, bloody, and dark forces.

Élosu declares that the struggle takes place in consciences and not on the streets. For my part, I say the struggle *first* takes place in consciences, *and then* on the street.

C. *The revolution is not an idea that found bayonets; it's an idea that smashed bayonets.*

I rectify:

"The revolution is an idea that found bayonets in order to smash bayonets."

For me, this simple rectification suffices to drive out error and reestablish the truth.

Come now, Élosu. What revolution is it a matter of? And which bayonets will it smash?

I think that it well and truly is to do with that revolution that will abolish the two enemies of all forms of liberation: the capitalist regime that engenders exploitation and the state that inevitably leads to oppression. When you speak of the liberating struggle I think that you are only speaking of that which will free, will liberate, all humans from that dual tyranny, capital and the state.

I would like to believe that we are in total agreement on this point and that the bayonets that, to speak a language free of any confusion, the revolution will smash are the violence, constraints, and the entire system of repression and massacre that the capitalist regime and the state, its armed accomplice, cause to weigh on the proletariat.

For the third time I ask you the question: Do you believe, can you believe that the two bandits armed to the teeth, capital and the state, will renounce, *without being absolutely forced to*, the armature of force that alone allows capital to exercise its plunder and the state to maintain its authority? Do you believe, can you believe, that ideas alone will succeed in smashing bayonets? Do you believe, can you believe, in the efficient force of the idea without its putting weapons in the hands that act?

Do you see, can you see a means of smashing the bayonets upon which the state and capital rely and by which they defend their usurpations and crimes, a method that would exclude the use of other bayonets in the hands of their enemies?

Do you hope, can you reasonably hope that in order to knock down the walls of that new Jericho that is the state it will suffice to bear with great pomp the arc of the alliance preceded by seven priests sounding the trumpet and escorted by a silently praying crowd?

It is impossible that you have such a hope. So then isn't one thing or the other necessary?

Either wait for the miracle to be renewed and, in this case, it means putting off for centuries the revolution that, without bayonets, will smash bayonets; or resolve to find bayonets for the smashing of bayonets.

D. *Authoritarian, war-like, and Caesarian, Sorel never claimed to adhere to the libertarian ideal. He felt, assuming he didn't know, that violence is not anarchist.*

This is how Élosu ends his study of Sorel and Sorelism, and it is in these terms that in the name of the anarchist ideal he, without any restrictions, condemns the resort to violence.

There is no need for exceptional perspicacity to understand that, between Élosu and the anarchist I am, the entire debate resides in these few words: "Violence is not anarchist."

Élosu rather hastily asserted that violence is not anarchist and, if he is reasoning in what can be called the absolute, if he is limiting himself to the realm of philosophical speculation and if, refusing to deal with reality he is also taking the pure idea of anarchism in itself into account, he is not wrong in declaring that "violence is not anarchist." For, specifically and intrinsically, anarchism is not violent, in the same way that violence is not specifically, intrinsically anarchist.

On the exclusively speculative plane, I would gladly go further than Élosu: I would not limit myself to saying like him that violence is not anarchist: I would affirm that violence is anti-anarchist.

Our ideal consists in establishing a social environment from which all prescriptions and repression exercised by force or constraint will be eliminated. Anarchism realized means the application of the woolly motto of the abbey of Thélème: *fais ce que veux* [do what you like].

Being a libertarian means not wanting to be either master or slave or leader who gives orders or a soldier who obeys. It means finding the authority that is exercised and whoever puts up with it equal objects of horror. It means accepting no violence and practicing none against oneself or others.

It is thus certain that speculatively, if it is exercised or submitted to, violence is anti-anarchist.

The proof for this can be found in our determination—as sincere as it is ardent—to forever smash organized violence erected into a means of government. This determination, common to all anarchists, cannot be doubted: it is resoundingly, unquestionably asserted in our war cry against the state no matter what the form, label, constitution, juridical basis, or organization. This is the point where the split clearly, cleanly, and brutally occurs; the split between those who are anarchists and those who are not.

But doing away with the state and all the manifestations of violence by which the authority principle it incarnates is practically affirmed, is the task of tomorrow, of a tomorrow from which we are separated by a lapse of time that it is impossible to fix. While waiting for this abolition of the state, the generating force and synthesis of legalized violence, it is appropriate to concern ourselves with today, that is, with the period of bitter struggle, of ferocious battle that will necessarily precede and, when the time comes, that will bring about the collapse of violence, the sole method of government.

I know libertarians for whom the social problem is and is only a moral problem, a problem of conscience. They believe that in order to live as an anarchist it is not indispensable that, on the historical plane, the anarchist ideal be socially realized. They intend to bring to the social problem as many isolated solutions as there are individuals. They consider that individual education is alone in being capable of forming beings morally libertarian and materially free. Therefore it is right to extend the benefits of individual education to all men and women, and that the surest and best method—if not the quickest—to wrest the authority they enjoy from those who make the laws (and who, in applying them, command) is to wrest the habit of submitting, the respect for legality, and the cult of masters from those who obey.

These libertarians declare themselves satisfied when they have as far as possible made their own revolution. As for the social revolution, whose object and result are the liberation of everyone in the social realm through the collapse of the capitalist regime and the abolition of authority, they go so far as to be almost totally uninterested in it. At the very most they are determined to aspire, to sigh, to hope, et cetera.

My own anarchism is less strictly personal and more active. It doesn't envision, even more, it considers unrealizable a liberation that would be limited to myself alone. I feel too strongly that "I am a man and nothing that has to do with humanity is foreign or indifferent to me" for me not to be attached to our common liberation.[1] I know that my individual liberation is indissolubly connected and subordinated to the freeing of all my brothers in humanity and that it is conditioned and measured by the emancipation of all.

Finally, I know that this common emancipation, indispensable to my own, can only result from a shared act, a collective effort, a concerted and mass action; an act, effort, and action that will make and will be the social revolution.

Anarchists are kindhearted, affectionate, and sensitive. For this reason, they hate violence. If it were possible for them to hope that they would realize through kindness and persuasion their vision of universal peace, mutual assistance, and free agreement they would repudiate any recourse to violence and would energetically combat even the idea of such recourse.

But as practical men interested in accomplishing things, whatever their self-interested and ignorant detractors might say, anarchists do not believe in the magical virtue, the miraculous power of persuasion and kindness. They have the well-thought-out certainty that in order to make their admirable dream a living reality it is first necessary to be done with the world of greed, lies, and domination, on the ruins of which they will construct the libertarian city. It is their conviction that in order to smash the forces of exploitation and oppression, it will be necessary to employ violence.

This conviction rests on the impartial study of history, on the example of nature, and the lessons of reason.

History—and I am not speaking of the history that the sycophants of triumphant force and despotic power have written, but of that for which the people have dug the furrows over the slow course of centuries—teaches us that the tears and blood of the disinherited have

---

1. "Homo sum: humani nil a me alienum puto," Terrance, *Heauton Timorumenos* (The Self-Tormentor) Act I, scene 1, c 170–160 B.C.E.

streamed abundantly in these furrows; that in these furrows are heaped the wounded bodies of the countless heroic victims of revolt; that every reform, improvement, and amelioration was the wage of bloody battles pitting the oppressed against the oppressors; that the masters have never renounced a scrap of their tyrannical power; that the rich have never abandoned a portion of their thefts, a fraction of their privileges unless the revolutionary action of the enslaved and the despoiled forced them to surrender to the threat, the intimidation of paroxysmal popular force; that only riots, insurrections, and bloody revolutions have at all lightened the weight of the chains that the mighty place on the weak, the big on the little, and leaders on subjects.

This is the lesson of the close and impartial study of history.

Nature unites its great voice to that of history in placing before our eyes the endless spectacle of violence breaking the resistance that forms an obstacle to the birth and development of the forces of transformation and constant renewal that are part of the eternal evolution of beings and things.

It is the labor that, with an ineluctable slowness, is produced in the depths of the oceans or the entrails of the land and that, after having occurred imperceptibly and unobservably, suddenly asserts itself in fearsome geological convulsions burning things down, flooding, overturning, pulling down, leveling, razing here and building there.

It is, in volcanic regions, the mass of matter set ablaze that, after having shaken the mountain with ever more frequent, ever more powerful tremors, violently cuts a path to the crater and vomits up maelstroms of fire.

It is the sub-soil furrowed with infiltrations that, meeting up, gradually form a layer of water, exert violent pressure on the earth's crust and, brutally crashing through the surface, cause the spring to spurt.

It is the child who, after having developed for nine months in its mother's womb, escapes from the maternal prison, causing its walls to burst, opening, tearing, and crushing all that opposes its passage as it is born in pain and the spilling of blood.

Finally, the data of reason confirm those of nature and history.

Elementary and simple reason proclaims that it is pure madness to count on the good will of governments and the rich; that both the latter and the former, considering that their privileges are only fair and that their safeguarding is indispensable to the public good, consider all those who attempt to dispossess them of power and fortune to be criminal, and treat them as such. If they surround themselves with police, gendarmes, and soldiers it is in order to launch them at the least revolt against their class enemies. And if by chance it happens that they consent to slice off the least little bit from the profits of their exploitation and domination it's only in order to cut their losses and save the rest. But they will never consent to lose everything, and consequently it will sooner or later be necessary to tear it from them by force. This is what reason says, in this in agreement on all points with nature and history.

It is left for me to indicate the nature of the violence that anarchists are forced to envision as a regrettable but ineluctable fate, owed to the needs of the struggle they are engaged in and that they are unshakably determined to carry out without let up until they reach their goal.

It is André Calomel who will respond:

"If violence were only to serve us to repel violence, if we did not assign it positive goals, it would be just as well for us to renounce participating in the social movement as anarchists; it would be just as well to engage in its educationist task or to rally to the authoritarian principles of a transitional period. For I do not confuse anarchist violence with public force. Anarchist violence is not justified by a right; it does not create laws; it does not judicially condemn; it does not have official representatives; it is not exercised either by agents or commissars, even if they are of the people; it is not granted respect either in schools or tribunals; it does not establish, it unleashes; it does not stop the revolution, it causes it to march ever forward; it does not defend society against the attacks of the individual, it is the act of the individual asserting his will to live in well-being and freedom" (*Le Libertaire*, no. 201, first page, sixth column).

It is the indomitable and pure militant Malatesta who has taken upon himself to speak to us:

> Violence is only too necessary if we are to resist enemy violence, and we must preach it and prepare it if we don't want the current conditions of disguised slavery in which the great majority of humanity

lives to persist and worsen. But it contains within itself the peril of transforming the revolution into a brutal melee, without the light of an ideal or the possibility of beneficial results. This is why it is necessary to insist on the moral goals of the movement and on the need, on the duty, to contain the violence within the limits of strict necessity.

We do not say that violence is good when we employ it and bad when the other side employs it against us. We say that violence is justifiable, good, moral, and is a duty when it is employed for the defense of oneself and others against the pretentions of the violent and that it is bad, it is "immoral" if it serves to violate the liberty of others.

We are not pacifists, because peace is impossible if it is not wanted by the two parties.

We consider violence a necessity and a duty for defense, but only for defense. Naturally, it is not just a question of defense against material, direct, immediate attack, but against all the institutions that hold men in slavery through violence.

We are against fascism and we want it to be defeated by opposing greater violence to its violence. And above all, we are against all governments, which are permanent violence.

But our violence must be the resistance of men against brutes and not the ferocious struggle of beasts against beasts.

ALL THE VIOLENCE NEEDED TO WIN, BUT NOTHING MORE OR WORSE.

(*Le Reveil de Genève*, no. 602, p. 4, columns 1 and 2).

I have not exhausted the arguments I could oppose to Élosu's thesis: there is so much to say about such a subject.

I could justify resorting to anarchist violence based on considerations of legitimate defense.

I could demonstrate that in propagating the spirit of revolt in its many expressions, including armed revolt, I remain faithful to the most distant origins of the anarchist movement and its steadfast tradition.

I could prove that the violence exercised daily by all governments is of a ferocity that could never surpass that whose need we proclaim, and that it causes misery, suffering, and deaths that could never equal the most ferociously unleashed anarchist violence.

I could cite the example of the surgeon who, to save the entire body, practices the ablation of a member and who no one thinks of accusing of cruelty.

I could cite this lapidary declaration, this cynical but precise admission known to all: between the supporters and the enemies of the current regime there is only the question of force!

But this refutation of the thesis supported by Élosu is already too long and I hope it will appear decisive to the readers of this encyclopedia.

—SÉBASTIEN FAURE

Vulture (from the Latin *vultur*)   Zoological: Bird of prey of the family vulturides.

Slang: Monsieur Vulture. Usurer. "Merciless landlord." (*Larousse Dictionary*)

This is precisely, in two words, the briefest definition of the maleficent bird we would like to speak of.

There's no need to expand upon the feathered bird. It is well enough known as an ugly bird that feeds on animal or human carrion that its eye is able to pick out from on high, and which its extraordinary sense of smell allows it to delight in in advance from afar by the strong odor of putrefaction that attracts it. After having flown through the air a few seconds it falls greedily on its prey and, with its powerful hooked beak, it quickly tears apart the corpse, feeds on it, and flees. For the vulture is not the eagle: it is cowardly and fearful—nature made it that way—and never attacks a living being on its own. It prefers risk-free carrion to fresh flesh of any danger. Its morality is cowardly and bourgeois, as we know it to be for most landlords. And so we contest nothing and are completely in agreement with what is in the *Larousse*: "Monsieur Vulture. Usurer. Merciless landlord."

The worst of them all are those who live off the misery of the poor. The latter pay poorly, but isn't there a reason for this? If individually we meet tenants who pay with difficulty one or the other of the rental payments owed annually to Monsieur Vulture, it's because in the home of the little tenant, the working-class tenant, the working couple with or without children, there are perpetual calamities: illness, unemployment, births, deaths.

He has a special mindset, this Monsieur Vulture. He doesn't care if sickness, which is frequent among his poverty-stricken tenants, is caused by the poor hygienic conditions of the place, which is usually unhealthy and filthy. The cubic amount of air needed per inhabitant of a lodging is of no concern to him. All he appreciates in the architect under his orders is his talent for making use of empty space and fitting the greatest number people possible in the tightest space possible. He is not concerned if there is room to move about within the apartment, where the air is unquestionably often, if not always, too rare and always polluted by the uncomfortable, insalubrious disposition of the rooms that make up a low-rent lodging, which is always too expensive for what it is.

In the working-class neighborhoods and the housing projects of small and large cities, "under the blue sky of our France," everywhere there is nothing but heaps of stone and plaster where light doesn't enter, where the humidity is high, and where only the lives of vile and harmful parasites prosper.

The working-class family, Monsieur Vulture's primary victim, wears itself out, exhausts itself all its life to make him wealthy. Several families, and sometimes several generations thus maintain that horrible bird: the merciless and rapacious landlord. He must be paid in full and on time, for the law is at his disposal: it is made for him alone and against his tenants. And those who apply that law, or those laws, all serve him docilely, as do those who wrote them and voted on them. They must be submitted to willingly or by force.

Monsieur Vulture has never counted the murders of which he is the direct or indirect author. Workers prostitute themselves body and soul, submitting to the wishes and authority of a boss, to low wages, to humiliation, to arbitrary power, to the shameful demands of a stupid and insolent exploiter who shamelessly exploits and pressures them so they can be housed, have a shelter in which they can hole up. It is in order to have and keep a shelter that women toil day and night in factories at whatever the cost and that young girls prostitute themselves once twice, three times, and then forever if a life of pleasure provides them more well-being and tranquility, if not charm, than a life of poverty.

Monsieur Vulture knows all this, but he lives off it and sometimes dies from its plethora. For he is not pushed to suicide.

People wonder why it is that Monsieur Vulture is so anxious to hold on to buildings with many tenants paying little, rarely paying, or not paying their rent at all.

It's simple: quantity makes up for quality. A hundred tenants paying low rent bring in more than a handful of tenants in bourgeois lodgings, and they are much less demanding. Low-rent tenants wear out more quickly in the murderous buildings of the criminal Monsieur Vulture. Tenants pass, the building remains.

The ignoble war of 1914–1918, unintentionally had the unquestionable utility of wiping out a few pestilential buildings where several generations of unfortunates lived and died. They managed to pay their killers, those good bourgeois landlords! The latter did all they could to avoid living in their slum buildings, or even in the neighborhoods in which they were located.

Where are they, the fugitives who didn't want to die beneath the rubble of the buildings the Germans (or the French) bombed? Perhaps they died during the exodus? Perhaps they went on to make other merchants happy, other exploiters, other landlords in other places.

They changed location, but they probably didn't change their fate.

As for Monsieur Vulture, whose building was destroyed, he patriotically did an accounting of his misfortune. And the grateful fatherland copiously compensated him for his sacrifice by compensating him amply for the loss of his building. If it was worth a few thousand francs he received a few tens of thousands of francs, in the same way that the pillaged factories, the luxurious chateaux, and the vast residences were rebuilt in a generous and modern fashion and are worth in millions what they were once worth in thousands of francs. Ah yes, for a few owners the war was a good, a very good affair. Monsieur Vulture was not forgotten in the patriotic compensations.

Before the war, the Vultures complained loudly (all the while skillfully and odiously making their calculations) of the profits from their buildings.

And so, before August 2, 1914 they had to pay a tax on household garbage. They complained of it but easily made up for it. Was the tax 2o francs? In that case, they raised the rent 20 francs for every apartment (each building containing 20, 50, or 100 tenants). Such were the ruses of Monsieur Vulture, who knew how to play loser wins and never lost.

Before the war there was a certain amount of popular agitation against the rise in rents.

Lodgings and apartments were empty, uninhabited for years on end, Monsieur Vulture preferring not to rent rather than rent without an increase. At the same time there were entire families, large families put out on the streets because in several arrondissements all of the landlords followed this good example. One Monsieur Vulture had raised his rents and evicted the recalcitrant; another Vulture didn't want any children, et cetera.

It was horrible to see poor people thrown out in the street with their wretched furniture (when they had any) and their miserable rags, shivering with cold. No vulture was any different from any other.

The prefecture of police didn't know where to go first and its amiable and courteous personnel had a way of throwing out those guilty of being poor and telling them to keep moving.

There was already a tenants' union. There was also a team of good souls who knew how to carry out a move in the dead of night.

This was when Comrade Cochon arrived.[1] He introduced the tenants' unions to the salutary method of direct action, used by the working-class in its struggle against the bosses and which was fervently advocated by the syndicalist militants of the pre-war revolutionary CGT, whose goal was the suppression of bosses and wage labor.

This amazing Cochon became very popular in Paris and the suburbs because of his methodical fashion of organizing demonstrations that made the exploits of landlords unpopular, in which bailiffs, police inspectors, gendarmes, and agents of public order collaborated. Watch out you vultures!

Cochon knew how not to view things dramatically. Imperturbably calm, he negotiated with the authorities of the bourgeois order and discretely installed Monsieur Vulture's homeless in unoccupied buildings.

But things didn't always go so easily. But for Cochon and his activity there was the encouragement of the crowds and the assistance of a few wealthy and well-known personalities, happy to participate in actions in support of justice and solidarity.

As could be predicted, the press took sides for and against and, in one or another of the ways it does things, its publicity favored comrade Cochon's actions and initiative. Every time he carried out an action he gathered around him an ever-greater crowd, and Monsieur Vulture blanched with impotent rage before the powerlessness of the police, who had orders not to aggravate the situation with brutality. Instead,

1. Georges Cochon (1879–1959). Revolutionary syndicalist and organizer of a large and militant tenant union, activity he began when he himself was about to be evicted.

they settled for maintaining order and protecting M. Cochon's procession that, to the sound of a marching band, led the unfortunates driven out by Monsieur Vulture's rapacity to provisional but safe shelter. The popular crowd, which remained spectators, was unsparing in its applause for M. Cochin and its boos for Monsieur Vulture.

The Noisemakers of Saint-Polycarpe, as Cochin's band was called, caused the representatives of the law to momentarily retreat. People laughed, they mocked, but they thought how odious it was that a landlord could throw out of their homes entire families unable to pay their rent as a result of illness or unemployment all in the name of the law. A certain press mounted a campaign against Monsieur Vulture. There were interpellations in the Chamber of Deputies, bills were proposed, and parliamentary commissions established. The government, badly embarrassed, fearing to offend public opinion by coups de force against the troublemaker Cochon and his companions, took measures that were nevertheless effective. There was no lack of slander. With the assistance of the press, through insinuations and denunciation, the vilest rumors were spread about Cochon and his friends. It's easy to imagine all that was said. It mattered little whether it was true or not, as long as it was likely. All of this is part of the bourgeois order. Even so, Cochon's stunts did Monsieur Vulture quite a bit of harm.

But since then the Vulture has had his revenge. The war was his final test and he's made up for lost ground. His old properties didn't suffer and if for a few years they weren't profitable, they've gained in value since and continue to do so.

During its first days the Paris Commune issued several decrees. One of them, that of March 29, 1871, wounded the heart of the Versailles government, for it vigorously affected its most sacred sentiment: property.

The landlords, the VULTURES, were defended by bourgeois government incarnate, M. Thiers himself, who promised vengeance at the tribune of the Chamber in Versailles.

THE PARIS COMMUNE

Considering that labor, industry, and commerce have borne all the charges of the war, it is only just that property make its share of sacrifices to the country.

DECREES:

Article 1—A general refund of all rents paid for October 1870 and January and April 1871 will be made to all tenants.

Art. 2—All sums paid by tenants during these nine months will be chargeable to the coming rent payments.

Art. 3—Refunds will also be made for rents paid for furnished rooms.

Art. 4—All leases can be terminated at the will of the tenant for a period of six months, dating from the present decree.

Art. 5—All departure notices will be prorogued for three months at the demand of the tenant.

Hôtel de Ville, March 29, 1871

This was truly an act of justice, of a kind carried out only during revolutionary periods.

Otherwise they are nothing but false promises and quickly forgotten verbal declarations. We saw this clearly after the war of 1914–1918. "The victors of the war of Right and Civilization," the puppet Clemenceau said, "those heroes, have rights over us." And indeed, they had the right to shut their mouths, to submit to the high cost of living, and to pay Monsieur Vulture, whose property they had protected. Medals and crosses for the wounded; privileges and priority on public transport; wretched pensions and vile and stupid fawning at the monuments to the dead.

Finally, vis-à-vis Monsieur Vulture, the survivor, the person who fled the war's dangers, is today like yesterday nothing but a profitable porker, like any other shirking or draft-dodging tenant. The *poilu* serves as a theme for the exploiters of everything that can perpetuate the crimes engendered by the false ideas of national glory and infernal and delirious patriotism.

The war did not impoverish landlords: it simplified and amplified their means of enriching themselves. It would be pointless to demonstrate this, for everyone knows how difficult it is to comfortably lodge people who live off their daily labor on their after-tax wages.

It's not war that kills the crows and the vultures, rather it fattens and multiplies them. Only a social revolution will annihilate them. In the meanwhile, as Eugène Pottier said:

How much of our flesh grows fat!
 But if the crows, the vultures,
Disappears one fine day,
The sun will still shine!

These words from the "Internationale" date from June 1871, and
since then the crows and vultures have not yet disappeared. In the form
of the grotesque and rapacious Monsieur Vulture the bourgeoisie rules.

In Paris in 1882, Eugène Pottier, the author of the "Interna-
tionale," wrote a revolutionary song he dedicated to Citizen Paul
Lafargue, which he called "The Eighth." It is a true to life portrait of
Monsieur Vulture.

Here is the song:

You, the terror of this poor world,
Monsieur Vulture, Monsieur Vulture!
Bill in hand you make your rounds.
Already the eighth! Already your day!
Vulture!
So this man created the earth,
Bricks, iron, and wood!
No, this man is a landlord,
The rent's due every three months.
He's a tough character,
Tougher than any other creditor.
He can sell your furniture,
Send a bailiff to throw us out,
In accordance with the dry and gruff law.
Women in labor and the dying, too bad if he kicks you onto the
street.
Vagabonds are swept up.
When joblessness and illness
Already sadden our homes,
Like an epidemic, a raise in rent
Falls on us.
For ten years, life flows in,
In his quarter of vacant lots;

He alone pocketing the profits,
He increases his revenue.
He mixed in with our vain tears, our vain sweat,
All his mortar.
It's the purest blood of our veins
That he received in rent all over town,
A rapid remedy is required,
Vulture is ferocious and subtle:
But if he pushes poverty to the limit,
How will things end?
The poor need shelter,
We are tired just as we are hungry.
Shouldn't housing be taxed
The same way as bread?
Usury has its tragic hours,
Foulon teaches you, my loves,[2]
How we promenade at the end of a pike
The pale head of the vultures.
You, the terror of this poor world,
Monsieur Vulture! Monsieur Vulture!
Receipt in hand, you make your rounds,
Already the eighth! Already your day!
Vulture!

—Paris 1882. Eugène Pottier.

Yes, a rapid remedy is required and we have to decide to apply
it. Once again, the people must count on themselves for this. When
as high-flying a bird as the vulture ravages a country one immediately
resolves to kill it. So the people should have killed good Monsieur Vulture a long time ago!

—Georges Yvetot

2. Joseph-François Foulon (1715–1789). Intendant General of Finance at the
time of the outbreak of the French Revolution, after feeling Paris on July 14, 1789
he was captured by the people, hung, and when the rope broke, beheaded, and his
head paraded on a pike.

War (and the anarchist point of view) A congress called the Congress on Peace Through the Young was held from August 17 to August 22 in Bierville, France.[1] Thirty nations were represented there by 5,000 delegates. But apart from a few rare delegates belonging to parties of the revolutionary vanguard, all the delegates belonged to the capitalist bourgeoisie. Fervent wishes for peace were deposed and accepted. Stirring indictments of war were pronounced and enthusiastically received. A few methods favorable to the fight against war were proposed and voted on. Various measures aimed at advancing the advent of peace were proposed and consented to. But the heart of the debate was not even touched upon. We can even say that in this era of rival and unleashed imperialisms not one delegate pronounced the decisive words that needed to be heard on the fundamental and profound causes of every armed conflict. All those purely sentimental pacifists limited themselves to stigmatizing the horrors of war and celebrating the beauties of peace. Not a single one expressed the conviction that war is inherent to the political, economic, and moral regime flowing from the authority principle. It is this truth that I wanted to cast a light on; it is this unpardonable lacuna I wanted to fill in in the following letter, which I addressed on August 20, 1926 to the 5,000 attendees.

***

Sirs:

You propose laying down the bases of peace through the young.

Working for peace is one of the most august and urgent labors imaginable, and appealing to youth means wisely entrusting the future with the care of realizing this magnificent work.

1. Congresses for peace were held annually between 1921–1932 in the town of Bierville, organized by the progressive Catholic Marc Sangnier.

Like hell, sirs, you are paved with excellent intentions, and it could occur to no one to refuse you the homage these admirable intentions deserve.

But allow a man of some experience and who for many years has fervently and fearfully pondered the problem of peace to honestly and directly tell you the results of his long cogitations.

Firstly, am I teaching you something you didn't know by telling you I've never met anyone—man or woman—who declares himself to be for war in principle? I'm neither thinking nor saying that no one wants, appeals to, or desires war. I'm simply saying that no one dares *in time of peace* affirm that he is the enemy of peace and a partisan of war.

What is more, war would be more catastrophic than it was in the past. The accursed war of 1914–1918 left such horrible memories that every man's conscience instinctively envisages the return of such a catastrophe as a horrific calamity and, instinctively as well, all express their desire for peace.

Hatred of war, love of peace. If we search people's hearts these are the two sentiments we would find in almost all of them.

It would thus be pointless and useless to assemble you in your hundreds and thousands in a congress if you were to limit yourselves to asserting you are supporters of peace, to cheering, to singing hymns, and to organizing solemn and grandiose ceremonies in support of peace.

I don't do you the insult, sirs, of thinking that this is your entire program.

Your program should have and certainly does have as its goal studying and deciding on the practical methods appropriate:

1. For preventing war.

2. For establishing a regime of stable and if possible, definitive peace.

This is how the question of peace is posed. The rest is nothing but stagecraft, décor, solemnity, loquacity, attitude, and pose lacking in sincerity, courage, precise meaning, and without influence on the events from which will emerge tomorrow either war or peace.

And so it is above all, and even solely, a question of preventing war. One method alone offers itself to any thinking being. This method consists in honestly seeking the real, profound, essential, and fundamental cause of wars, and this cause having been discovered, working with all one's strength at its suppression.

It is obvious that as long as the cause hasn't been abolished the effect will persist.

In certain circumstances it will be possible to prevent an imminent conflict and defer its outbreak. But this purely fleeting victory will in no way strengthen the cause of peace, the latter remaining at the mercy of the morrow.

It is thus indispensable and of primary concern to discover the real and essential cause of war in order to publicly denounce, combat, and put an end to this cause.

Well, sirs, this cause is now known and for the past half century the anarchists have tirelessly denounced it without it having been possible to deny they are right.

That cause is the authority principle. A principle that, on one hand, causes conflicts to emerge, and on the other resolves them, can only resolve them, through force, pressure, violence, and war, the indispensable corollaries of authority.

For it is authority in its present economic form, capitalism, that incites envy, encourages cupidity, unleashes competition, and causes rival and rampant imperialisms to set them to battle each other.

And it is authority in its current political form, the state, which, working hand in hand with capital, maneuvers diplomatically and acts militarily according to the plan drawn by international capital. Then, when the moment comes, it prepares, excites, and drives sentiments, decrees mobilization, declares war, opens hostilities, establishes censorship, represses insubordination, and imprisons or executes those courageous men who, having declared themselves against war in time of peace (which is frequent and risk-free), persist in declaring themselves against war in time of war (which is rare and dangerous).

I repeat, sirs, in our time the cause of all wars is authority, capital, and the state.

There are only two choices. Either you will frankly, honestly, valiantly, and tirelessly continue to seek until you discover the cause the anarchists point out to you, in which case you will not leave here without having committed to denouncing that cause and to fight it by all the means in your power, until it has been totally and definitively obliterated.

Or else, retreating before the immensity, the difficulties, the dangers, and the consequences of the implacable struggle against authority, you stop half-way or perhaps even after the first steps. In this case, I tell you clearly sirs and without any hesitation, so certain am I of what I am saying: you will leave Bierville having done nothing and doing nothing afterward that can prevent the war of tomorrow and establishing peace on foundations in any way solid.

What is more, sirs, if you are truly and sincerely determined enemies of war and irreducible partisans of peace, if you aren't so only in words and half-heartedly, but rather from the bottom of your hearts, you will not go your separate ways without having all signed the following vow: "I swear, with all my heart and all my mind, to henceforth dedicate all my efforts to the victory of peace and if, even so, war were to break out, I solemnly swear to answer any mobilization order with a formal refusal. I swear not to take part, either at the front or in the rear, either directly or indirectly in hostilities. Whatever the risks, I commit to fighting against the continuation of killing and in favor of immediate peace."

Sirs: If this double decision I just spoke of were to be issued by this congress: the struggle against authority (the state and capital), the source of all wars, and the unanimous and sacred vow to categorically refuse to take any part in hostilities. Well then, sirs, what an impact on the four corners of the globe your assembly at Bierville will have had! And what a mortal blow you will have delivered against ignoble war and what a giant step you'll have taken in the cause of peace! (Sébastien Faure)

***

Several anarchist comrades made the trip from Paris to Bierville to distribute this letter, a large number of copies of which were printed, to the attendees. But the false apostles of bourgeois pacifism prohibited their distribution and expelled the distributors. We had presumed this would happen, for we knew that many statesmen and heads of political parties, as well as priests and pastors, merchants and industrialists, and perhaps even—O terrible hypocrisy!—manufacturers of cannons, munitions, and implements of war were taking part in the congress. We were sure before getting here that despite the fuss in the world press nothing would come of this congress other than comedy, verbiage, the symbolic wedding of the flags of all nations, oratorical pomp, congratulations, embraces, and assorted nonsense of no practical consequence. The event confirmed our predictions.

Peace will not come from on high, but from below. The interests of the owning class and the rulers of all countries who are the safeguard of their privileges, and the maintenance of the social regime of which they are the cynical beneficiaries, demand that the regime of armed peace from which war inevitably and periodically emanates must go on.

Only the abolition of the authority principle, the cause of war, can put an end to the effect. The peoples of the world are beginning to understand that war is folly and a crime: folly on the part of the peoples who agree to make it, even though they could die in it, and crime on the part of the rulers who live off it.

The proletarians of all nationalities are called on to more clearly realize this truth, which in our time is attaining the brilliance of the obvious. When this truth will have sufficiently penetrated the consciousness of the crowds horribly sacrificed on the fields of carnage, then and only then will war disappear, because the anger of the laboring masses, in killing authority, will with the same blow kill war.

—Sébastien Faure

Zeal n. (from the Greek *zelos*, ardor, eagerness.) Zeal is the active ardor deployed in support of a cause, an idea, or a person one particularly loves. If ancient and foolish religions continue to prosper and if ignoble political parties attract a large clientele, it is because they have enthusiastic recruiters whose proselytizing spirit is contagious. Because they allow themselves to be guided by sentiment and not by reason, most men are less sensitive to intellectual arguments than to emotional motivation.

To be sure, we deplore the fact that cold, naked truth has so few lovers even in our time of scientific progress, and people continue to prefer misleading fables and myths to the rigid conclusions imposed by impartial observation and logical deduction. Let us hope that one day just causes will triumph through the force of rational evidence alone. But in order to hasten this happy time, a labor of individual and collective education imposes itself that requires much zeal and disinterest on the part of its protagonists. A zeal quite different from the incoherent and disordered agitations whose results have usually been negative. A zeal that refuses to resort to constraint, as our adversaries so often do, and that remains respectful of the freedom of others. But a methodical, thought out, tenacious zeal that never leaves the field clear for the enemies of truth, and whose persistence overcomes seemingly unsurmountable obstacles.

Personal example, benevolent understanding, and kindness often more surely win over spirits than do violent critiques, sudden accesses of ill humor, and petty and endless discussion. Nevertheless, harshness is sometimes appropriate, and one must occasionally know when to respond strongly. Misunderstood or untimely zeal harms a cause far more than it serves it. Alongside adversaries in bad faith there is room for sincere contradictors who should not be put off by the sour-tempered bitterness of ill-considered statements.

Those who spend their lives criticizing others without ever doing anything themselves accomplish a negative labor that is not without its use. Nevertheless, when opinions breathe malevolence or partisanship they do not increase the prestige of those who express them. We must not discourage enterprising and bold men who expend themselves for a labor that is fertile and noble, even if we esteem it preferable to personally fold our arms.

—L. Barbedette

AK Press is small, in terms of staff and resources, but we also manage to be one of the world's most productive anarchist publishing houses. We publish close to twenty books every year, and distribute thousands of other titles published by like-minded independent presses and projects from around the globe. We're entirely worker-run and democratically managed. We operate without a corporate structure—no boss, no managers, no bullshit.

The Friends of AK program is a way you can directly contribute to the continued existence of AK Press, and ensure that we're able to keep publishing books like this one! Friends pay $25 a month directly into our publishing account ($30 for Canada, $35 for international), and receive a copy of every book AK Press publishes for the duration of their membership! Friends also receive a discount on anything they order from our website or buy at a table: 50% on AK titles, and 20% on everything else. We have a Friends of AK ebook program as well: $15 a month gets you an electronic copy of every book we publish for the duration of your membership. You can even sponsor a very discounted membership for someone in prison.

Email FRIENDSOFAK@AKPRESS.ORG for more info, or visit the Friends of AK Press website: HTTPS://WWW.AKPRESS.ORG/FRIENDS.HTML.

There are always great book projects in the works—so sign up now to become a Friend of AK Press, and let the presses roll!